The Long Public Life of a Short Private Poem

SQUARE ONE
First-Order Questions in the Humanities

Series Editor: **PAUL A. KOTTMAN**

THE LONG PUBLIC LIFE OF A SHORT PRIVATE POEM

Reading and Remembering Thomas Wyatt

Peter Murphy

STANFORD UNIVERSITY PRESS
Stanford, California

STANFORD UNIVERSITY PRESS
Stanford, California

Printed in the United States of America on acid-free, archival-quality paper

Library of Congress Cataloging-in-Publication Data
Names: Murphy, Peter, author.
Title: The long public life of a short private poem : reading and remembering
Thomas Wyatt / Peter Murphy.
Description: Stanford, California : Stanford University Press, 2019. |
Series: Square one : first-order questions in the humanities |
Includes bibliographical references and index.
Identifiers: LCCN 2019005085 (print) | LCCN 2019006186 (ebook) |
ISBN 9781503609297 (e-book) | ISBN 9781503607002(cloth :alk. paper) |
ISBN 9781503609280 (pbk. :alk. paper)
Subjects: LCSH: Wyatt, Thomas, Sir, 1503?–1542. They flee from me. |
Wyatt, Thomas, Sir, 1503?–1542—Appreciation—History. | Sonnets, English—
History and criticism. | Poetry—History and criticism—Theory, etc.
Classification: LCC PR2402.T483 (ebook) | LCC PR2402.T483 M87 2019 (print) |
DDC 821/.2--dc23
LC record available athttps://lccn.loc.gov/2019005085

Cover design: Michel Vrana

Typeset by Kevin Barrett Kane in 10/14 Minion

Because of Audrey

Contents

"Which words should we remember, and which words should we forget?"

Peter Murphy poses this first-order question about midway through the book. By the time it arrives, the reader has been taught to hear that the emphasis falls on the word *should*. Murphy is not just asking *which* words we remember or why; he asks whether our remembrance—shot through with contingency, fragility, and loss—connotes anything of value.

As the title of this book confesses, the following pages offer many words about a few words: Wyatt's 1530s poem "They Flee from Me." Although this confession might be taken to admit an ill-fittingness between the central concern of Murphy's book and its form, I think that in fact the reverse is true. I see this book as—among other things—a meditation on a form that literary criticism might take in response to the needs of a five-hundred-year-old poem. Indeed, one of the remarkable things that comes to light in Murphy's book is that Wyatt's readers and critics, editors and students turn out not to be the only ones with needs. The poem itself emerges as an object of shared concern, something that has been cared for and valued in different ways over the past five centuries.

Poems are not only imaginative creations, writes Murphy—they "lead full physical lives, subject to the winds and the weather, exerting their own force on the world." Unlike most things made by human beings, "They Flee from Me" has not been used up, discarded, or thrown away. Given the length of time that has passed, it seems implausible to attribute the poem's survival wholly to a "projection" of value on the part of different audiences or consumers—as if the poem's canonization reflected nothing more than engrained, stubborn cultural preferences. And it seems equally implausible to think of Wyatt's poem as simply standing the test of time, like a sturdy monument resisting the ravages of decay. Rather, one is tempted to say with Murphy, the poem has *matured* over time, revealing to us its potential to surprise or delight or provoke, far downstream from its historical context of origin.

In this sense, at least, Murphy is a materialist critic—but of a very special kind. Whereas a conventional literary history of Wyatt's poem and its reception might tell a developmental story, about how the poem's meaning and worth have become clearer, more revelatory, Murphy instead follows the historical contingencies and shifts to which critical judgments about Wyatt could never do justice, but to which they are nevertheless bound. While there is, Murphy suggests, something redemptive in the uncorking of Wyatt's poem, the reception of Wyatt's poem is not only a redemption story but also a reaction to the poem as a kind of disturbance—as if the history of the poem's reception were the slow, unpredictable ripening of the poem itself, as it makes its way toward our shared judgment of it.

If my uncorking analogy is apt—that is, if the promise of redemption that adheres in the maturation of Wyatt's poem, and its material disruption of idealized historical "progress," is not unlike the anticipation of enjoying of an aged wine—then this is not because certain objects manage to stand the test of time. It is because they stand the test of their own maturation, in our judgment.

Murphy never forgets that none of this could have been foreordained or foreseen by Wyatt and his contemporaries. The poem *could* have been lost forever, like the countless other words that have fallen into oblivion. But the period of time during which the poem has been preserved, with increased intensity over the past two and half centuries, also suggests a special connection between the fate of Wyatt's poem and the concerns of modern aesthetics—in particular, of modern literary studies. Murphy's attention to this is one of the most suggestive aspects of his book, because in this way he manages to connect the fate of this single poem to issues of broad, shared concern.

"In a universe that seems always to be accelerating toward chaos," writes Murphy, "little islands of order like this poem are a consolation to the spirit, and so we love them." From this, a further observation might follow: appreciation of Wyatt's achievement has risen alongside our appreciation, after Kant, that judgments of taste do not simply descend from cognitive criteria but rather arise from our senses. Much in our current situation, in literary studies, too—as Murphy's account of Wyatt's poem shows—follows from our inability to leave behind the sensuous, irredeemably idiosyncratic aspects of our taste. Which is to say: A key task of modern literary criticism—and modern aesthetics, and of Wyatt's poem, too—is to respond to the failure of transcendence, the finitude of sensuous life, with whatever validity our judgments of taste achieve.

Thanks to the all-preserving amber of the Internet, words nowadays risk becoming forgettable, not by being paid insufficient attention, but by being undeletable. Perhaps Murphy's book, like Wyatt's poem, can begin to be read as an elegy for the poem itself.

Acknowledgments

I wrote this book over a period of almost twenty years; vast numbers of friends, family, students, colleagues, and institutions have had the opportunity to help me with it. This number includes lots of people no longer with us, reaching back through the centuries. To all of you, living and dead, thank you. Since the book itself is partly about the role of spiritual and intellectual debts in learning, please also take what follows as a beginning remittance on the debt. As I say, toward the end: learning of the kind this book explores is fundamentally social.

Some people and institutions need specific thanks. My students will recognize the Mode, which I created in collaboration with them. The environment provided by Williams College is the fundamental support and context of this book, and everything else I do. Several friends have helped in very specific ways, some repeatedly and over long stretches of time: Steve Harty, Paul Park, Chris Pye, Christian Thorne, and Emily Vasiliauskus. Sarah Trudgeon and Aaron Thier read the manuscript at a crucial moment, and I believe I finished it only because of their encouragement. Sarah, in particular, has played a central role in both the making and the finishing. I quite literally could not have done it without her. Faith Wilson Stein and the production staff at Stanford have been both highly competent and also very nice; my copy editor, Elisabeth Magnus, deserves special thanks for her sympathy with and her disciplining of the idiosyncrasies of my style. The staffs of the Williams College and Yale University Libraries have been core resources in almost everything; I owe additional thanks to the Harvard Libraries and the Cornell University Libraries, and to librarians, generally, present and past. The British Library holds the Keys, of course, and so they even get parts of the book devoted to their work. My anonymous readers at Stanford Press will recognize many of their pointed, sympathetic, and exceptionally helpful remarks in what follows. The end result is of course not their fault.

Finally, my editor at Stanford Press, Emily-Jane Cohen, picked my profoundly unsolicited book out of the welter of stuff she receives every day and took it on, in spite of its idiosyncrasies. I'll remember that moment forever.

Proem

No doubt there are many good poems only one person ever knows about. Such poems could be a consolation and a pleasure to their makers, and might be subtle cultural objects in their own right, but readers of poetry have nothing to do with them. Such poems might be important, but only in a private way. To become important in any other way, poems must become shared objects in the material world, and their existence as objects is a fundamental feature of our experience of them.

Poems we can know about are physical as well as conceptual objects, and so they lead full physical lives, subject to the winds and the weather, exerting their own force on the world, containing within themselves associations with a myriad of other objects, with people, and with the broad forces of history. Poems are ideas, and they are also ink. The inkiness of poems allies them with the crumbling material world, but their ideas can make them seem permanent, free of time's grip.

Like the Great House turned hotel, the conceptual space marked out by a poem inevitably gets reoccupied as time goes on. Or: like the old iron that becomes a doorstop, poems get used for different purposes, and the variety of these purposes increases as poems escape the glowering eyes of their makers. The iron was meant to be an iron, but it also makes a great doorstop. What is more, as the centuries unfurl, the reasons for bothering to reuse and reoccupy old poems become more difficult to articulate. Why be interested in an old box of (someone else's) feelings when you have so many boxes and feelings of your own? The Great House might become a hotel, or it might become a field of wildflowers. The old poem has infinite opportunities to vanish.

This book is about what poetry is and what poetry has been used for, as enacted in the trip through time of a single poem: Thomas Wyatt's "They Flee from Me," first composed in the 1530s, in Henry VIII's court, and currently, five hundred years later, a popular resident of both anthologies and literature courses. In spite of and because of its inkiness, "They Flee from Me" has been remembered, but remembering it has also included a lot of forgetting and losing, and all sorts of human frailty and strengths—life and death and fire and clear-sighted calm. "They Flee from Me" makes a good object for this story, since the poem itself is about just these things: remembering, and forgetting, and frailty, and strength.

They flee from me, that sometime did me seek
With naked foot stalking in my chamber.
I have seen them gentle, tame and meek,
That now are wild and do not remember
That sometime they put themself in danger
To take bread at my hand; and now they range,
Busily seeking with a continual change.

Thanked be fortune it hath been otherwise
Twenty times better, but once in special,
In thin array after a pleasant guise
When her loose gown from her shoulders did fall,
And she me caught in her arms long and small,
Therewithall sweetly did me kiss
And softly said dear heart, how like you this?

It was no dream: I lay broad waking.
But all is turned thorough my gentleness
Into a strange fashion of forsaking
And I have leave to go of her goodness,
And she also, to use newfangleness.
But since that I so kindly am served
I would fain know what she hath deserved.

The Long Public Life of a Short Private Poem

PART I

Thomas Wyatt Writes a Poem and Shows It to Others

Getting Oriented

"They Flee from Me" begins its object-life beautifully and evocatively. It was written into a book Thomas Wyatt owned and carried around with him, sometime around 1535. Today, the page on which it appears looks like this:

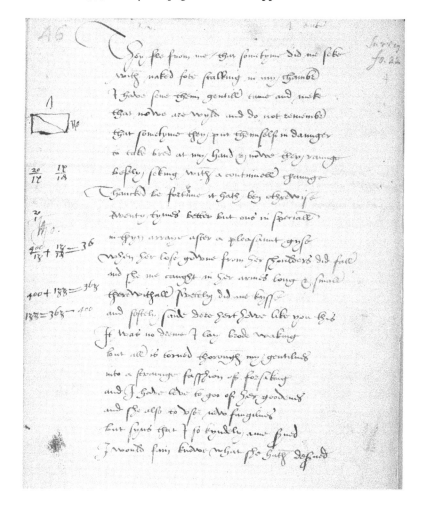

The book containing the page of which this is an image is stuffed full of writing, much of it put into the book before 1540. The old scripts make it almost indecipherable for the reader without the relevant specialized knowledge. There are many layers of time and owners present. Pages that have poems centered on the page also frequently show, in the margins, or written right over the poems, some selection of the following: numbers, arithmetic of an obscure and occasionally flawed sort, geometric figures, geometric proofs or expositions; long periods of prose, written in a very dense seventeenth-century hand; Hebrew words, or whole paragraphs of Hebrew; sermons; moral tags in Latin, repeated and translated; doggerel rhyme, scrawls, doodles, recipes for headache cures. On what is frequently the bottom temporal layer, poems: some written out very neatly, one poem to a page, almost always without a title. Some are clearly working drafts, in a comfortable scrawl, with words crossed out and others substituted.

That "They Flee from Me" and its book have survived the nearly infinite chances for destruction they have experienced in their long life together is wonderful, even astonishing. During that time the book has changed from a personal possession into an old object people forgot or did not value (except for the blank spaces left in it, good for doodling), and then into a sort of international treasure, locked up in the British Library and immensely valuable. In its almost five hundred years of life many people, known and unknown, have held it, turned its pages, slung it into bags and boxes; it has been forgotten for years and years, remembered, and forgotten again. It has been bound and rebound. It has been carted about by aristocrats and clerics and ordinary citizens.

The page on which "They Flee from Me" appears has a certain heft and feel, a texture, and a bookish, pleasant scent. Many people, known and unknown, have touched it over the long centuries. Someone other than Thomas Wyatt wrote the poem down, probably after being told to do so by Thomas Wyatt. That is, from a manufacturing point of view, it was "finished": made, found to be good, or good enough, and so written out in this beautiful script, on nice paper. There was not at first anything else other than the poem on the page, and at a time when paper was expensive and blank paper not always at hand, this is notable. The poem was already special to someone: to Wyatt, if to no one else, and in a plain way to his secretary, who earned his keep by writing it down. Imagination can be aided by eliminating some of the signs of time:

They fle from me / that sometyme did me seke
with naked fote stalking in my chambre
I have sene theim gentill tame and meke
that nowe are wyld and do not remembre
that sometyme they put theimself in daunger
to take bred at my hand & nowe they raunge
besely seking with a continuell chaunge
Thancked be fortune it hath bene otherwise
twenty tymes better but ons in speciall
in thyn arraye after a pleasaunt gyse
when her lose gowne from her shoulders did fall
and she me caught in her armes long & small
therewithall swetely did me kysse
and softely saide dere hert howe like you this
It was no dreme I lay brode waking
but all is torned thorough my gentilnes
into a straunge fasshion of forsaking
and I have leve to goo of her goodenes
and she also to vse new fangilnes
but syns that I so kyndely ame serued
I would fain knowe what she hath deserued

The script is called the "Secretary Hand." Members of Thomas Wyatt's circle—that is, most of the members of the most powerful social caste in Henry VIII's England, around 1530—would have been taught how to write the Secretary Hand, among others, though most people would not have perfected it in the way Wyatt's secretary has. The Secretary Hand was the basic script of public life in this period, used for letters, memos, and some sorts of important documents. This script, and especially this secretary's pure, beautiful version of it, signals that the words and the text were being entered on a public stage. Whatever the poem was before Wyatt's secretary wrote it down (perhaps just thoughts inside Wyatt's head), this embodiment not only makes it possible for others to interact with the poem but also marks it as something its maker(s) *expected* others to interact with. It is a kind of publication.

This page is a physical presence, as Thomas Wyatt himself was once, though through good fortune it has lasted rather longer. Wyatt passed away, and the page could too. This is not true in the same way of the poem the ink spells out. One material embodiment of the poem is on this page, but it is also, now, spelled out on countless other pages, physical and virtual, distributed through the whole world. It also has an immaterial form in the memories of living people. This immaterial form could also perish, along with the earth, but it is not present in the same way the paper-poem is present. Each time a poem takes shape as a material object, it descends from out of the abstract, immaterial space where it lives with all words and all things made from words. The material poem can appear in Times New Roman 12-point type on my screen, or in the same type on my printed page, or in neat Tudor script in a photograph of an old piece of paper—or on the once-new paper itself.

The first task, in beginning to follow out the long story of the life of the poem, is to understand better what kind of object it is. What is the nature of its inky, physical life, on this old page, in this old book? And what is the nature of its conceptual life? What is a "poem" in 1535?

"Tho."

It is just to the left of the poem, amid the math: an abbreviation for "Thomas," in an italic script, in Wyatt's own hand. Nearly five hundred years ago, Wyatt looked over this page, which had been written by an employee, and approved it, standing in a bright room overlooking the fields of Kent, or while on a diplomatic mission in Spain: or somewhere else. He did this before October 1542, when he died on the road to Falmouth from a fever, and after 1503, when he was born.

We can only imagine why Wyatt's mark might be there. Such a signature in a manuscript of Tudor poems is extremely rare; manuscripts of Tudor poems are extremely rare themselves. Since the poem was written out by someone other than Wyatt, and since that same person wrote out the first fifty or so pages of the book in which it is contained, it seems plausible that Wyatt assigned this writing as a task and then looked over the finished work at some future point and initialed it. On other pages Wyatt changes poems written out by his secretary: crossing out or scribbling over words, writing in new, rather messier words. In the case of "They Flee from Me," all we really know is that Wyatt was there, looking at this page.

That is, when he initials it, Wyatt himself looks at his poem as an object, a small thing he has made but someone else has written. It is out of his head and has taken its place in the world. Clearly Wyatt wanted this to happen. In 1535 poetry was work a highly respectable person might engage in, work that could be done more or less capably and that produced objects other people received familiarly and expectantly. This poem was part of Wyatt's daily business, just as the letters he wrote to Henry were part of his business; indeed, we can identify the "Tho." as Wyatt's by comparing it with the writing in his letters.

Wyatt's initials connect this page and this poem to the busy and deadly world of Henry's court, and to the life of a man.

Tho. Wiatt Knight

Here is the man, caught by another hand in Henry's court, that of Henry's favorite artist and decorative handyman, Hans Holbein:

This image, which has its own long story of preservation and transmission, has much the same power as Wyatt's signature. It tells us (it helps us imagine) that once, in some real place, Thomas Wyatt, a real person, sat in front of Hans Holbein, an exquisitely trained and immensely talented artist, and Holbein drew these lines, guiding them by looking at the person sitting in front of him. On that day Wyatt's beard (might have) curled in just this way; on that day some stray hairs peeked out from under his cap. Holbein omits the details of Wyatt's cap. He perhaps meant to simply remember them, but he long ago turned to dust (along with the cap).

Did Wyatt look this way as he looked down at the page with his poem on it, just before he scribbled his approval there? What was he thinking? Did he recall its writing with fondness or regret? Did he recall the moment of writing it at all? Did he think of the applause with which it was received, or the silence? Perhaps he meditated on a lover in his past, perhaps on a lover in the present; perhaps on no lovers at all. He might have thought about the day he wrote it, the way the pen felt, the weather that day, the ways in which his fortune had turned, for better or worse, since that day. He might, at that moment, have been safe within the sturdy and quiet walls of his castle in Kent; he might have been within the hard walls of Henry's Tower, uncertain of his fate, thinking about friends (Anne Boleyn, say) recently executed in the courtyard below.

In any case, it is interesting and salutary to ponder the possibility that Wyatt looked down on his poem of love and regret with the hard, canny, and hooded eyes Holbein recorded here: no soft light of memory shining through, no delicate self-consciousness disturbing the surface. These are the eyes and face of a capable and controlled man. A diplomat, a shrewd and calculating advocate of his King's interests, and his own.

Birth

Wyatt's invention and materialization of this poem was mostly a transformation of already existing culture: already existing poems, inherited forms, popular subjects for poems, ways of thinking common in Henry's court. In other words, there is a lot in this poem Wyatt did not make up. Wyatt's circle would have encountered such poems every day. Many of these poems were carefully allusive and fancy, as this one is, and many of them were constructed in very similar ways. The subject matter, love and regret (to put it generally), was by far the most common subject of short poems in this period, and for several centuries previous. The form of the poem, called rhyme royal, had been a common form (in English and French) for centuries.

Wyatt may, in fact, have made this poem by translating someone else's poem. Wyatt was very interested in translation and did a lot of it, although no one has ever found another version of this poem. He also might have started by thinking generally about someone else's description of someone else's inconstant heart, in French, Spanish or Italian, all of which he knew, and then, finding it fit him in some way, adapted that description into English.

Perhaps he didn't translate some old poem or adapt an old thought but simply had his head turned by an interesting or evocative old word ("newfangleness," for instance, which he would have found in Chaucer), and then his poem grew out of that word and its context, since it fit with other things he was thinking about. Perhaps it sprang to life all at once in Wyatt's head, and he simply wrote the poem out one London spring morning in the 1530s; perhaps he didn't need to write it down, since he could remember it perfectly well. Perhaps, during one of the carefully orchestrated and complicated gatherings of the inhabitants of Henry's court, Wyatt put this all together suddenly, from pieces lying about in the air or in his memory, as an entertainment for the men and women that made up his business and social circle.

Whatever the truth might be—whatever actually happened—the birth of this poem is bound to be either entirely or partly invisible. It might involve saying words, or doodling a bit, or writing out words here and there; it might involve writing a different but closely related poem out entirely and then changing that poem. Some still-existing pieces of paper show Wyatt doing this with other poems, but not this one. Inventing this poem might involve just thinking, so that the first time it appeared in the world it would already have been finished: writing it out, in this case, would be clothing it in the visible as a way of getting it out of his head. Reciting would make the poem material in another way. If Wyatt himself recited it, the very first writing out of the poem could easily have been done by someone other than Wyatt, by someone listening to him.

Like all language-objects, and certainly like all poems, Wyatt's poem is a new thing when it comes into being, and it is an old thing too. There hadn't ever been something exactly like this poem before at the moment Wyatt made it (this is still true even if he did translate a poem from some other language), but there were many already existing poems a lot like it. It would have felt new to the people who first encountered it, in ways I will come to, but "They Flee from Me" also sat comfortably within their Circle, new and deeply familiar at the same time.

Some Details

Like many of Wyatt's poems, "They Flee from Me" gives the distinct feel of doing several things at once. Its first stanza is an evocative meditation on a shift of fortune:

> They flee from me, that sometime did me seek
> With naked foot stalking in my chamber.
> I have seen them gentle, tame and meek,
> That now are wild and do not remember
> That sometime they put themself in danger
> To take bread at my hand; and now they range,
> Busily seeking with a continual change.

What are the beings that range with such interesting, distant busy-ness? Wyatt doesn't say. Certainly there is not much here to associate these formerly tame companions with women, or with the "she" that is to appear in the second stanza. With their naked feet and their stalking, their gentleness and their eating of bread from the hand, they are distinctly birdlike, but they are not specifically birdlike. They are full of life, and an interesting sort of life. They have shown themselves capable of gentle meekness, and they have shown a sort of delicious open intimacy, taking food from a (potentially) grasping hand, but they have also shown an energetic independence that puts the speaker in the poem in his place, as only one of a number of things in the world they are interested in. They seek continually for—something—and the poet has put himself, in retrospect, on the list of things they have sought. Their energetic exploration makes them different from the seemingly chamber-bound poet, who, since he does not seek with them, has been left behind.

The second stanza takes the meditation on this life-turn and tells a story to illustrate it: but the poet simply and without drama substitutes a woman, and a deliciously erotic encounter, for the multiple flighty presences of the first stanza:

> Thanked be fortune it hath been otherwise
> Twenty times better, but once in special,
> In thin array after a pleasant guise
> When her loose gown from her shoulders did fall,
> And she me caught in her arms long and small,
> Therewithall sweetly did me kiss
> And softly said dear heart, how like you this?

> (To Tudor speakers "small" meant, among other familiar things, "thin." Wyatt might have encountered the phrase "long and small" in old poems.)

The poet still looks back in time from his chamber, but he has turned away from the window on the outside where they range, away from a distant perspective, to a distinct and compelling memory of an encounter that might have taken place there, in the chamber. Because this stanza does not mention the birdlike creatures of the first stanza, those creatures turn (in retrospect) into metaphor, a way of talking about the sad distance the poet feels from the intimate immediacy described in this stanza.

In particular, "she" mixes together the bewitching submission and independence that the formerly tame feeders demonstrated. She gives herself to the poet, but she also takes him (in her arms); she has the lead in this encounter. In her implied, evocative nakedness, she is submissive; in her forwardness, she is energetic, independent. He takes her in his gaze, but when she catches him he submits. This quick story is a fantasy of intimacy and personal exposure, two people opening themselves to each other, both of them defenseless and both of them active.

Using the metaphor from the first stanza: the potential energy and danger in the open hand, tameness exposed in the hand of power, gives urgency to this encounter, where both people take from the other's hand, and both leave the hand open, relaxed, unflexed.

The third stanza turns back to the lonely window on the dismally distant and unresponsive Outside:

> It was no dream: I lay broad waking.
> But all is turned thorough my gentleness
> Into a strange fashion of forsaking
> And I have leave to go of her goodness,
> And she also, to use newfangleness.
> But since that I so kindly am served
> I would fain know what she hath deserved.

He was awake, the poet says, awakening us, too, from the delicious dalliance of the second stanza. It was real, it was something that happened. Hard reality is the mode of this last stanza. No more metaphor, no more dreaming over memories. He has been abandoned, and the poet describes the reasons for this in subtle psychological terms, noticeably complicating the relatively open and simple emotional feel of the poem so far. He did not flex his hand to catch her—he was gentle, he says—and he has been repaid by her flight. "Newfangleness," the word from Chaucer, is (like "newfangled" today) uncomplimentary: overly attracted by novelty (and usually applied to faithless *men*).

Her independence, an erotic energy in the second stanza, has become plainer. She has taken flight, without regret or attachment, like the seekers of the first stanza. He is free to go, and she is also free, to use new ways, to take food from other hands. The beautiful and intimate agreement that allowed them to open to each other has been forgotten. No longer passive, the poet judges her, and analyzes himself, in his active description of his fate and her fate. He describes what looks like plain-sighted if unhappy understanding.

And then this unhappiness takes a turn in the final couplet, the last pair of lines, bound by their rhyme. A personality appears: call him Thomas Wyatt, a man who once lived and loved real women, and who served a capricious King. There is an animated intersection of meaning in the word "kindly." There is "in a nice way," certainly, but more so "unkindly," in bitterness of spirit. There is also a half-hearted admission that he might have deserved it, as in "payment in kind." There is also, finally, perhaps, a gendered accusation, as in "a woman [or man] is the kind of being who would. . ." Then this sullen, mixed bitterness turns nasty in the final line, with its interest in retribution, in its pettish refusal to say what she deserves, and in its implication that she at least deserves something worse than what he got.

So the bitterness is not simple disappointment, which makes it an interesting complaint instead of a simple complaint. Wyatt's suggestion that punishment might be in order is an attenuated and tardy flex of the hand, a suggestion of power that makes final sense of the poem's interest in power and defenselessness. He has closed himself up and pointed a finger. Why should she not range, go on to other interests? Only because the poet does not want her to. This arbitrary extension of power suddenly puts the woman where she might have been expected to be in the first place, considering it is 1530. Except she is not, she is gone, and the poet is only summoning the picture of his masculine rights in a sulky sort of way.

It is not at all clear he could punish her in some real way, some way other than this way, by saying these words. He gives no indication he could. In fact, he seems to just fling this idea out at the world, with a hope that someone else might take care of it for him. The suggestion of power is mostly a distant sort of smear, a gesture that calls up, in the end, passivity instead of active revenge. She might not have cared.

Wyatt and many other courtier-poets wrote many poems of disappointed love. The usual mode is complaint about the lack of interest on her part. These poems often now have an unpleasant air, since they constantly insist she has to pay attention to him simply because he says she should. She must respond to him, or she is "cruel." Indifference is not allowed to be indifference simply. "They Flee from Me" is almost this sort of story—except for its rendering of her independence as a desirable trait, and except for its brief but sharply drawn rendering of the existence of other, entirely independent selves. The poet is complaining, but something of this independence appeals to him. It bewitched him, once.

Wyatt presents this muddled state as a sort of self-consciousness. The thinking and remembering become unexpectedly complicated; in particular, the poem seems to be of two minds, as we say, both offended at her demonstration of independence and also attracted to it, admitting that this independence contributed to her attraction in the first place. This thickened depiction of the self, which is routine to us, and which reaches an astonishing and expressive technical apogee in the poetry of Shakespeare and Donne, about seventy-five years on, is very unusual in the poetry of Henry's time. In fact, it really appears only in certain sonnets by Wyatt, in some poetry by his friend and protégé Henry Howard, the Earl of Surrey, and in this poem.

(At Least) Two Poems in One

"Irony," officially speaking, means "saying one thing and meaning its opposite," so we might want to use that word to describe Wyatt's use of the word "kindly" as both "kindly" and "unkindly." That doesn't get it all, though, since Wyatt really does mean he was *both* kindly and unkindly used, and he has also filled that doubling out with the other meanings. We understand the fullness of "kindly" through reading in tone, imagining a speaker who says it in the way we say such things when we want our listeners to get more than one meaning. Some of Wyatt's other poems are much denser in this way, requiring us to keep many meanings in mind as we read along, as many of Shakespeare's sonnets do.

The multiple meanings create poems vibrating alongside each other. Reading the poem in its most general sense requires us to keep at least two versions in our minds. In one, say, he is treated kindly; in another he is treated unkindly. Since in truth (in retrospect especially) Wyatt feels several ways at once, we might think of the multiple versions as semitransparent layers, one on top of the other. The experience of the poem is looking through them all at once.

Why Wyatt Wrote It, and What It Means

The Inevitable Unknowable

Is it possible to know exactly what the words in this poem mean? Five hundred years is a long time, and language has changed substantially since then. A lot of our ability to know what the poem says rides on this question: "kindly"; "new-fangleness"; "served"; "deserved." Much scholarly energy has been expended on this kind of question; the results of this scholarship, like the *Oxford English Dictionary*, are now everyday resources. Some questions remain: How much of a sexual air does the word "served" have, for instance, in Tudor usage, in Wyatt's language? By and large the language in this poem feels fairly well behaved to modern ears; more well behaved, in fact, than the language in some other Wyatt poems, and many other poems of the period.

But is it possible to know that while the word "stalking" seems to mean mostly "to walk softly" to Tudor speakers of English, Thomas Wyatt, one particular person, used the word in this way? Maybe for purely personal reasons "stalking" had a scary, hunted feel to Wyatt and he used it with this feel in mind. This is a worry about words, but it derives from a deeper uncertainty about what we can know about the thinking of others. How do I know Thomas Wyatt's interior life was so much like my own that I can apply words like "bitterness" to it with confidence? Is it clear that his experience of erotic life was enough like mine that I can calibrate his thoughts through my thoughts in the ways I have suggested? Wyatt's poem seems to reach for and describe certain emotional commonalties, shared features of human life, but how can we be sure that Wyatt does share these features with us, that the situation in this poem is not something wholly different, described in words that are now like a code whose key has been lost?

Imagining the work "They Flee from Me" was designed to do—imagining any specific moment in cultural history—might be a pleasure, the pleasure of historical speculation, but it might also create anxiety and hesitation. We have the authoritative stamp of Wyatt's initials, his mark of satisfaction, but in raising the small details of this poem's functioning from the dead, error is a certainty. The unrecorded past is lost, pure and simple.

Seeing into the souls of other people is difficult in just the same way. Gestures, words, poems might help, but they can show only so much, and after they run out we are left to ourselves. This loneliness is one of the things Wyatt's poem is about: what it is like when other people baffle us, leaving us to brood on what they meant. The past, and other people, are reanimated in Wyatt's poem, but, paradoxically, as partly unknowable things. It is hard to say exactly what others are thinking, and this causes us trouble all the time.

That is: Wyatt, thinking about (his) life, and we, trying to recover Wyatt's thinking, touch the same blank spot, feel the same anxiety about the limits of what we can know (about other people). So that is the point of reference, the reason we do go on, the reason we don't just leave an old thing like "They Flee from Me" behind. It all seems rather familiar. With this somewhat cold comfort in hand, I'll go on. Why did Wyatt write this poem? What work would it have done for him in his daily life? What would others have thought about it? What did Wyatt mean by it?

Rhyme Royal

The culture of Henry's court had a place for this poem, since its subject matter, speaking generally, was familiar, and because it was short and written in rhyme-royal stanzas: a seven-line stanza, with lines of ten syllables rhyming ababbcc. Rhyme royal was already an old, well-used meter in Wyatt's time. It was, above all, and especially in the context of a love poem, the stanza of Chaucer's long poem *Troilus and Criseyde,* a perennial favorite in court circles. Rhyme royal was used by upper-class poets and was associated with court, clerical, and wealthy circles.

The rhyme-royal stanza has content. Wyatt's stanzas were already speaking to his audience and to him before he voiced any of the actual words in those stanzas. What the form of the stanza by itself says is very hard to hear now, at our great distance, but certainly Wyatt's potential audience had already read many poems in rhyme royal, and those poems were all very much like one another. Just looking at the stanza, before reading it, Wyatt's audience would already have had quite specific expectations of what the poem would be about. These expectations would have been almost entirely independent of Thomas Wyatt, nor could he impose any real control on this message. The stanza is the most obvious part of the poem Wyatt did not think up. He takes his form from the past, from previous poems, and in so doing dissolves some of himself and some of his voice in the chorus of Poetry, what people have already said and read.

The filtering of the personal through an inherited, continuing culture is the very essence of lyric poetry. Poetry as Wyatt knew it, that is: writing in a deeply familiar form about deeply familiar subjects using familiar kinds of words. A lyric like "They Flee from Me" is at root a performance of well-understood models, and fundamentally a calibration between what is being said now, in the poem, and what has already been said in other poems. From a certain point of view, taking the heavy inheritance of poetic form into account, Wyatt has very little freedom. His lines need to be of a certain length; the last words in each line must be of a certain sort (to keep up the rhyme); his vocabulary is largely provided for him by a long tradition. His subject matter is also provided for him, though a little less sharply.

The ways in which inherited poetic traditions direct what Wyatt may do derives from a kind of agreement between Wyatt, his circle of listeners, and that tradition. This agreement is the source of culture: shared ways of talking and writing and doing things. There is not usually any moment of agreement or decision in the formation of culture, in exactly the same way individual speakers do not usually decide in any active way what any particular word means.

Within the hothouse exchanges of Henry's court culture, Wyatt could, in principle, write in any sort of form, use any vocabulary, talk about anything. But without participating in and performing some part of culture, he would be speaking a private language. Taking inherited convention and culture as I have described it, everything about his poem announces its public nature. "They Flee from Me" is highly interactive, intimately and already tied to its audience and to the history of audiences and poets stretching out behind it. This is especially worth noting, in our time, because the intimacy of what the poem actually says can tempt us to forget it. It might seem Wyatt is "just talking."

Especially in the twentieth century, great artists are often depicted as confronting and breaking apart old forms in a titanic effort of self-assertion. This has been true of some of the art of recent times, but not all of it, and it is much less true of older art. For Wyatt, the prescribed form of the short lyric offered both restriction and opportunity. He had to do certain things in order to make his poem recognizable as a poem to his audience, but this confinement in the small space of the rhyme royal also ensured he would benefit from the sharp ears and eyes of his audience. If a line ran to eleven syllables—or eight—his audience would notice, and would ask why. If his treatment of the pains of love and fortune departed from the common, his audience would notice. In compensation for the weight of their elegant chains, the rules Wyatt accepted in writing this poem marked out a small, brightly lit space where delicate shadings, slight verbal movements of meaning and sound, and carefully delineated psychology would all be highly visible and carefully scrutinized.

Old and New

Generally speaking, a member of Wyatt's audience hearing or reading the three rhyme-royal stanzas of "They Flee from Me" would have looked forward to an elegant, compressed, and witty discussion of the fortunes of love and life, a discussion that pursued some meditation on the nature of women, using various expressions and metaphors he or she already knew and enjoyed. Such a person would have been surprised to find anything else.

An example from Wyatt's poetic past will make what "They Flee from Me" actually is more concrete. Here are two stanzas (the middle two of four total) from a fifteenth-century lyric quite possibly by a person called the Duke of Suffolk. It is impossible to say whether Wyatt knew it or no, but it is representative of a class of poems Wyatt certainly would have known. I have (mostly) modernized spelling:

> Me-think thou art unkind, as in this case,
> To suffer me so long a while endure
> So great a pain without mercy or grace,
> Which grieved me right sore, I thee ensure
> And syth thou knowest I am that creature
> That would be favored by thy gentleness,
> Why wilt thou not withstonde mine heaviness?
>
> What causeth thee to be mine adversary?
> I have not done that which should displease,
> And yet thou art to mine intent contrary,
> Which maketh now my sorrows to increase;
> And sith thou wost my heart is not in ease
> But ever in trouble without sykernesse,
> Why wilt thou not wythstande mine heaviness?

("Wythstande" and "withstonde" are the same word; it means "to prevent, or deny"; "sykernesse," related to our "security," means "safety, or security.")

Suffolk's poem is a stolid example of the Standard Poem Wyatt was working with in accepting, from the past, many of the formal features we find in "They Flee from Me." Suffolk's poem is rhyme royal in steady, plain lines of ten syllables. The rhymes fall where they should. Like most poems of this sort, the stanzas end with a repeated line, a feature that recalls the origin of such poems in song (these lines are a sort of vestigial refrain). The speaker complains of his ill fortune and asks for relief. This complaint is done with a certain literalness, by listing individual complaints. From a distance, this poem is almost exactly like "They Flee from Me."

But from up close the differences are plain: a faint but credible echo of a possible contemporary reaction to Wyatt's poem. The vocabulary of Wyatt's poem is very much like Suffolk's (even down to the rhymes on long words ending in

"esse"), but in spite of this, Wyatt's total effect is much more fluent, much more
evocative, much less perfunctory. Perhaps the intervening one hundred years have
drawn Wyatt's usage that much nearer our own; in any case, Wyatt's poem seems
more comfortable within its confines. The Duke's words have been whipped into
obedience to the form—though not without skill—and so they are rather stiff in
their march through the lines. Wyatt's words flex and speak "naturally," as if they
don't really notice their participation in an old stanza form.

Beyond the verbal differences, the poems treat their subjects very differently. Suffolk's method is a list of complaints: here's what's wrong, here's how I
feel about it. The poem does not, however, show details about the personality
feeling these things. Wyatt's poem has only one complaint, but it turns that
one complaint over in an intensely realized way. Wyatt's poem complains very
personally, even idiosyncratically, and asks us to visualize and sympathize with
very specific emotional states. The first three lines of Wyatt's poem provide more
individuality than the whole of the Duke's poem.

Underneath the fluency—perhaps, in a counterintuitive way, contributing
to it—Wyatt's lines are less disciplined about the rules. They are less predictable
in their length (they have nine or ten syllables usually: one line has eight, one
has eleven) and less steady in their rhythm. The syntax of the sentences does
not match the ends of the lines very often, a noticeable difference from the older
poem. A couple of the rhymes sound slightly off to our ears.

Most importantly, most noticeably, Wyatt's poem has turned the list of complaints into an intensely drawn and evocative drama. The irregularity of the lines
comes along with this drama. It is as if the lines are being pushed around by the
strong feelings, as if the poet is writing them Now, while feeling them, as if the
words are pouring out as he sits in distress at that moment, escaping some of
the disciplines of form. Wyatt produces this disturbed feel by slightly disturbing
the expectations created by his inherited form.

Repetition is the governing principle of the Duke of Suffolk's poem, and
of almost all English lyrics previous to Wyatt. Whatever psychological drama
these previous poems depict is confined by the method of continuous return
to a central idea or formulation. In Suffolk's poem, it is the line "Why wilt thou
not wythstande mine heaviness?" The repetitive lyric mode is a fundamentally
nondramatic mode—nothing really happens—and the repetitive poet is more
interested in decorative surface than emotional depth. The poet's mind is not
developed or explored as a subtly organized or especially interesting place. It is
described by listing out its contents.

Such a poem need not be clunky or unpleasant, as two stanzas of another Wyatt poem demonstrate:

> My lute awake! perform the last
> Labour that thou and I shall waste,
> And end that I have now begun;
> For when this song is sung and past,
> My lute be still, for I have done.

> As to be heard where ear is none,
> As lead to grave in marble stone,
> My song may pierce her heart as soon;
> Should we then sigh or sing or moan?
> No, no, my lute, for I have done.

There is a grace and fluency of language in this poem like that in "They Flee from Me," though without the intensity of the latter. Here the language does not seem forced into repetition: the stanzas accept repetition and rhyme gratefully, as beautiful ways of designing the thought. They even vary it a little, emphasizing their easy relationship to form. These stanzas are not enslaved to form: they make obedience fun.

"They Flee from Me" substitutes linguistic and psychological drama for repetition and listing. But if this is a disturbance of form, the disturbance is accomplished from the inside, since Wyatt's poem obeys (for the most part) the rules that govern traditional rhyme royal. The older poetic mode is discovered in this poem (and some other Wyatt poems) to have a sort of false or disappearing bottom: underneath the patterned surface a considerable depth appears, falling away into the mystery of (Wyatt's?) self. In other words, in compensation for the loss of the decorative surface Wyatt gives us psychological depth. This is accomplished through the quick and feeling drama he describes and through the idiosyncratic flexibility of the lines as they unfold. The final couplet puts a point to the whole thing: summarizing, in a way, as a final line would in the old mode, but twisting too, adding a dark and uncertain coloring to the meditation that preceded it.

In short, "They Flee from Me" does not foreground linguistic and emotional control as its primary accomplishment. It is not asserting its settled, conventional design as a partner to a settled understanding of the poet's emotional situation. Inside the rule following of "They Flee from Me" is uncertainty. Wyatt does not make the feeling in his poem exactly clear, and he implies, since he is obviously capable of subtle self-reflection, that in fact he doesn't quite know. He is not done working it out, and the poem depicts the process of working, instead of presenting a finished set of complaints and conclusions.

And so "They Flee from Me" is a virtuoso performance. Wyatt thoroughly acknowledges the past, the source of his form, and this acknowledgment tells his reader that like a great athlete he accepts and is grateful for the opportunity for expression the rules have provided for him. This is not a disrespectful performance: it is a subtle performance. By accepting the confines of rhyme royal Wyatt enables the finest of nuances, since his audience would have been able to detect them. The old is made new without the destruction of the old. It is like a magic trick. Out of the traditionally shaped hat of the rhyme royal Wyatt pulls the rabbit of (his) self, and since the hat seems too small to contain his substantial bulk, his audience (might have) applauded with delight.

All expressive culture characterized by inherited form and rules works in this same way. The fifteen-year-old player of video games is attuned to the smallest deviation from his expectations; the listener devoted to contemporary music knows when the smallest new thing is happening. This environment of intense familiarity is the foundation of live culture and living forms. Such is the environment into which Wyatt introduced his poem.

Punctuation

Transcribed out of the difficult old script into our own printed letters, the poem looks like this:

> They fle from me / that sometyme did me seke
> with naked fote stalking in my chambr
> I have sene theim gentill tame and meke
> that nowe are wyld and do not remembr
> that sometyme they put theimself in daunger
> to take bred at my hand & now they raunge
> besely seking with a continuall chaunge
> Thancked be fortune it hath ben othrewise
> twenty tymes better but ons in speciall
> in thyn arraye after a pleasaunt gyse
> when her lose gowne from her shoulders did fall
> and she me caught in her armes long & small
> therewithall swetely did me kysse

and softely saide dere hert howe like you this
It was no dreme I lay brode waking
but all is torned thorough my gentilnes
into a straunge fasshion of forsaking
and I have leve to goo of her goodenes
and she also to vse new fangilnes
but syns that I so kyndely am serued
I would fain knowe what she hath deserued

Writing the poem out this way makes it easier to read than the copy of the page in Wyatt's book, but there are still difficulties and strangeness; it begins to look more like the copy I put at the beginning but retains some striking differences. There is, for instance, only one mark of punctuation, a "virgule," a small slash in the first line of the MS, which is usually transcribed as a comma.

For the modern reader the lack of punctuation is no small thing, especially in a poem with such a personal feel, a poem mimicking, in a broad way, a person talking to someone or to himself. Marks of punctuation, in modern usage, are important signals for the way something is meant to be said in silent or sounded performance and, in many cases, how meaning is being made and distributed. "?" marks a questioning tone, and it marks the grammatical question itself. Periods tell us to pause, briefly gathering the meaning of the sentence we just finished: they also tell us a unit of meaning has been completed and another is about to begin. And so on.

The poem on the manuscript page asks us to assign the performance part of the content by actually reading and understanding all the words. Only the stanza divisions (marked by capital letters) provide guidance. It is a bit like a musical score. Some of how the poem goes, and what it means, is up to the reader. It needs to be performed, even when being read silently. It has to be *understood*: for instance, that the words "dere hert howe like you this" follow the word "saide," and so are a quotation, and are said by the "she" of this stanza. "It was no dreme" does not belong to her, even though it is conceivable she says this too: partly because it makes less sense than giving these words to the poet, and partly because "It" begins a new stanza, and so, in parallel with the transition between the first and second stanzas, the scene of the previous stanza has come to an end and a new scene (continued "talking" by the poet) has begun.

So this version of the poem has less written out than a typical modern version. The missing punctuation represents, in a very simple and very noticeable way, the parts of the poem that are lost to time: the turn of Wyatt's head, the tone of the words she says to him. The words written out on Wyatt's page record a sort of basic structure, to which live people have always added live, performed touches. In the modern version, an editor (a person I will come to, later) has added these touches with inserted marks of punctuation.

The absence of punctuation makes a big difference, but how important is this difference? I will consider this more thoroughly as I follow our poem on through the centuries. For the moment I will simply declare this loss of information unavoidable, one of the results of time's continual passing. Wyatt, his gestures and his way of speaking all passed away: his lovers and friends, and Henry VIII, and Anne Boleyn, are all dead.

It is impossible to be certain about the relationship between our performance of this poem (whether we do it ourselves or let the editor help us) and a performance by Wyatt, say, in 1537. We can only do our best, putting quotation marks where they seem to be needed, learning as best we can about this long-ago world. Large cannons of scholarship must be trained on this delicate cultural songbird before we can even decide what letters are written on the page, who wrote them, and who invented them.

Indirection

Wyatt does not say who "she" is, and he does not say, exactly, what "they" are who roam so seductively in the first stanza. Some poets, still not telling, will award their lover an abstract name. In another poem, Wyatt addresses "Phillis," a Greek name taken from the long tradition of lover's poetry, and Wyatt is conceivably using this name as a cover for a real person. But here there is not even that sort of general specificity. They roam; she takes him in her arms; he grows bitter. Wyatt is careful with his naming, indicating only that Something is there, not exactly who or what, and this is interesting, since in other ways he is so direct and intimate, telling us details about himself and about his lover.

The Duke of Suffolk's poem is also indirect. The manuscript in which we find it titles it simply "Compleynt." It could be a lover who has abandoned the poet: or it could be good fortune, either as an abstraction or as personified in his sovereign (for instance). Wyatt's indirection is very clearly of this old type, but Wyatt's inflection of the momentum of poetic history makes it different. The intensified, personal drama in "They Flee from Me" sharply emphasizes Wyatt's refusal to name names. Wyatt makes his resistance to naming feel like more than a poetic habit, since he gives everything *but* the name. He shows her arms, her feelings, her seductive ways, her independence; he describes her in both intimate and real-feeling ways, but he doesn't say her name.

The suggestive distance in Wyatt's little drama is partly the result of the intervening five hundred years, but it is mostly the result of the indirection of the poem itself, its evocative summoning of nouns into an abstract space that encourages imagining (almost) anything about them. The poem was already not telling Who Did It when Wyatt's secretary wrote out the fair copy for his master's approval.

What Wyatt Meant

Poetry was a basic counter in the daily life of the courtier in Henry's court. Its performance, frequently as song accompanied by music, was a basic staple of interaction and a common public event. That these poems were so frequently about love and courtship derives primarily from long traditions in court life (and hence literary life) in which power, and ambition for power, are represented as love relationships between men and women. This inherited mode was naturalized, of course, by the sincere interest people have in love and by the frequency with which people fall in love.

Such poetry could serve many different functions at once. It could declare the actual love of one person for another in beautiful and evocative ways; it could add a sophisticated luster to a poet who was capable of describing himself or his loved one beautifully and evocatively. Poetry could advance the career of a courtier by demonstrating his facility with language, his knowledge of old books and literature, his social tact. A poem could flatter those in power with compliments made easier to accept by being targeted at some fictional person; poems could make such compliments directly. A courtier could complain about ill fortune or bad treatment in ways made safer by being hidden as complaints about fictional love disappointments; a poet could rehearse events in his personal life or at court in a style that cushioned their reality by distancing such events into fiction and decorating them with fancy, abstract, and traditional language. A poet could construct a public persona through poems, presenting himself as manly, superior to women, inferior to particular women, or emotional in accepted and closely prescribed ways.

In particular, during this time, poetry was an especially effective mode for courtiers and other public personalities to declare what sort of mixture of independence and subservience the powerful would find in them. Poems about love relationships, naturally full of discussions of dominance, service, and submission, were easily adapted to this task.

Poetry in Henry's court performed, in other words, the same functions cultural objects in general have always performed, but with a force and focus peculiar to us, since we don't typically use poetry in this way. Whatever Wyatt was after, it was likely to have been quite specific. The circle he was writing for was, by our standards, extremely small and mutually entwined. As he was composing, Wyatt could probably have named almost all the people likely to soon encounter his poem in its oral or written form: on the order of tens. If etching interesting new patterns into the already detailed surface of the rhyme-royal poem seems a little like working in code, then at least he had a group of people around him who knew the code. This group would have been intimately acquainted with the details of Wyatt's personal life, so if there had been a lover who had abandoned him, or if Henry had twitched the reins in a new and arbitrary direction, Wyatt's audience would have known (something) about it.

That is: in reading or listening, this poem's nearly total indirection would have produced not bafflement but the delicious, cozy tickle that comes from being In the Know. "They Flee from Me" takes advantage of energized intimacy by rewarding those who know and (necessarily) excluding those who do not. The reward is a personal disclosure on the part of an interesting man. I am Thomas Wyatt, the poem says: these are my skills, these are (or might be) my woes, my raw thoughts, my frustrations and hopes. But in this poem self-assertion, of the sort required from an ambitious courtier, is also elegantly placed within the curiously self-deprecating tale the poem actually tells, a story that does not reflect simple glory on the teller.

This self-presentation (might well have) had power at court. Several messages are being sent. Wyatt shows himself to be "deep witted" (as was said of him after his death), a person capable of finely divided states of feeling and thought. He also shows himself willing to tell tales, so people working with him at court would have to stay alert and prepare to appear in a poem after the fact. He shows himself capable of an unpleasant and potentially troublesome sort of bitterness, the sort of bitterness that might make victims if given the means or the opportunity. He also shows himself capable of a beautiful sort of restraint at the same time. Bitterness, yes, and the details of the bedroom, sure, but no names, nothing to hang a trial on, nothing to lose your head over, just the scent reality leaves behind after exiting the room by the window or the door. And yet more: in his mastery of the traditional language of the court, in his easy mix of obedience and innovation, he makes himself an arbiter of taste, a "maker," to use the old term, of language and culture.

Imagine that terrifying man Henry VIII (or someone else, but someone looking for evidence), leafing through this book as Wyatt sat in the Tower (for the second time) in early 1541, accused of treason by a former diplomatic colleague, lamenting the fall of his longtime protector Thomas Cromwell, who some months previously had been beheaded in the courtyard, supposedly saying Wyatt's name with his last breath. Looking over the poems, Henry would see nothing to incriminate Wyatt directly in anything. He would see Wyatt's keen self-awareness, Wyatt's understanding of his change in fortune, his bitterness and his regret and his "gentleness." But Henry would also see Wyatt's talent for indirection, for veiled threat, for elegant language and sharp discernment: the skills of a diplomat. He would be able to admire Wyatt's fluent command of the traditions and language of the court, traditions Henry valued very highly and in which he played an active, creative part. He would see Wyatt's delight in simultaneous subservience and mastery.

He (or someone else) would see, in other words, a formidable man, a useful man, a complicated and intriguing man: a man capable of the subtlest tasks, a man worth having around.

Influence, Effluence

The future is hidden, and the past disappears behind us. We can sometimes control a moment, and certainly one of the pleasures of poems like "They Flee from Me" is the control they exert and exude, the small victory they post over time and isolation. Wyatt may insist on uncertainty, but he does it carefully and eloquently. His poem is about how confusing other people can be and how obscure the world sometimes feels, but it is not itself confused. It says what happened. It knows that much, and it keeps this particular present from disappearing in time. When Wyatt writes "Tho.," he is celebrating his small victory over confusion, forgetting, and the chaos of everyday life.

In marking the poem as Right, as finished, Wyatt fends off and cancels other, perhaps hypothetical versions of the poem that would be wrong. Not any of those, he says: *this* one. But even as Wyatt stamps this version with his approval, culture has caught his poem up and is whirling it away from him. In making his poem visible to others, in making it an object in the world, Wyatt has ensured it will escape him.

Sharing and the Manuscript World

Mary Howard and Her Friends

Mary Howard, sister of Wyatt's protégé Henry Howard, Earl of Surrey, member of one of the most powerful families in England, and wife to Henry Fitzroy, illegitimate son of Henry VIII, had a manuscript in which she and her friends wrote down poems. It is now a small, elegantly bound book; it was initially, perhaps, like Wyatt's book, an unbound set of blank pages, assembled in the early 1530s. Eventually it was full of poems, many of them by Thomas Wyatt, written down by many different hands (none of these hands are Wyatt's). At some point, perhaps relatively soon, the book passed on to Mary's friend Margaret Douglas, niece to Henry VIII and grandmother to James I. During the 1530s, Margaret Douglas was briefly, and secretly, married to Thomas Howard, Mary's half uncle. This book is now usually called the "Devonshire Manuscript," after one of its (much later) homes; its current home is the British Library, where it is "Add MS 17492."

The circle of friends who used this book participated in the full, deadly array of the pains and pleasures of Henry's reign; they were at its very center and epicenter. They were closely associated with Anne Boleyn (Mary Howard was Anne's cousin), and the year that brought her execution (1536) saw Wyatt captive in the Tower as one of her suspected lovers. Wyatt's sister was also there, attending Anne. The year 1536 also saw the death of Henry Fitzroy, Mary Howard's husband, and Margaret Douglas and Thomas Howard imprisoned for their secret marriage (Thomas Howard died in the Tower a year later).

The poems this circle included in the book are typical of the time, full of complaints about changing fortune, full of faithless lovers and steadfast hearts, constructed out of the language of the court and traditional court poetry, and marked by the basic indirection and lack of naming visible in Wyatt's poem. The deep conventionality of this poetry might tempt us to forget what interest naming names would have, in the volatile circumstances of their lives, what a faithless lover could mean and do, and what cost might be paid for faith. When Anne Boleyn, her brother and others were arrested, they were asked for names, for details of assignations, for proof of steadfast love or fickle affection. Death attended on the answers. Wyatt escaped, as did Margaret Douglas, but since most of the charges were invented anyway, it isn't clear why.

This circle was using poetry as a part of their daily lives. They could have used it as a consolation or a comfort; it may be that they used it as a sort of light entertainment. Poetry was undoubtedly part of the continuous jockeying for power and favor that was their daily business. A poem like "They Flee From Me" would not, of course, offer them comfort of a simple sort. It dramatizes the kinds of events that at least in theory led to Anne's execution, but it does not offer wisdom or consolation. It describes a wandering lover and rehearses a troubled way of thinking that could also describe the vengeful Henry as he pursued his vendetta against the Boleyns.

Many pages in the Devonshire Manuscript are devoted to the relationship between Lord Thomas Howard and Margaret Douglas, containing many poems and extracts expressing their steadfast love and their faithful devotion during their imprisonment. It turns out several of these "poems" are actually extracts from older poems; one of them (on 29v), for instance, consists of a few stanzas taken from the fourth book of Chaucer's *Troilus and Criseyde*, with Criseyde's name erased and space left by the copyist to replace it with another's (presumably Margaret's, but it wasn't filled in). The stanza is, of course, rhyme royal:

The space for Lady Margaret's name is in the fifth line: "Syns ye [Criseyde] and me have fully brought / Into your grace. . . . " This poetic carpentry demonstrates perfectly and crisply the role poetry played in Henrician culture. *Troilus and Criseyde* is a very long poem and was much admired by this set of people. It had recently reappeared in William Thynne's edition of Chaucer in 1532. In Chaucer's poem Troilus is bewailing his fate and protesting his faithfulness. Margaret Douglas and Thomas Howard were real people, and their trials and imprisonment quite real. Troilus is an imaginary character, his lover a fiction, his woes an invention, his faithfulness an abstract ideal: and these inventions are woven together in a very involved and deeply conventional story set in an ancient and distant past. The user of poetry responsible for this stanza's extraction on this page (Thomas Howard, say, giving orders to a secretary, in the Tower with him, or someone else) knew all that, and yet he wanted to merge his thoughts with the language of the old poem in this way.

This extraction and very slight adaptation is a minor version of what Wyatt does. Howard and Margaret inflect tradition in their direction, make it say something about them. They show themselves (to others using the book, and to themselves) to be part of an ongoing and evolving culture. They demonstrate not only their faithfulness to each other but also their elegance, their literate feelings, their mastery of an inherited culture, and the faith they have in that culture as a vehicle for their feelings. In the face of Henry's declaration that their secret marriage was not legal (Margaret was a plausible heir to the crown: she needed Henry's permission to marry) and the abrupt removal of their court status, they declare who they are. They are lovers, yes, and steadfast; but they are also courtly virtuosos, declaring their worth and claiming their contested, tenuous place in the structure of power.

Another Home

In other places in the book we now call the Devonshire Manuscript, poems are put to work in plainer ways. Another member of the circle and user of the book, Mary Shelton (whose Aunt Madge was briefly Henry's mistress in the last days of Anne Boleyn, and who was herself the lover of the Earl of Surrey's friend Thomas Clere), marks several poems in ways that appear to be preparations for performances of various sorts, including singing. So the book was also, at some point, used as a kind of handbook for courtly life, a source of the small structures of emotions and words around which important parts of court life were built. Many poems in Wyatt's book were copied into this book, as on these pages, 69v–70r as the British Library now counts them:

"They Flee from Me" begins at the bottom left and continues onto the right-hand page. Transcribing into our letters out of the old hand yields this:

Theye fle from me that some tyme ded me seke
wᵗ nakid fote stalking yn my chamber /
I have sene theim bothe gentill tame and meke
that now are wyld and do not remembre
that some tyme theye put them self in daunger
to take brede at my hand and nowe theye Rainge,
beselye seking contynuall change /
Thanckid be fortune yt hath bene othrewise
twentye tymes better / but ons in esspiall
in thyne arraye / after a pleᵃsaunt guise
when her loose gowne from her shulders ded fall
and she me caught in her armes long and small
but therewᵗall swetely she ded me kysse
and softelye saide dere herte how lyke you this
yt was no dreame · for I laye brod waking

but all is toᶠnid thorowe my gentilness
ynto a sraunge fasshen of forsaking
and I have leve to parte of her goodness
and she likewise to vse newfangleness
but sins yᵗ I so gentillye am seruid·
what think you bye this yᵗ she hat deserued /

Is this "They Flee from Me"? Yes, certainly, but there are several differences from the poem in Wyatt's book. Some of these differences seem important immediately, like the substitution of "gentillye" for "kyndely" in the second-to-last line, and the wholesale rewriting of the last line. Less immediate but still noticeable is the way in which Wyatt's characteristic rhythmic movement has been smoothed away by deletions and additions. The lines now all have ten syllables, and the places where Wyatt's poem most obviously accumulates over some emotional and rhythmic hitch are gone, as in the fifteenth line, where the "for" now helps us over the deep pause. There is much to say about this new, obviously very closely related poem, the simplest of which is that the poem Wyatt wrote has left home and commenced a life away from its maker.

It is now an object and a conceptual structure unsponsored by Wyatt's initials, or his voice and his hooded eyes. It is a house for thought and can be modified to fit the current user, in the same way the copyist took the stanzas from Chaucer and blanked out Criseyde's name. This is not how Wyatt wanted the poem to be at the moment he signed his initials. In our own day, if the poem had been stamped with the modern authorization of copyright, the changes made might even be considered a kind of crime, a disturbance of the author's intellectual property. This was not even remotely true in Tudor England. The practice of changing poems as they circulated from hand to hand in these manuscripts was not only common but highly valued as one of the activities the poems made possible. Readers—users—would change poems because they wanted to.

Wyatt stamps one particular version of his poem with his initials, and this is interesting and very unusual. His authorization is in the same category as his quirky personalizing of the genre of the love lyric in "They Flee from Me." There is more of him in his poems than expected, but in spite of this unusual interest in authenticity, Wyatt was a central figure in a culture that shared poems continually. He would not have been surprised to see his poem (if he ever saw it) quietly adapted to the taste or purposes of the compilers of this book.

The Poem, Out and About

The beautiful sheet on which "They Flee from Me" appears in Thomas Wyatt's book, marked with the simple "Tho.," makes it doubtful that he was behind the changes we find in the Devonshire Manuscript. He certainly approved of the version in his book, and there is nothing to offset this certainty. Besides, the changes in the Devonshire version result in a poem that seems somewhat unlike him and the poems known (through his mark) to have been finished under his eye. It is impossible to say with any certainty who did make the changes, though we can name some of those who might have seen them (Margaret Douglas, Mary Howard, Mary Shelton, and a few others—perhaps the Earl of Surrey). Whoever it was, they had something in mind. It is carefully and purposefully done. Why did they make these particular changes? What effect were they after?

The smoothing out of the rhythm is striking. In a plain way, Wyatt's variable metrics are his most intimate effect, the characteristic of his poetry that most identifies him. He seems to have been quite committed to this effect and took some pains to build it in. The poetry of Henry Howard, the Earl of Surrey (Mary's brother), closely associated with Wyatt's in later eras, is famously smoother than Wyatt's. Later readers admire Howard for accomplishing this smoothness, for "improving" Wyatt's methods. The Devonshire version of our poem is the first evidence of an improving method, of the imposition of a taste that will characterize the great Elizabethan flowering of lyric a few decades on. So this change looks to the future; but since these changes are made by someone who knew Wyatt, who was his clear contemporary, these changes also emphasize that it is not only later readers who would perceive Wyatt's curiously assertive individuality. With history between us, and with Elizabethan verse doing the mediating, we notice the seemingly purposeful roughness of Wyatt's poetry: but so did his friends.

Replacing "kyndely" with "gentillye" is striking. "Gentillye" ties this moment, when the poet's bitterness appears most clearly, to his description of himself as treating his lover with "gentilnes" a few lines earlier, and to the "gentill" beings of the first stanza. The sarcastic edge remains, but the mood is made more simply poetic, since it makes the way she has treated him symmetrical with way he treated her. Wyatt's idiosyncratic accumulation of meaning in "kyndely" is replaced by a word more clearly part of a poetic design. The person who made this replacement had a sharp ear. The intent, personal aggravation of "kyndely" seems to have been experienced as a kind of clog; this change clears the slowdown and smooths the structure of the poem as a whole.

The substantial change to the last line is a bit more puzzling, since it does not make for a totally different sense than the original: it seems, at first, mostly just a different wording. It is more "countable" metrically, with its succession of ten (rather than nine) alternating syllables, but it is not particularly smooth in effect. It pointedly avoids the three plunks of "would fain knowe," a distinctly Wyatt-like effect. It also avoids the "I" in Wyatt's painfully direct final voicing of (uncertain) feeling, and this was perhaps what the Changer was after.

In a general way these changes make the poem less distinctive and less noticeably the voice of Thomas Wyatt. They remove some of the ways through which Wyatt made his poem embody "actual" feeling, the ways in which he built in the immediacy that makes the poem seem so much like the real effusion of a real person. These changes make the poem slightly more general. They make the poem slightly easier for someone other than Wyatt to use.

Indirection, as a style and a way of poetic thinking in poetry in English, begins here in the dangerous courts of England, where a misspoken name or an unguarded bitter accusation could lead to disaster. Indirection is a natural solution to the high-stakes game of saying what you feel—something the courtly lover was bound by tradition to do—without losing your head. Wyatt's indirection in "They Flee from Me" deflects the poem quietly and compellingly toward himself. The changes of Mary Howard and her friends equally quietly de-deflect it. They make it slightly easier to insert some other Self into the lonely chamber Wyatt builds and inhabits.

At the center of the courtier's art, and at the heart of the worldview of the social circle this book inhabited, is an understanding that all will be overheard and used. Wyatt writes his poem knowing it will be overheard; it is introspection, but introspection rehearsed in front of an audience. It was written *so that* it might be overheard. He runs down his arch list of complaint, confession, and error so indirectly that no one will be called out by it or will feel so immediately exposed that action will be necessary. He indicts her, but he also identifies with her. Wyatt might even score some points (with someone) by being so publicly clever about private agony, so good at negotiating and describing the deadly ins and outs of court life. What looks to us like an intimately personal poetic style is also fundamentally a public style, a way of doing a certain sort of public work.

Wyatt distinguishes himself by the slight twist he gives to the deeply conventional lyric of courtly love. While this twist toward a subtle picture of the self becomes the very quality that most distinguishes the long history of lyric in

English, it was a new trick for Wyatt's audience. And so someone notices: the poem in Mary Howard's book has been slightly untwisted.

That "They Flee from Me" was put into Mary Howard's book at all indicates it was not taken as a simple anomaly. Wyatt was a celebrated poet, and so whatever effort his readers had to make in order to use his poetry, they were clearly able and willing to do it. Beyond this, while the changes in the poem make it less intensely personal, it is still dramatically personal: its intimacy is in all its parts, and eradicating that quality would leave very little of what Wyatt put in. That was not the aim of the person who put it in Mary Howard's book. This person liked the poem, found it interesting and useful in the daily life this book accompanied (with some small changes).

The Smudge

At the beginning of our poem as it is entered in Mary Howard's book, between the first two lines, is a smudge. If you take out the book itself, turn to this page, and look through a magnifying glass, you can see it for what it is. It is a fingerprint, that well-known, court-verified marker of individuality.

Sometime in the 1530s a person wrote out "They Flee from Me" on this page, and in the process got ink on her finger and left this print. It identifies someone, but without the finger, long since turned to dust, we cannot say who. All we see is this sign of individuality, a mark showing us that Someone was here, writing, thinking. It is a heart-rending trace of the lost world of this poem.

This fingerprint is an appropriate mark of the peculiar nature of "They Flee from Me." Much Tudor poetry is literally unidentifiable: we don't know who wrote it with any reliability, and it is noticeably undistinguished stylistically. It is poetry made from the seamless voice of court traditions. Wyatt's poetry is sometimes different, marked with his personality and his idiosyncrasies, and his friends and general contemporaries felt the need to clean some of it off.

The specific identity we detect in Wyatt's poems, his fingerprint, will bother people reading his poems for a long time.

Yours or Mine?

The lyric poem in English is being created in Wyatt's poetry, and especially in a poem like "They Flee from Me." Born out of the intimately shared culture of Henry's court into a world where the border between the personal and the public was especially fluid, this poem, in its two versions, looks like a working-out-in-progress of the fundamental nature of the short poem. Deeply personal, the poem is picked up and used by other people for (presumably) personal purposes. Is the poem in Mary Howard's book Wyatt's poem still, or is it now someone else's? This question is a practical version of a more fundamental one: When we read and think about the poem, is the emotion and thought in it Wyatt's or ours?

Both, it is relatively easy to say, partly because we have the history of poetry behind us. The slight tensions between the versions in Wyatt's book and in Mary Howard's book indicate that Wyatt and his audience did not find balancing between self and other easy or intuitive. If this seems slightly clumsy of them, they compensate by taking poetry very seriously on a daily basis. The worry over the personal nature of Wyatt's poem indicates its interest and points to the vitality of poetry in this culture. The performance of the self in Tudor poetry is *interesting*.

Behind the changes in Mary Howard's book are some of the fundamental purposes and qualities of the short poem in English and some of the distinctive ways in which this poetry has been put to use. The sharing of intimate reflection in poems became common, over the centuries, and evidence suggests we now find painstakingly intimate, overtly sincere personal revelations interesting, at least in poetry. Familiarity obscures how it happened, and, more particularly, how it is done: how personal feeling is turned into public property by using traditional and familiar modes, creating a shared emotional form we fit ourselves into as we read.

"They Flee from Me" and its contexts show how it was done. The feeling and thought in the poem are packaged in a carefully made semitraditional box so someone else can make it theirs. They are also interestingly and intently personalized, and Wyatt's audience noticed this and made slight, careful adjustments. That most modern editions of Wyatt have returned to the text of the poem Wyatt initialed suggests that we find it easier to fit ourselves into poems and that we no longer need to cushion our contact with the personal as the users of Mary Howard's book did.

Putting aside contemporary notions of intellectual property, and shrugging off even Thomas Wyatt's authorization of one version, a full description of our poem, at this point in its career, would include both versions, and others that have no doubt been lost over the centuries. The poem's variety is a sign of its vitality and its utility.

The Elite

"They Flee from Me" is part of a conversation among the wealthiest and most powerful people in Henry's England. There were important and powerful people who were not part of this circle, but Wyatt's circle was at the very center of inherited Tudor power. Taking Holbein's series of portrait drawings, done throughout the 1530s, as an idiosyncratic sort of census, there were about one hundred people in this immediate social set. All of the important people I have mentioned so far (except Chaucer) are connected together by birth or marriage. They could all be included in a relatively simple family tree.

I could—I probably should—describe the poetry of Wyatt and other courtiers as a self-satisfied code spoken by this elite group. The form of the poems, and the traditional vocabulary they deploy, amount to a kind of dialect, learned by these few, shared among them, and used only by them. In this sense their practice of poetry is the celebration and rehearsal of a code separating Insiders from Outsiders. The primary source of this kind of practice is the need to articulate and celebrate inherited court culture and the values court culture entailed, as a way of maintaining them. The poems in Mary Howard's book are thus both proof of courtly accomplishment and also models for that accomplishment: a handbook, in the plainest sense. So when "They Flee from Me" escaped from Wyatt's supervision and took up residence with Mary Howard and her friends, it had not really gone very far. It moved within a very clearly and even carefully defined area defined by the boundaries of inherited court culture. Even the notion of this (small) movement was built in from the start.

At this point, our poem's whole life is inside this elite world. If you wished to read or hear Wyatt's poems in 1540, you would need to look inside Mary Howard's book (or its equivalent; there were very likely other similar books about), or you would need to attend one of the functions for which Mary Shelton marked certain of the poems to be sung. If you were not part of this circle, or related to someone within, it simply could not be done. None of these poems were published in the modern sense, none were meant to be seen by people who could not with some immediacy understand them, and this restriction would not have bothered Thomas Wyatt.

The expressive modes of Tudor lyric poetry are built from the details of a relatively arcane cultural inheritance. Without this inheritance, and an energetic and attentive shared sense of its relevance, these poems simply could not be born, and the space for them in culture would not exist either. Their very substance is built from inclusion and its evil twin, exclusion.

Other Tudor circles had their forms: popular songs (ballads among them, at this time) were incubated and created within nonliterate communities; delicate religious forms thrived among the choirs of the Universities: and so on. All of these depend for their conception on some set of shared conventions, the private language spoken by people inside a group to others inside that group. But

Wyatt's circle coincided with the exercise of power and was accessible only to the very wealthiest and best-educated people in England. Understanding this poetry depended on books and education, still very rare and expensive cultural commodities, and on European forms, accessible only to those who could learn those languages and travel. Only the ruling elite had these things, knew these things, and had these opportunities.

The association of the short expressive English lyric with the social elite turns out to be an enduring one. This association will not weaken until education and access to deep literacy become something other than a monopoly of the elite. The association with social elites continually qualifies what the lyric does and how it will be treated as time goes on.

A social elite associated with the exercise of power in Henry's England invented the short lyric. They invented it for themselves and shared it enthusiastically among themselves. They did not want to share it with others.

Death, Sleep, Forgetting

The two books now called the Egerton Manuscript (Wyatt's book) and the Devonshire Manuscript (Mary Howard's book) cast a wonderfully bright light onto the birth and early life of "They Flee from Me." In these books, in the life they echo and record, this poem is seen leading an active life, hand in hand with the daily life of its creator and his friends, the people he created it for.

Thomas Wyatt, rehabilitated after the fall of his friend and protector Thomas Cromwell (for a decade the most powerful of Henry's inner circle), died suddenly from a fever in the midst of his ambassadorial duties in 1542, when he was still a young man. At least he met his death through natural causes. From the mid-1530s on, the mortality rate among men (and occasionally women) close to Henry is quite appalling. Death and the scattering of families that follows upon death decimate the group that shared these poems. Its terminus might be put in 1547, when Henry Howard was executed, or 1554, when Wyatt's son was beheaded. Henry Howard, the other truly accomplished poet in this circle, whose graceful elegy marks Wyatt's death, was one of the last people Henry killed: his father, the Duke of Norfolk, survived because Henry VIII himself died before he could kill Norfolk too. Wyatt's son, called by history Thomas Wyatt the Younger, was at the center of the plot to put Lady Jane Grey on the throne in 1554, over which plot he too lost his head. It is quite possible his father's poetry book accompanied Wyatt the Younger during his last days in the Tower, on what could have been its second or even third visit, the first being in 1540 (and/or 1536) with his father.

People pass away, along with their feelings, their way of talking, the hopes and harmonies that made up their days: their things pass away too, their houses fall down, their books turn to dust. Sometimes their children pass away and so even their genetic descent to the future is cut short. The vital, terrifying, and thrilling way of life into which Wyatt introduced "They Flee from Me" passed away like everything else, hurried off the stage by executions and the change of regimes, by decrepitude, by Henry's Reformation, by the flames of Queen Mary's reign.

In the 1550s the object-part of the poem is just sitting there. The poet that would fain knowe what she hath deserved has been dead for fifteen years, but his "I" remains written out in the pages of these books. Their leaves lie compressed, one poem on top of another, the work of a lifetime collected into an inch or so of paper. These books are no longer handbooks for daily life. The writing in them has turned into memorials of that life.

As a memorial, the energy of our poem has been reversed. Instead of being generated by a way of life, it now generates that life, if an eye or ear will come to read or hear. Most everything has been washed away by time except the hardest bits, the words themselves and the tiny structure of meaning they can create within their elegant and now outmoded box. Some of the life of Thomas Wyatt and his friends is now compressed in there, saved, but asleep as long as no one is using the poems.

Its immediate work done, the poem is now poised between life and death. It mediates the memory of Wyatt: words of that dead man, words that at this time can still speak to (be seen by) people who remember Wyatt, who spoke to him, perhaps loved or hated him, if they know where to look. This attachment of the words to Wyatt the man depends (in 1555) entirely on living memory, since in their books the two versions of the poem are not labeled as Wyatt's in any way that someone who did not already know them to be Wyatt's would find it easy to decode. Even "Tho." doesn't say much if we don't know Thomas already: there are a lot of Toms. The books are also by now relatively far away from their origins and original owners, and their original purpose is being diluted daily by other people's needs and the inclusion of other sorts of material. The object itself, the poem as written in the physical books, is dangerously close to insignificance, to the kind of invisibility that leads to destruction.

Why did it not vanish into time, like all speaking? It is a dense and intense description of the feelings of a dead person. Even when we dignify it further by making it the record of the complicated exchanges of power and identity of its world, it still describes a small event in a dead past.

That it does not vanish, that people have not wanted it to vanish, is a sign that the poem contains something other than the voice of a person talking to himself and his friends. It is a sign of the poem's capacity to talk to people *other* than the poet and his friends, in worlds far away in space and time. The lyric is not fully formed as long as it stays in the hands of its creators, and this first limited natal stage is what is dying away as "They Flee from Me" quietly lives on in the two books. Only after a sleep and a forgetting, after its everyday functioning has passed away, does the lyric become the powerful expressive mode we inherit.

Overhearing, Indirection, and Outsiders

To whom is he speaking when he begins, "They flee from me. . . . "? To his audience, certainly, but that describes the outside of the poem, its presence in an actual world putting the poem to use. The poem itself does not dramatize this speaking directly by addressing the audience, as many an older poem does: "listen, lordlings, and you will hear. . . . "

Wyatt's poem does not dramatize the hearing because his poem is meant to be overheard, not heard. We are listening in. The poet is speaking to himself, in a way people sometimes do speak (or write) to themselves, though perhaps in an unusually detailed way. He is speaking to himself in the way Hamlet, seventy years later, speaks to himself when he says, "To be or not to be. . . . " The high artificiality of the moment (rhymed words and counted syllables, conventional vocabulary) paradoxically heightens its seeming sincerity. The artificiality becomes a sign of the sincerity of the expression because it makes clear that Wyatt has thought hard about it, that this is serious. It is not a randomly selected part of an ongoing inner monologue. This is a staged, coherent overhearing, an overhearing of private thought adapted and shaped so it makes sense and then dramatized—turned into a story—so it feels like the sudden outpouring of feeling.

We can overhear Wyatt because, knowing that we are (someone is) listening, he talks in a special way, and when the poem was written, people really were listening, for good and for ill. The poem's indirection, the way specific persons are represented only as "she" and "he," is important for our ability to overhear. The protection provided by this abstraction turns out to make the poem ready for travel. There are many products of in-circles, of court cultures, that are not this way and so get lost in time because we really have lost the keys to their codes.

In the midst of its sleep, captive in the two books, "They Flee from Me" is simply waiting for new eyes and ears. It was written knowing it would be overheard, and the deep indirection of its reference turns out to only make it easier for Outsiders to imagine their way into the scene the poem represents: a paradoxical side effect of its adaptation to the deadly intimacy of its birthplace.

Summary: The Language of the Self

All court culture, all in-circles all over the world, have created and still create intricate rituals and protocols of communication and representation; often, all over the world, these have taken the form of poetry. The language and forms of Tudor poetry, which are a shared inheritance for the members of Henry's court, allow the users of Tudor court poetry to talk to each other in a special, intimate way. At every level this poetry is made from shared elements of culture. It does not, precisely, belong to its authors or speakers. The authors borrow words and forms for the moment, putting them to use in specific but not-really-new ways. The poetry Wyatt inherited (and changed) was a group possession, and its job was to connect author and listeners, and listeners with other listeners, through the medium of shared culture and group identity.

Wyatt's special talent, and his innovation, was for performing this group culture with a fascinating mixture of shared values and idiosyncratic inflection. His poems carried the messages of the shared culture, but they also carried with them a fine grain of personal feeling. He found (specific) ways of making his poems both functionally shared and intensely personal. So there is paradox at the heart of the kind of poetry that Wyatt invented and that we inherit from him. Through an intensification of the personal, private feel of the poetry, Wyatt made his poems a better, more exciting medium for the exchange of thought between his friends. By becoming more private, his poems become more social.

It also appears his audience found this effect somewhat disconcerting as well as fascinating. The small changes Mary Howard's circle made to "They Flee from Me" lessen the charge of individuality a bit. Their changes turn down the intensity. They don't turn it down all the way. What is left is still different from the poetry Wyatt inherited.

When they are written down, these poems take their place in the material world, along with all other objects. They become self-sufficient, and they become capable of wandering away from their makers. This is another unforeseen side effect, the side effect of writing, almost the opposite of the original intent.

Through the side effects of objecthood, combined with the side effects of its fundamental indirection, "They Flee from Me" becomes capable of outliving its immediate function, its makers, and its world. Asleep in its books, the poem is also ready to jump. First, and most importantly, it jumps to a printer named

Richard Tottel. From the printed page, "They Flee from Me" will travel the globe. It was written to be overheard, and it was.

The World of Print
Release

Richard Tottel was a maker of books who was well known in his day, long-lived and very successful. He printed many books (most of them law books), but we remember him primarily for just one, first published in 1557, the book often called *Tottel's Miscellany*, but actually carrying the title *Songes and Sonettes, written by the ryght honorable Lorde Henry Haward late Earle of Surrey, and other.* "They Flee from Me"—or, rather, another version of it—awakens from its sleep by appearing in this book, in a section labeled as the poems of Wyatt.

Between 1547, when Surrey was beheaded after a residence in the Tower and his property was divided among his enemies, and 1557, when Tottel's book appeared, the Tower welcomed many large groups of distinguished people, many of them associated with either the house of Seymour or the Howard family. Henry Howard lost his life in the conflict between these families over the form the Regency would take after the death of Henry VIII. It is possible that Thomas Wyatt's book passed from Thomas Wyatt to his son and thence to Henry Howard (they were close friends), and from Howard to a man named John Harington, a loyal retainer of the Seymour family, as part of the spoils distributed after Howard's execution. It would make for a bitterly interesting story. Hard to say: but by the late 1550s the book seems to be in the hands of John Harrington, a veteran of Henry's court and a friend of Thomas Wyatt's son. Harington and Wyatt the Younger were both confined in the Tower after the rebellion in 1554; the Seymours and Howards were now united in opposition to Mary. John Harington used Wyatt's book, and it remained in the hands of the Harington family for more than two hundred years.

The Tower serves, during Tudor times, as a curious sort of anticourt, where those out of favor gather together with a lot of leisure time on their hands. As happens during tumultuous times, those out of favor look almost exactly like those in favor; only the location of their rooms tells the difference. And so in 1554 many distinguished and literate people (John Harington was one of Henry VIII's favorite musicians) gathered together in the Tower, a melancholy reproduction of the court they had hoped to displace, composing and reciting poetry. There is a continuing culture here: for much of the older poetry on hand either was itself composed in the Tower or was closely associated with the trials of people like Wyatt the Elder and Surrey, both of whom had been confined there.

In any case, from out of the mixture of people, memories, and loyalties going in and out of the fatal gates of the Tower at this time appears, in 1557, the collection of poems published by Richard Tottel. Through all their changing fortunes the Howards and the Wyatts remained powerful families, and it is conceivable one of them may have taken offense at the transformation from private to public property Tottel accomplishes. This is a risk Tottel had clearly either worked through or simply accepted. Judging from the poems in the book, Tottel seems to have had (or had access to) Wyatt's book, almost certainly; beyond that, the sources are mysterious and perhaps quite numerous.

Tottel's Miscellany is an important book. It helped form the taste of a very distinguished generation, the Elizabethan lyric poets, and it in effect created, in a broad way, the genre of the lyric poem as we know it. Insofar as the history of culture can be described as containing big events, the publication of Tottel's collection of poems was a Big Event: everything changed (everything to do with poetry). But the reason why this book changed everything is deeper than might at first appear. For when we focus on "the publication of these poems," it turns out that the critical part is not the stuff itself, the poems, but rather what has happened to them: publication.

Tottel's book is not simply the demonstration of a way of making poetry many people had not seen before (though it is that) but also the disclosure of a whole way of life, a way of thinking, a whole world that had been unavailable before, closed off within the walls of the court and within the covers of personal books. When Tottel published these poems, the privately held practice of courtly poetry, an activity pursued by the members of a group for their own entertainment, benefit, and pleasure, written down for their own purposes in their books, became a public commodity.

I don't think it diminishes the book to imagine the contribution a salacious sort of voyeurism made to its popularity. There was a famous name on its cover— the Earl of Surrey was quickly being turned into a sort of cult figure of courtly perfection—and the name of a recently executed and potentially heroic figure (Thomas Wyatt the Younger) inside, though the name belonged to that figure's father. The subject matter of the poems appears to be of a most intimate sort, and of a personal sort, but also general enough to be decipherable. Tottel's book contains many meditations on changing fortune, on love, loss, and despair, meditations that could be felt in specific ways by readers witnessing and participating in the terrors and shifting ground of Mary's last months. It was, in other words, juicy stuff, seemingly about important and exalted personalities, provided to an audience in a highly receptive state. They were informed enough to feel the content of the poems, remembering or knowing the names, but removed enough to believe almost anything about them.

Tales from High Life always have much the same charge, though the definition of "high" changes a bit. Even in our own topsy-turvy day such tales still need to be stolen somehow. They need to find their way out of the closed circles that generate and live their content; they need to be overheard somehow by someone in contact with both worlds, both the inside and the outside. This was even more true in Tudor times, when the circle of the elite was almost entirely closed off by wealth and literacy, among other powerful forces. Some people—and John Harington at least fits the description—who had a foot in both the high and the middle could conceivably carry something from the one to the other. Since personal property (the manuscript books) was at issue and famous and dangerous names were at the source, this transmission was not without its hazards. High life is exciting partly because it is actually dangerous, and in the Tudor era offending the wrong person could mean death.

We don't know who edited the poems for publication (it may have been Harington; it may have been one of the poets included, Nicholas Grimald; it may have been someone else) and we don't know who wrote the Preface to the book. For simplicity's sake I will name the people or person who did these things as "Richard Tottel." Tottel's Preface shows the stress of the project, both its danger and its unprecedented nature. It contains the description of a literature writ small, and so I will give the whole thing (with matters eased somewhat by modernized spelling):

> That to have well written in verse, yea and in small parcels, deserveth great praise, the works of diverse Latins, Italians, and other, do prove sufficiently. That our tongue is able in that kind to do as praiseworthy as the rest, the honorable style of the noble Earl of Surrey, and the weightiness of the deepwitted Sir Tomas Wyat the Elders verse, with several graces in sundry good English writers, do show abundantly. It resteth now (gentle reader) that thou think it not evil done, to publish, to the honor of the English tongue, and for profit of the studious of English eloquence, those works which the ungentle hoarders up of such treasure have heretofore envied thee. And for this point (good reader) thine own profit and pleasure, in these presently, and more hereafter, shall answer for my defense. If perhaps some mislike the stateliness of style removed from the rude skill of common ears: I ask help of their learned friends, the authors of this work: And

I exhort the unlearned, by reading to learn to be more skillful, and to purge that swinelike grossness, that maketh the sweet marjoram not smell to their delight.

All seems new here. Tottel even takes time to pick out the size of the poems with a little flourish: "yea, and in small parcels." In a way no one would have to after him, Tottel has to say why he is doing it: why he is publishing these records of an intimate circle of the past, why the poems might be interesting, why he is justified in kidnapping them from their private sanctuary and putting them on display, why, even though they will appear to be arcane and artificial, the reader should pay attention to and even like them. The instability or exposure of his position between high and regular life is neatly packed into the little Wyatt-like turn on "ungentle," in which he implies that the literally Gentle (the gentlefolk) are ungentle (unkind? selfish?) for keeping their accomplishments to themselves.

This is anxious play. Why should he insult the sources he is celebrating in his book? He looks especially uncertain when he descends moments later into typically rough sixteenth-century abuse of the very people on whose behalf he has rescued these poems, the (potentially) disgruntled common readers, cheerfully referring to their "swinelike grossness." In the end, the plain justification Tottel presents is both confusing and plain: the hoarders of these poems may be ungentle, but the swinelike reader can become more like them—as that reader must or should want to do—by reading their poems. Tottel's conceptual disorientation is entirely understandable. He is using other people's material, but what he does with this material amounts to a major creative act.

The poems become entirely different things when they appear in Tottel's book. Their shape is (largely) the same, but their function and their place in culture have changed fundamentally. They are no longer materials out of which a courtly way of life is built, or a career inflected, or a grab for power or status accomplished: all of this, even for Tottel, becomes a matter for historical reconstruction. Tottel's printing erases the last connections, which are the physical traces of objects: ink, writing, fingerprints, the paper, the material reality of the manuscripts, touched and carried by the creators. When a person holds Wyatt's book, she holds a thing Wyatt himself once held.

A printed book is completely different thing. The pages of the printed book show the trace of a printing press instead of a hand, and the letters are entirely standardized, repeating themselves precisely each time they appear. This generalized space, unmarked by the traces of individual people, creates new needs. Removed from the world that remembered them (the people who could say whose poems were whose), and from the pen's trace of individuality, Tottel must organize the book by labeling poems with their maker and by grouping them together. "Wyatt" becomes the label for a group of poems instead of a man. The book is finished when it is printed. It does not invite new arrangements or interpolations. It is a product, to be purchased.

Tottel gives the poems titles. We may not have noticed they did not have titles, before, but the lack of titling is as plain a characteristic in the manuscript books as the lack of punctuation. We can imagine the title, the "name" of the poem, was, like the punctuation, part of the continuing world of performance and personal contact. Why give it a title? "It is Wyatt's poem, the one that. . ." After printing, the poems are set loose into abstract space, without obvious origin or destination. They must be labeled, so as to make up for the lack of a personal introduction.

Reborn, and Captured

"They Flee from Me" appears a little way into the Wyatt section of Tottel's book:

When her loose gowne did from her shoulders fall,
And she me caught in her armes long and small,
And therwithall, so swetely did me kysse,
And softly sayd: deare hart, how like you this?
     It was no dreame: for I lay broade awakyng.
But all is turnde now through my gentlenesse,
Into a bitter fashion of forsakyng:
And I haue leaue to go of her goodnesse,
And she also to vse newfanglenesse.
But, sins that I vnkyndly so am serued:
How like you this, what hath she now deserued?

To a ladie to answere directly
          with yea or nay.   Madame

This is not handwriting, but it is old print (called "black-letter"), so it is still
helpful to transcribe it into our letters:

The louer sheweth how he is
forsaken of such as he somtime enioyed.

They flee from me, that somtime did me seke
With naked fote stalkyng within my chamber.
Once haue I seen them gentle, tame, and meke,
That now are wild, and do not once remember
That sometyme they haue put them selues in danger,
To take bread at my hand, and now they range,
Busily sekyng in continuall change.
Thanked be fortune, it hath bene otherwise
Twenty tymes better: but once especiall,
In thinne aray, after a pleasant gyse,
When her loose gowne did from her shoulders fall,
And she me caught in her armes long and small,
And therwithall, so swetely did me kysse,
And softly sayd: deare hart, how like you this?
It was no dreame: for I lay broade awakyng.
But all is turnde now through my gentlenesse.
Into a bitter fashion of forsakyng:

And I haue leaue to go of her goodnesse,
And she also to vse newfanglenesse.
But, sins that I vnkyndly so am serued:
How like you this, what hath she now deserued?

Our poem's escape from manuscript is emphasized by the title, both by its simple existence and in its content: not "Wyatt sheweth. . ." but "The lover sheweth. . ." No One is showing how he is forsaken; or Anyone is. The house of thought is ready for occupation by all lovers who may come to read; the door stands open (or partway open).

I pass over most of the changes from the poem in Wyatt's book, since by and large they strongly resemble the changes made in Mary Howard's book, smoothing out Wyatt's characteristically rough style. The thorough punctuation is entirely new, but not surprising, since Tottel needs to compensate for the loss of the performed environment. This is much less a score to be performed, much more a total product, a cultural commodity ready for general delivery.

The last two lines have again received renovation. The last line has been completely altered, as in Mary Howard's book; and in the previous line, the "kyndely," replaced in Mary Howard's book with "gentillye," has been changed to "unkyndly." This is a big change.

Gone is the bitter, prosaic, nearly-powerless snarl of the poem Wyatt approved, and the tangled encounter of the different senses of "kyndely." In Wyatt's poem this encounter is important, since in certain ways she really did treat him kindly, and he can very nearly admit it. That he can't really admit it is the source of the snarl. Even if we are offended by this erasure (on behalf of Thomas Wyatt, dead and unable to take offense, in 1557 as now), we should also remember that the psychological depth of this poem, the quality that makes it different and special, does not depend entirely on the multiplicity of "kyndely." But the psychological density of the poem in Wyatt's book is summarized and brought to a point in that word, in its tone and its several meanings.

Tottel's poem has been directed down one of the verbal paths created by Wyatt's multiple-mindedness. It has been directed down the least personal, or the least deeply personal: in Tottel's poem, Wyatt (or what we now must call "the speaker of the poem," since Tottel has called him "the lover") says what he is thinking, and he is thinking just one thing. His lover has been unkind. He is still a little mean, a little vengeful, but not particularly. The new last line, the airy chattiness of "How like you this, what hath she now deserued?" matches the simplification of the emotional state of the speaker.

The twisted, thickened personality of the poem is thus lost. Much is retained, especially the emotional and evocative texture of the first two stanzas, which is most of the poem's seductive power. But the small twists, the signatures of the man who made it, have been eased away. The not-yet-completed thinking of the nearly self-aware poet has been replaced by certainty. This is still our poem: it would be overly pedantic not to recognize the magnetically personal meditations of the first two stanzas. But Tottel has grabbed Wyatt's poem hard enough to hold it in just one of its states. Tottel's poem is one of the possible poems contained within the poem in Wyatt's book, one of the psychological states Wyatt depicted.

Given Tottel's purpose, we should not be surprised at his restriction of the ranging emotion of our poem. The poem's multiplicity connects it to a real person, feeling a peculiarly real way. The people who entered the poem in Mary Howard's book knew Wyatt and knew his life, his way of being. They were bothered, a little, by his poetic technique, and so smoothed out the poem's roughness. We have some sign that the snarl in the second-to-last line also bothered them a little, since they tinkered with the word, but "gentillye" snarls too, if more decoratively than "kyndely," and it retains the multiplicity of Wyatt's poem.

Tottel did not know Wyatt. He did not tremble before Henry VIII, he did not sit and sing with Thomas Wyatt or Anne Boleyn or Mary Howard; he might even have resented the power and authority wielded by this ruling elite and its descendants. The materials out of which "They Flee from Me" was made were not his. He had no use for the reminder, in the last two lines, of the intense individuality of the speaker, for the remnant of voice that has been written out there. This poem is now spoken by "the lover," so the last lines needed more generality, not to mention fewer complications. The poem is being put into general circulation, and it is as if it needs to be smoothed over so as to pass more easily from hand to hand, from head to head. So, in keeping with the practice of the time, Tottel changed it.

The poem has had to change on its journey into the wide world of print; some of the intensity of self it carried has been removed. The busy seeking of the self Wyatt depicts and carries out in the poem has been tied up, locked into one place. The vibrating thing, the poem whose arc through the life of Wyatt's circle is recorded in Wyatt's book and the Devonshire Manuscript, has been frozen in the fixity of print, and Tottel's restriction of the emotional range of the poem matches this fate perfectly. The poem as Wyatt made it remains too intense for use. It must be filtered, some of the resonance taken out, before it can be taken up by Tottel and his readers.

Thomas Wyatt, that subtle man, the idiosyncratically accomplished poet, the useful if proudly individual servant of power, is now a little more dead than he was before. But in spite of the changes, in spite of its death and resurrection, his poem is more vital than ever. It is probably true that in the first month after publication more people read it than had read it in all of its previous life.

Order, Reference, Memory

Tottel's book was a hit: a new edition was required within a few weeks, and there would be six more before the end of the century. These successive editions differ from each other in various ways, which will cause later readers much confusion (the differences are largely "mistakes," a notion I will return to). The second edition, which followed so closely on the heels of the first, contains an important difference. At the back there is a "Table," which lists the first lines of the poems alphabetically, with a reference to the page on which the poems appear. There are also page numbers.

Such a table—or rather, the idea of including such a table—is interesting, partly for the idea, and partly because the table's sudden appearance emphasizes its absence in the first edition. From the perspective created by the second, the first edition retained in a distant way one of the features of the manuscripts from which it selected its materials. It gives no guidance to the wandering reader, beyond labeling the sections as devoted to Surrey, Wyatt, and Other; and even these labels come at the *end* of the sections. It has no index or "table"; it does not even have page numbers. If a new reader picked up the first edition looking for "They Flee from Me" (having heard it, or having seen it in some circulating manuscript), the only thing to be done would be to look through the pages, examining each poem. The first edition expects the reader to get to know the book and its contents.

In this there is a trace of the familiar relationship the owner of a manuscript has with its order and its materials. Picking up the manuscript, before a performance, in need of refreshment or consolation, she finds a particular poem in the same way she finds the book in her room, or her room itself: by knowing where it is already. A manuscript is a personal place. Like a house, it can change hands (we have seen this happen to Wyatt's book, and it will happen again), but each successive owner occupies it thoroughly, calls it his or hers, puts the furniture and the poems where he or she wants them. We do not provide maps at the door of our houses, and we do not rely on diagrams to find where our things are kept.

With the celebrity of the first edition, the poems from the old manuscripts Tottel had on hand circulated widely and gained their own various degrees of individual celebrity. Many people would have purchased or picked up the second edition because they had heard some of the poems in the course of their days. So they might come to the book with just a hint: "I think it begins 'They flee from. . .'" It is as if Tottel was at first beguiled by the deep individual personality of the manuscripts and reproduced their personal opacity to a small degree.

The popularity of the book woke him up, and the second edition is suddenly self-conscious about the strangers that are taking the book in their hands. Like a guide to a country house, once the home of families, and now a national trust, the table allows the book to be more easily used by people who don't already *know*.

Fame, and Silence

The most delightful marker of Tottel's fame, like a brightly colored ball floating on the mostly obscure stream of time, is a mention in Shakespeare's *The Merry Wives of Windsor*. Just as the play begins, Slender, who loves Mistress Page, looks for words with which to woo her and says to himself:

> *I had rather than forty shillings I had my Book of Songs and Sonnets here.*

For Elizabethan affairs of the heart, you can do no better than copy out of Tottel's book, especially when, like Slender, you suffer from a poverty of imagination or talent and cannot make good things up yourself.

It is hard to see the imaginary Slender making use of "They Flee from Me." It does not really fit (as we have seen) into the handbook format. "They Flee from Me" is not a complaint designed to move the hard heart of a mistress; nor is it a song designed to attract her in the first place, unless she is attracted to bitter and remaindered personalities. It is very similar to a "love poem," but mostly our poem is about Thomas Wyatt. What use would Slender have for Wyatt's (specific) troubles? Better to use some other poem from Tottel—perhaps the one that begins this way, from the "Uncertain Auctours" section:

> Like the Phoenix a bird most rare in sight
> With gold and purple that nature hath drest:
> Such she me seems in whom I most delight . . .

After Shakespeare's reference, there is mostly silence (to our ears, from what we can hear), about Tottel, about Wyatt, about Surrey, for a very long time.

Especially, perfect silence about our poem. Almost two centuries will pass before what we can hear will report someone noticing "They Flee from Me" in any particular way.

All that time, of course, copies of Tottel's *Songes and Sonettes* wander all around England, passing through (and sometimes staying in) both private libraries and the libraries of Oxford and Cambridge Universities. There are, at first, thousands of copies, but one by one they are lost, disregarded, damaged, and turn to dust. So while even now copies of Tottel are vastly—infinitely, we might say—more common than the copy of "They Flee from Me" with Wyatt's initials by the side, it still becomes a very rare book, and then is for all practical purposes forgotten. We can only imagine the thoughts of scattered readers as they puzzle out our poem through its black-letter, passing a rainy day in the library of a Great House in the country or waiting to go to a play on a winter's night in London. They would almost certainly have taken the book down by accident, or because of the interest of the old binding.

Would they notice the tiny deflection of the prevailing tone of the book that happens in our poem, how the Freezing and Flaming Lover, full of Daintie Wit, suddenly turns real, pettish, and confused?

A Quiet but Sturdy Life, in the Country

After the publication of its close relative in Tottel, the version of "They Flee from Me" initialed by Wyatt continues the life objects live, on its page in the book that was once Wyatt's. It goes where its book goes, lives and dies by the fate of this book. Because the later owners of Wyatt's book continued to use it, we can trace many elements of its quiet life. This is much less true of Mary Howard's book, which has its life, of course, but which contains less documentation of that life. Almost 300 years will pass before Wyatt's initialed version of our poem returns to public life. What is it doing all that time? This era has three parts. The first 150 years or so are a very busy period for the book that contains the poem, when the people using it remember the book but actively, pointedly forget the poem. In the second era, the next 100 years or so, the book itself is also forgotten. Then the book is brought back into public life; and then the poem. I will deal with these eras in order. The first is the period in which the poem is forgotten and devalued. And why not? Of what use is a dead person's description of a momentary and complicated inner moment?

Memorial

Returning, then, to 1554, Wyatt's book is now the property of John Harington, often called "of Stepney" or "the Elder," to distinguish him from his son, Sir John Harington, who had a visible and checkered career in Elizabeth's court.

Wyatt was well known for his translations of the "Penitential Psalms," a selection of David's psalms frequently gathered together in the sixteenth century: Wyatt's translations were printed in 1549, well before his other poems. They appear in Wyatt's own hand late in his book. John Harington read and admired these translations while languishing, maybe, in the Tower, and marked both his admiration and their presence by copying into the book (on the page before the Psalms begin) the following small poem, as a combination signpost, celebration, and tombstone:

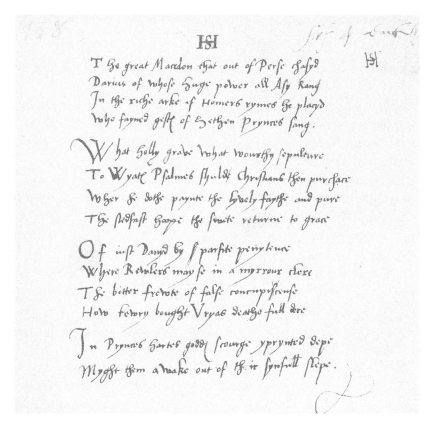

This poem also appears (with, of course, some small differences) in Tottel:

Praise of certain psalmes of David, translated by sir. T. w. the elder.

The great Macedon, that out of Persie chased

Darius, of whose huge power all Asie rong,

In the rich ark dan Homers rimes he placed,

Who fayned gestes of heathen princes song.

What holy grave? what worthy sepulture

To Wiattes Psalmes should Christians then purchase?

Where he doth paint the lively faith, and pure,

The stedfast hope, the swete returne to grace

Of just David, by perfite penitence.

Where rulers may se in a mirrour clere

The bitter frute of false concupiscence:

How Iewry bought Urias death full dere.

In princes hartes gods scourge imprinted depe,

Ought them awake, out of their sinfull slepe.

Harington put the quasi-coronet of initials ("HS") at the top to show that this lovely poem was by the quasi-royal Henry Howard, the Earl of Surrey. Surrey may have written this poem to stand at the beginning the printed edition of Wyatt's translations; but he was executed before that book appeared.

In his poem, Surrey asks: What sort of monument should we "purchase" for Wyatt's poems? Alexander (the "Great Macedon") put Homer's poems in a richly decorated box, the "ark" in Surrey's poem. Two millennia later, the glorious Box of the British Library is a container rivaling Alexander's, a suitable Ark even for writings much more important than the small poems of Wyatt. Under close guard, the book itself, the precious volume now known as MS 2711, the Egerton Manuscript of Tudor poetry, has also become its own Ark. The ancient paper makes an evocative and rich house for the poems that find their home there, and Wyatt's handwriting is a decoration of fitting splendor.

John Harington the Elder clearly did not feel this way about the book he inherited from Wyatt. It is not yet an Ark. You can tell because he writes in it. Much of what Harington writes refers to Wyatt and his poetry, but the fact remains he writes in the book with freedom. He may remember Wyatt fondly, or even greatly admire and revere Wyatt's legacy, but Harington still writes in what used to be Wyatt's book. Wyatt's poems and memory are in it, but in a daily, personal, and nonsacred way. Harington clearly does not feel he is

disturbing the past or Wyatt's soul by fooling around with a book that used
to belong to him.

For instance, it is possible it was Harington who wrote this bit, faintly present
at the top of the page on which our poem appears:

Hard to figure, in the old script, but it says "1 ent," the "ent" being short for
"enter." This seems to have been part of a nascent classification scheme. Harington writes this mark on pages containing short lyrics; he writes "2 ent." on
pages containing 14-line sonnets, on up to "6 ent" (which marks prose letters).
He was up to something, but exactly what is not clear. He was thinking (about
Wyatt's poems).

The book that had been Wyatt's is still a live location in the mid 1550s, with
poems valuable to its current owner being entered at will. With Harington's additions Wyatt's book begins to look more like Mary Howard's book and less like
a personal book. Harington is furnishing the house to his taste, and part of what
he wants to put in his house are tasteful memorials to Wyatt's memory. Surrey's
poem is a fancy funerary urn with a mixture of Surrey's and Wyatt's ashes inside.
Part of its function is simply its existence as a poem by Surrey, a famous person,
and in some minds a martyr to tyranny (Harington was in the Tower as a result
of his distant participation in the 1554 rebellion against Mary).

Since it seems very likely he would have at least met Wyatt, Harington is
recording and celebrating his own memory of Wyatt by hailing Wyatt's shadow
in a formal way. Surrey's memorial poem records and celebrates Surrey's memory
of Wyatt; intently personal, but, in the old Indirect way, Surrey's poem is also
about the bad behavior and repentance of Princes, and so it is also a covert protest, or two covert protests. It might have been a protest (by Surrey) against the
concupiscence of Henry; and since its language is general, writing it down here
might be a protest by Harington against Mary's murderous reign.

Harington takes advantage of a blank page in the book, a page Wyatt simply skipped, to interpolate (posthumous) praise for Wyatt by (the now-dead)

Surrey. The retrospect created by Surrey's poem is physically before or "earlier" than Wyatt's Psalms: next, in the book, is Wyatt himself, struggling over the texts of his Psalm translations, crossing out words, remaking. As always, in the shared private space of the manuscript, the final result is a group effort. Harington uses Surrey's poem to create a last "section" in the book, which creates an emotional structure as well. The "first" section of the book is (now) poems about love and changing fortune; the "last" section, marked off by Surrey's poem, is about regret.

Harington's creation of structure also points up a potential biographical trace within the book, since "ending" with the Psalms might fit beautifully into a manuscript that begins with Wyatt's poems about love and lovers. The Psalms he translates are about error, regret, and the hope for forgiveness: they are reflections on the follies and hazards of youth. They happen to be on the last pages writers of the sixteenth century used; these poems of regret also come at the temporal end of the book's exciting career through dangerous and troubled times. By placing Surrey's poem before them, by "introducing" Wyatt's translations of the Psalms, Harington gives the book a sort of narrative shape. Error before repentance, youth before age. Wyatt's poems of court life, of seduction and love, come first. Repentance comes later, and last.

It may be that the Psalms come near the end because Wyatt wrote them near the end of his life, perhaps during his second sojourn in the Tower. Maybe, but Wyatt didn't know he was to be felled by a fever in mid-gallop. In the structure Harington creates, it *looks* that way: Wyatt's retrospect comes at the end, after folly, after experience, after youth, and just before death. It might be true. More important is the picture of the small poems this perspective creates, the sense that they are the things of a light youth, to be followed, eventually, in the wisdom of age, by poems like the Psalms.

Ownership, of Books and the Past

To Harington the poems and their pages—the poems, that is, as physical presences in this book—are not precious objects or unique survivors; the book is not yet an Ark voyaging on the flood of dissolving time. It is a place where poems have been captured, where copies of them are being kept for convenience or for the purposes of an expressive design. Other things can or should be added: the poem by Surrey, along with a couple of other things, like the transcript of a letter of advice from Wyatt to his son. These items complete the book as Harington wants it to be.

When John Harington the Elder writes in the book, it is not because he has not thought about the precious value of the present and the melancholy truth of the past. It is because he is not yet living in the future. The past stretches out behind him, but he is connected to it, and he regards it as his. He can write out his entries in his present, comfortable with his continuation of a past that has led to him. He assumes his role is to continue time, to hand it to his own son, to the next owners. The past needs neither safeguarding or recovery: it is right here (in this book).

This is a healthy attitude. There is life in Harington's engagement with the material in Wyatt's, now his, book. If you don't like this old part of your house, call the contractor and make it over to your taste. It is your house, and you have to live your life, and the past, after all, is just a succession of other present moments exactly like the current one, each one as valuable (for its own reasons) as the next. Harington values the past, and he seems to have had a taste for memorials. We owe the preservation of our poem to him, in part. But he is not worshipping the past as a thing apart, and so this is also simple luck. He could just as easily have used it to light the fire.

John Harington the Elder died in 1582. He served Elizabeth faithfully, especially in the years just before Mary's death, when Elizabeth was in mortal danger from her own ambitions and the ambitions others had for her. She rewarded him. He had a son, who became Sir John Harington; Elizabeth was his Godmother.

Sir John Harington; and John Harington MP, JP

Sir John Harington was born in 1561, just after the accession of Elizabeth, into a family very much in Elizabeth's heart and care. He grew up to be a wit and a poet, a writer of diverse prose tracts, and a not very good soldier. He was, in other words, a courtier, and he resembled Sir Thomas Wyatt in a broad way, in the shape of his daily business. Everything had changed, and Elizabeth's world was very different from Henry's. But Elizabeth was fond of Henry's example, and her court regenerated in a self-conscious way many features of Henry's court.

Sir John alternately annoyed and charmed Elizabeth, and James I after her, sometimes being welcome at court, sometimes being sent away to his estates at Kelston, near Bath, a manor house his father obtained from his wife. Elizabeth once visited Kelston, and Sir John spent a great deal of money and attention making it fit for that visit. On one of his journeys from London to Kelston, sometime, somehow, in favor or disgrace, Wyatt's book, now belonging to Sir John, came along and took up residence in the Harington family library.

In some circles Sir John is best known as the inventor of a kind of flush toilet, around which he structured a scurrilous satire called *The Metamorphosis of Ajax.* Elizabeth is said to have installed one in one of her houses. In others circles he is the translator of Ariosto's *Orlando Furioso.* He is also the transporter of our poem, and its book, from London to (psychologically) distant Somerset. At some point he added his own translations of the Penitential Psalms to the book. Sir John might have done this while he sat in his house after one of his dismissals, his luxurious equivalent of time in the Tower.

He was the father of many children, one of whom was named—to the continuing confusion and aggravation of later interested parties—John Harington. This next John Harington wrote the math that sits next to our poem, and many other things, in the book he inherited from his father. Born in the heart of Elizabeth's reign, in 1589, this John Harington died in 1653, in ripe old age, serving the Commonwealth he had worked hard to establish. He was a Puritan, a Parliamentarian, and, it seems, a political moderate.

John Harington MP was a busy member of the governing class, a successful lawyer, a careful supervisor of his substantial estates, and an important participant in local and national government. He was a serious man, and in the sober conduct of his life, his love of sermonizing and moralizing, no one could be more unlike his father, the sparkling and sportive Elizabethan wit, the lover of poetry and cultural pastimes. He does resemble his father in his intellectual accomplishments. He knew Latin, Greek, and Hebrew, for instance, and seems to have been teaching himself Arabic late in life. He and his father are also similar in the amount of time they spent writing.

Sir John translated poetry and wrote prose satire and mordant satirical epigrams after the style of Martial, among other things. His son the member of Parliament wrote speeches, sermons, math problems, and legal memoranda. He also kept a diary, which has survived and is currently housed not far from Wyatt's book in the British Library. Harington's diary, a rare kind of item, is an important source of information about the daily life of a member of Parliament in this era. After him the family is mostly obscured from us by the dusty lens of time (as always, they were not obscure to themselves).

In the course of his days this John Harington practically filled up the book containing our poem. He clearly was not even remotely interested in what was already there; he was interested in the substantial amount of blank paper still to be found between and among the existing entries. There are very few pages that do not show traces of his having been there.

Math, and a Remnant of Thought

John Harington MP was a busy and important man. He used the book extensively in his daily business, writing out copies of addresses to juries and official business, as well as personal meditations and problems: things he might need to look at later. To Harington the book was just bound paper he wrote on. He probably wished its previous owners hadn't written so much into it, especially the poet with the questionable morals and a prodigal disregard for the expense of paper. Sometime during his life, probably in the 1630s or '40s (since that is when it seems he used the book most intensively), this sober John Harington did the math in the margin next to "They Flee from Me," leaving the page looking like this:

Though it looks a bit obscure, it is not too hard, in a plain way, to see what John Harington was up to in his left-hand margin, a thin strip of mostly blank paper that suited his mood one day (he didn't use the larger blank spot at the bottom). He was doing algebra, in part, and really quite straightforward algebra. The system of algebra Harington used is called the "Cossicke system"; the variables (the symbols) are called "Cossicke numbers." This squiggle $\mathcal{Z}$ is not an eight; it is a delightfully clear version of the Cossicke symbol for "an unknown number squared." We would write it x^2. The symbol $\mathcal{B}$ is a placeholder, a version of "1," which the Cossicke system includes. Modern systems don't have any real equivalent.

The symbol $\mathcal{V}$ is the unknown quantity to be discovered: we would write it "x." Robert Recorde, who introduced the Cossicke system of notation to England, called it "the dark position." Though a middle-school subject for us, the notion of variables was difficult to get across at first (like the notion of the zero, also gaining general acceptance at this time). People were bothered by the idea of writing down a number while not knowing what quantity it represented. Recorde led his readers over this symbolic blank: "It may be thought to be a rule of wonderful invention that teacheth a man at the first word to name a true number before he knoweth resolutely what he hath named."

(Recorde wrote this in his book the *Whetstone of Witte*. It was published in 1557, a few months after Tottel published his poetry collection. Recorde wrote some of the first math textbooks in English. His Arithmetic, called the *Grounde of Artes*, was still being reprinted in the late seventeenth century. For various reasons, it seems unlikely that Harington had actually read *The Whetstone of Witte*, but he could have, since he inhabited a house with a library that began in the era of its publication. It would seem more likely one of his tutors had read it, or one of his tutors' tutors. The Cossicke system was being replaced in the 1630s. Harington was old-fashioned.)

The larger purpose of Harington's problem is obscure, however. He may have been working out a problem involving what Recorde called "diametrall numbers." *The Whetstone of Witte* has many diagrams like the one Harington draws at the top. In any case Harington's equation has no real solutions, which may be why there is no more math on this page. You need imaginary numbers to get at the solution to this problem, and no one had yet imagined them.

So: a man, an important, highly educated man, a working member of the governing elite, sits down in front of a page that clearly, to him, is blank paper, even though a one-hundred-year-old poem is already written there. He works through a problem, and his writing records the process of his thinking. At the end, he has come to no clear solution. Why he did so is lost to us; but the writing tells us about his encounter with his problem.

This sounds a lot like "They Flee from Me." How similar is it, really?

Algebra Is a Set of Rules Inherited from the Past, and a Sort of Power

That is: In what ways is writing down math-thinking using a set of rules inherited from the past similar to, and different from, writing down feelings in a poem, using a set of forms, words, and metaphors inherited from the past?

A few people can do algebra easily and intuitively, but most of us can't. We lose track of where we are and get confused. Writing out the steps fixes our thinking and allows us to hold our own against the flux of time rushing through our heads. We can look back (at the top of the page, at the past) and say: that is what I was thinking then, and this is how I got to where I am now. The writing keeps extra information from infecting what we are doing. It keeps things straight. The algebraist does not write out all her thoughts: just the thoughts that seem right and that advance the task of solving the problem.

For most of us the writing down is also *part* of the thinking, not simply a record of thinking accomplished. When John Harington writes $\check{\gamma}\check{\gamma}$, he is manipulating symbols (distributing x^2 through the terms of the equation) according to a rule he learned about this sort of operation. When he carries out this operation, the rule tells him to write the two symbols next to each other; this means the same thing as x^4. He need not think out why this works, or how: he just follows the rule for this operation that accompanies the Cossicke system of algebra.

Some of the thinking, in other words, has already been done (by Robert Recorde, say) and contained inside the Cossicke system of algebra. The set of symbols and the associated rules for their manipulation do some of Harington's thinking for him. He just has to follow the rules. When one does a problem in this way, writing out the steps according to a set of rules, thinking becomes symbiotic with the representation of thinking: some of the thinking is done by the writing. The system does it for us, and we don't have to think it all out every time.

By associating symbols with ideas and the manipulation of symbols with mathematical operations, an algebra allows for these operations to be written down quickly, and for a group of people to talk with each other more easily than would otherwise be possible, since they have agreed beforehand on lots of meanings they do not have to re-explain each time. The establishment of consistent and widely accepted notational conventions was one of the great accomplishments of Renaissance mathematics. Part of this accomplishment is conceptual, and part of it is social: getting people to agree.

In most lives, knowing a system of algebra makes certain kinds of thinking possible. Some people invent systems, thinking the thoughts first and then recording those thoughts in a new conventional system, but most of us learn the way of thinking by learning the conventional systems other people invent. Knowing a system of mathematical symbols and operations was an accomplishment and a rare thing in England when Recorde wrote his book. It amounted to a marketable expertise that mathematicians of the time sold in various situations, as tutors or as consultants of a sort.

An algebra is an especially tangible intellectual inheritance, and an inheritance we know we want, since it so obviously saves us the trouble of inventing it again. Mastering such a system underwrites other sorts of mastery, and so Recorde's book is a distributor and creator of power. People who read it could do more afterwards. They could move on to other things, and they did move on, to number theory, calculus, rockets, quantum mechanics.

In this way knowledge grows. Knowledge is power, and knowledge is also one of the objects on which knowledge can exert its power. In the conceptual world, the rich get richer, as long as they don't forget to pass things forward.

Poetry's Rules as a Way of Thinking

So: the math next to our poem can be described in almost exactly the same terms as the poem. It is a thoughtful manipulation of a set of learned and shared rules for the purpose of finding out an answer to a problem, and that answer has eluded the writer.

The work an inherited poetic system does is much less well defined than the work of mathematical systems. Possible "operations" are much less clearly determined, even though the set of rules that governs any particular poetic moment can be quite specific and strict (use seven-line stanzas, alternating rhyme, these kinds of words, and so on). The source of the more extensive degrees of freedom in poetry is the space within the human soul, of course; that space appears tangibly in the great width of meaning words carry, a much greater width than the specifically defined meanings of mathematical symbols. The poetic system Wyatt inherited enforces a limited vocabulary, but even within a very limited set of words meaning can roam with some freedom and can move in new directions all of a sudden.

For instance, the tradition Wyatt was working within associated the Chaucerian word "gentlenesse" with the performance of the knightly virtues of the servant-lover: beautiful manners, beautiful humility, beautiful faithfulness. In "They Flee from Me" it turns slightly sour, becoming a (retrospective) name for a sort of weakness, a role the lover now regrets playing (in a way).

The poetic traditions Wyatt inherited also provided him with preestablished psychological categories (the distressed lover, the seductive but flighty mistress), and with a preset way of depicting personal and social issues through the dynamics of erotic relationships. Wyatt uses these presets very plainly: the abandonment he depicts in "They Flee from Me" crosses from love to bigger arenas. His distress and bitterness are erotic and social and political all at once.

Did convention also do some of the thinking for Wyatt, as it does for Harington when he writes out his math? A clean answer to this question would best be provided by Thomas Wyatt, the person who did the thinking, but he (like Harington) is not available for comment. Clearly, though, Wyatt fed his thinking through the rhyme royal and all its rules and associations. Many of these rules—about love, self-control, unhappiness—were also part of the broader world in which he grew up, making up part of the inherited culture that provided him with the ways he used to make sense of his world. In this way a substantial part of Wyatt's thinking about his subject was undoubtedly accomplished by the poetic and social systems he inhabited. In discussing the distress and pleasures our poem depicts, Wyatt already had on hand descriptions of amorous and psychological cause and effect delivered to him by the traditions of courtly love poetry. No doubt the ways of thinking and behaving associated with these descriptions also helped steer the original experience (or the imagining of an experience) in the first place.

But Wyatt found that the set of traditional poetic operations (sigh, complaint, demand for love) did not finish the problem: there was remaining work he wanted to do that the previous keepers of the rules did not imagine. The rules Wyatt inherits dictate a single-minded conclusion, but the rules he passes on allow for a dramatically deepened interior environment. Wyatt is like a creative mathematician who discovers further subtleties in the rules he or she inherits. After the inherited operations are run through, there is still something left over, and that something else is actually what "They Flee from Me" ends up being about.

Of course, Wyatt's accomplishment is visible only to those who understand the system of conventions he is manipulating. In order to see it, we (for instance) have to relearn his set of conventions, in exactly the same way we must learn Cossicke algebra in order to understand the math John Harington is doing in the margin.

Writing Out Poetry

To return: Is writing out a poem like writing out a math problem? Many poems, and our poem in particular, imitate the relationship that writing has to the thinker solving math problems. That is, poems often look as if the poet is figuring something out by writing. "They Flee from Me" looks like Brooding. It starts with a unsatisfying scene in the present, moves back to the past (as the brooding thinker might: effect to cause), and then returns to the present charged with conclusive, bitter, vaguely vengeful energy, the product of thinking out the connections between his present problem and his pleasant past.

The shaping of experience into a process or drama of thinking (first this, then that) is one way of describing the accomplishment of the poem and why someone might write it. It shapes the inevitably mostly chaotic psychological data deriving from a daily moment into a "problem."

The careful design of the poem tells us it is only an imitation of a train of thought, however. The words are fit into a carefully articulated pattern, the rhyme royal, a pattern that precedes the thinking (and the poet, for that matter), and the completion of this inherited pattern is one of the "accomplishments" of the poem. Like all interesting expressive culture that fulfills patterns and expectations, part of the effect of the poem is to create the feeling of miracle: the poet pretends the thinking just happened to come out in this shape.

That is, the poet speaks as if he is thinking it through and writing the thinking down on the way to his conclusion. Art appears in the pattern this thinking turns out to contain or express, in the fluency with which the poet links the apparently heartfelt and spontaneous expression of feeling with the preexisting pattern he has inherited and reproduced. In this way the poem makes the world resemble the math problem for a moment. In both cases writing (briefly) controls the chaos of the world. The written design excludes the extraneous, masters the inconsequential or irrelevant, and marches thought to a conclusion.

But of course our poem doesn't really finish its thinking, since it is of at least two minds; and so it also depicts the way the poet's inner life escapes from the formulas of explanation that the poem's inherited poetic system provided. The solution is unsatisfactory, and this unfinished quality is what communicates the actuality of the long-dead Thomas Wyatt so urgently.

"They Flee from Me" is not a conceptual dead end, as John Harington's math problem was to him, but it is not a solution like the solutions produced by better-behaved math problems either. It doesn't say what to do differently so that such situations may be avoided; it doesn't say what to do now that the episode has occurred. This is one of the puzzling features of the role it might have had in Henry's court: What does it *do* for the listener? It is the answer to the problem only if describing what the problem is constitutes an answer. Wyatt was especially good at describing what was bothering him.

More Writing: Diaries and Doodles

John Harington's diary records daily life's variety of events. Much of it is business, and potentially very interesting business. He records who said what on given days in Parliament, and some of those days were important days, when the future of his nation hung in the balance. Some of it is the deep inverse of important business: I wrote my wife, my toe exuded some "corrupt matter," I forgot my staff. I helped a friend's son, I was constipated.

Sometimes he seems to have decided what to write down by thinking about saving important moments for the future, either his own (who knew how all this conflict was to turn out?) or the nation's. But often it seems he was just writing things down as a sort of solace in itself. He was making himself and his experience slightly less mortal by turning it into an material object that could voyage with him on the stream of time.

Children also voyage with us; William was John Harington MP's son. Will used the book that used to be Thomas Wyatt's to practice his penmanship, under the direction of a tutor. He was a moderate student, and his attention wandered easily to the things that boys wander to, like dragons and dreams. (Was there only Will? Probably not. But I collect together all the youngsters using the book for their schoolwork and call them "Will." Will appears several times in John Harington's diary; once he loses his bag while traveling.)

He wrote his name in the book (and then someone scratched it out):

Will's tutor would sometimes write out a sample phrase, and Will would then try to imitate the hand of the tutor, or some other set hand (sometimes the alphabet, with uppercase and lowercase letters, would be written out in a top corner for easy reference). Some pages are completely filled with letters formed and unformed, and phrases like "fear the lord and depart from evil" repeated over and over:

For Will, writing it out is the simple point. He could have practiced something like "How like you this" (conveniently available on another page, in lovely capable script), but his tutor no doubt felt the boy he playfully calls "naughty" on the opposite page would do better writing out a morally improving maxim. In his Puritan world, "improving" means increasing one's capacity not for erotic self-reflection but rather for self-limitation, humility, and resistance to temptation. Will's neat letters (should, must) coincide with a neat moral formulation, both of which his tutor and father could only hope would coincide with the state of his soul. In this kind of education, the mechanics of writing merges with the mechanic of morals.

But Will was a boy, too, and so sometimes he practiced other things:

This monster haunts a page late in the manuscript, in this recumbent position, the horns on his knees threatening the poem above him: one of the Psalm translations of Will's grandfather Sir John. There can be great pleasure in making something like this. We imagine our monster, in its glory, and even though we can't draw very well, we still enjoy getting it out of our heads and into the world. There is a sad falling off of detail in the translation (we are not all Hans Holbein), but there is a parallel and sometimes compensatory reality, the thrill of seeing a thought inhabiting the world. Thinking is good, and satisfying, but sometimes we just need to see our thoughts looking back at us. We can imagine Will (tongue between his teeth) working out his monster while his Tutor is out of the room, rubbing his feet together in glee as they dangle off the too-tall chair.

Is Wyatt writing out his poem like Harington writing in his diary? Or like little Will, delightedly extracting something from his head? Yes: it is like Harington writing in his diary, since it records a moment simply because the poet found it important. And yes, it is like Will drawing his dragon: it is a design, a shaped thought, and Wyatt might well have produced a grown-up version of little Will's delight when he looked over what he had made.

Robert Recorde, Briefly

Recorde published the *Whetstone of Witte* in 1557, the same year that Tottel published his poetry. It turns out Recorde felt anxious, like Tottel, about printing his book, and his note about his worries bears a striking resemblance to Tottel's Preface. This is the beginning of Recorde's "Epistle Dedicatory":

> I will not, nor ought I to judge of my country, that learning here can have no liberty, but by aid of friendship, or strength of power. For as England did never want learned wits, so at this time I doubt not, but there be a great multitude, that desirously do embrace all kinds of knowledge, and friendly are affected towards the furtherance of it. And therefore I dare say, they cannot malice me, which am so willing to help the ignorant, according to my gift and simple talent.

He is working for and against the holders of Knowledge, engaging in a struggle very much like Tottel's conceptual wrestle with his Ungentle Hoarders. In mathematics, as in poetry, the mid-Renaissance culture of learning in England still depended mostly on people talking to one another, and printing remained an interesting but unusual and potentially troublesome disturbance of business as usual.

Printing the secrets of mathematics amounted to diluting a monopoly on a marketable skill. Recorde dedicated *The Whetstone of Witte* to the Muscovy Company, which had hired him as a consultant. If members of the Company had read Recorde's various books carefully, they might not have had to hire him. Recorde may not have minded this. He was a famous teacher at Oxford, famous for making mathematics available and interesting to all comers. In publishing *The Whetstone of Witte*, Recorde clearly feels as if he is breaking Guild rules, and his Preface is an attempt, like Tottel's, to both explain it and feel better about it.

Once someone sees the way to do it, you can't get it back. They know it, they can tell someone else, and your accomplishment (what you learned through hard labor) becomes general property. You will die, and eventually your book will crumble, but the knowledge will persist, as long as people keep trying to remember. Robert Recorde is forgotten, but algebra is not. Conceptual objects, like conventional systems, decay, but not in the same way physical objects do.

(Old) Poetry as a Form of Knowledge

What sort of importance can or should old poetry have to those who inherit it? For the moment, this good question is thrown into relief by the example of John Harington MP, who seems to have had no use at all for the poetry in his book. He used blank leaves in the book very extensively, but when he ran out he simply crossed out the lines of poetry so they would interfere less with his densely written prose. He worked out geometry problems by drawing lines right through the poems already written on the pages, as if they were invisible.

Perhaps this highly accomplished man, who entered into the book many charges to the juries over which he presided as a Justice of the Peace, who was partly a participant in and partly a contributing architect of the Civil Wars (along with his son, yet another John, a Captain), simply found these poems beneath his notice. Why would he be interested in the hot sighs of some long-dead and even then mostly conventional lover? It is easier to see the use and power of geometrical knowledge than the use of this record of past emotion. We all have our emotions; we are all experts in sadness and hope. A Justice of the Peace has many opportunities to witness despair and to adjudicate revenge and desire.

John Harington is long dead and the Civil Wars are long past; the many cases he decided were already forgotten three hundred years ago; the estate his geometry would have helped him survey has been resurveyed and has taken its place in a new world. Wyatt's poetry, meanwhile, lives in countless books and classrooms. So it may be hard for us to enter into his point of view, to see the vital importance of the work he records in his/Wyatt's book. But to him it was his world, and he wasn't thinking of us.

John Harington did not see the relevance of the old poetry in his daily life, and the arguments as to why this is reasonable are much easier to articulate than those that might work against it. There is no reason to assume John Harington did not value love, or good writing, or beauty, but he clearly found the records of a century-old articulate passion uninteresting. He also clearly felt no responsibility for the poems and the record of the past they represented. It was his book. He did as he wished with it. Poetry such as Wyatt wrote is small, on the page, and in the world. It seems far more likely it that would fade and become invisible—as it has, here, at this moment, in the middle of the seventeenth century—than that it would retain its vitality and interest.

In fact the poetry will start back into life, and John Harington's writing will become at least as invisible as Wyatt's poetry was to Harington. It is worth paying close attention as this happens, since Harington's forgetting, from a plain, everyday point of view, makes a lot of sense.

"They Flee from Me," Dead and Alive

The year is—let's say—1660, a momentous one in Britain's history. The King has returned; John Harington MP is dead; his son the Captain lives on. "They Flee from Me" sits on its page, accompanied as before by Wyatt's initials and now joined by Harington's math. As best as we can tell, no one is currently using the book; the blank space is almost entirely used up. It is shelved, somewhere in the library at Kelston.

The poem(s) we call "They Flee from Me" is (are) not doing anything. In the outside world, copies of Tottel's book still circulate, but just barely; these books, the very few still in existence, are mostly resting on shelves too. The version of the poem Thomas Wyatt had someone write out and then initialed with his approval has, especially pointedly, vanished from culture. The world in which it did its work has now receded not only into the past but out of memory. There is no Wyatt to use the poem for his own advancement (of various sorts); there is no John Harington the Elder to think about the world that has passed away; there is no witty Sir John and his talent for poetic expression. Because no person remembers the existence of this poem, it has no immaterial existence, and so it is now totally dependent on its status as part of a page in an old book, written or printed: on its status as a physical and relatively frail object.

Wyatt's initialed version has disappeared for what we might call family reasons. John Harington, or perhaps his son the Captain, puts the poem and its book away. We will not hear of it for another century, for two reasons. No one looks at it; but also no one looks *for* it. The obscurity of Tottel's book is somewhat more complicated. It is natural, of course, for older books to be forgotten, since new books are being made all the time. The new books have to go somewhere, and, if the past is not being systematically valued (as is routine in contemporary libraries), they go in front of the old ones. And even though print is easier to read, after a time the old words start to feel unfamiliar, requiring some sort of work to understand.

Still, since there are so many of any printed book, they are not simply put away, as what was once Wyatt's book is put away at Kelston. Printed books are, more precisely, forgotten. They are put away by many hands, neglected by many readers. Older books are forgotten when they lapse out of culture, when no one talks about them, when no one needs to refer to the objects they contain in order to keep some kind of cultural conversation going. Old printed books are forgotten when no one needs them.

People might not need an older book because they have a newer one. In the case of books of poetry, many, many of them had been published since Tottel's book. Any reader looking for poetry would not need to look as far as an old, obscure black-letter book. New books of poetry would have the additional advantage of presenting poems in contemporary language, poems created out of the culture of the moment instead of some obscure past. We might even say that our poem can be forgotten because so much of it has been carried forward in the new poetry. If, in 1660, you want the presentation of a modern, thickened self, read Donne, read the sonnets of Milton, strong inheritors of poetic precedent, strong inheritors of Wyatt's deepening of the form. Literary history, the forward movement by which older poetry turns into new poetry, carries Wyatt's innovations forward. Who needs older poetry? Who needs Cossicke algebra?

PART II

A Century of Learning, and the Invention of Literature

OVER THE COURSE OF THE EIGHTEENTH CENTURY, two things will be added to the page on which the version of "They Flee from Me" initialed by Thomas Wyatt sits: a page number in the upper left, and a note in the upper-right-hand corner, both in the same hand, and in pencil (along with the little "+" sign). Someone, in other words, visits, opens the book, turns to this place, and writes. The whole page then looks like this:

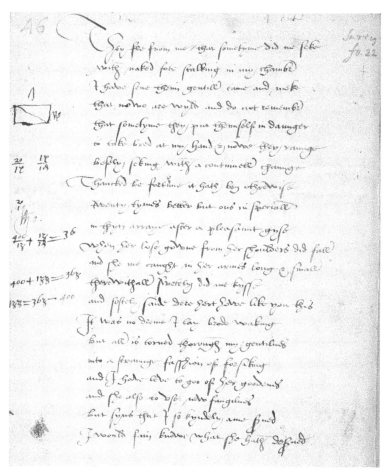

Which in fact is the way it still looks today.

The person who stops by and (however briefly) looks at the version of the poem Thomas Wyatt approved was named Thomas Percy. Percy was a dull, interesting, excitable, entirely staid exemplar of the whole of the century. What the note in the upper right says is that the poem on this page can be found in Tottel's book ("Surrey") on "folio 22." Which generates a simple, profound question: How did Thomas Percy know? The short answer is that it took the labor of hundreds of people over the whole of the eighteenth century. That labor, and especially Thomas Percy's, is the next part of the story. Along the way, another question (re)appears: Why did Percy care?

Groping in the Dark

The Dark Past

Thinking about old poetry in the later 1600s would not only have been unusual; it would also have been extremely difficult. If a member of the Harington family happened to look into Wyatt's book, he might (but probably wouldn't) come across the page on which our poem is located. On the surfaces of the pages in Wyatt's book the accretion of an already long life is present all at once. The past is entirely visible, but that visibility is precisely the problem. All is superficial and competing for attention: the past is overwhelmingly available but entirely unsorted. The chaotic experience of confronting time all at once can be summoned up by looking at a page not far from that on which "They Flee from Me" is written:

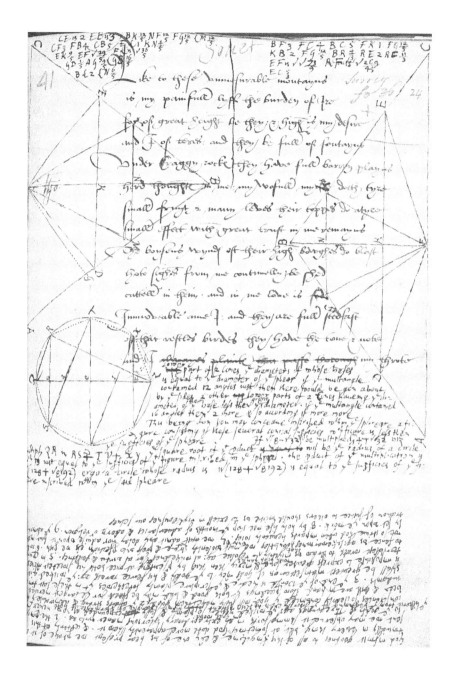

The familiar "Tho." is hidden under the apex of the triangle on the left: but is it over or under the triangle? Does it go with the poem or the prose? The Secretary Hand would be a clue, but it would have been nearly as opaque to our hypothetical Harington as it is to us. The unlettered archaeologist of the page can only dig down through time by imagining its depth. The ink could tell the tale, but the science of Ink is far in the future.

Let's say this Harington figured out there is a poem here: Wyatt's translation of an Italian poem that begins "Like to these unmeasureable mountains." What would he do next? He could not visit any libraries with a section of poetry books, and he doesn't know Italian. No truly public libraries existed, and private and University libraries had no cataloguing systems worth mentioning. You found books in them by already knowing where they were. He could not read a systematic history of English poetry. There was none in existence, and would not be for another hundred years. There were no books that collected together poetry from various periods. There were very few recent editions of older poetry: certainly no editions of Wyatt, but also no editions of any of the poets of the first half of the sixteenth century. Indeed, our imaginary Harington would have been hard pressed to find any person capable of naming any of the poets of the first half of the sixteenth century, even within the walls of Oxford and Cambridge. A few existed, as we will see shortly, but very few.

(There is a quite specific exception to this conundrum, George Puttenham's *The Arte of English Poesy*, published in 1589. This book contains a four- or five-poet history of pre-sixteenth-century poetry and specific appreciation of Wyatt and Surrey in particular: he reprints a bit of "unmeasureable mountains," in fact, out of Tottel. This book could even have been in the family library, since the imaginary Harington's grand- or great-grandfather Sir John is on record as being irritated by it. By the mid-seventeenth century it would have been even rarer than Tottel.)

Not being able to look much of anything up, our Harington would have to do it himself instead, which would not only be tedious or laborious: it might well be impossible. Old books in England were in private libraries, or in the semiprivate libraries of Oxford and Cambridge, and in the old way these libraries emphasized preservation over access. As Robert Recorde said, "Learning here can have no liberty, but by aid of friendship, or strength of power." In order to even begin browsing, one would need to know all sorts of people who would almost all be above this Harington's station, now well declined since his ancestors were on familiar terms with Kings and Queens (loss of this kind of access is what "decline" means).

Without the raw materials, without library catalogs, and without a strong conceptual mapping of the passage of culture through time, all this hypothetical Harington's work would be blind work. To nail down a name might take years: years of finding out where the great libraries were, asking for admission, and somehow traveling there. Once there, he would have to figure out what books were in the uncatalogued library, and then look into those books, one by one, with only the vaguest notion of what he was after anyway. It might take years of effort to meet and get on intimate terms with Cambridge or Oxford dons who knew about poetry and the books in the various libraries, and who might or might not be able to lend guidance, and might or might not be willing.

The history of poetry simply did not yet exist. The basic materials had yet to be found and read; the books containing those materials had yet to be sorted, in the most basic ways; organizational schemes and chronologies had yet to be tried out, disputed, and developed. Scholars did not find it easy to meet each other and know each other, and the most basic technologies of communication, the most basic technical vocabularies, the most basic stylistic rubrics, had yet to be born.

The Beginnings of History

Perhaps, through what would have to have been some kind of accident, our hypothetical hopeful scholar Mr. Harington might, as he began his project, have come across a copy of the *Theatrum Poetarum* by Edward Phillips, published in 1675, which contains hundreds of entries about poets ancient and modern (and, interestingly, female poets, toward the end). He would have had to keep his energy up while reading it, since it is not only organized alphabetically but organized alphabetically by *first* name. This is the whole of Phillips's entry about Thomas Wyatt:

> A Person of great esteem and reputation in the Reign of King Henry the Eighth; with whom for his honesty and singular parts; he was in high Favour; which nevertheless he had like to have lost about the Buisiness of Anne Bullein, had not his prudence brought him safely off. For his Translation of David's Psalms into English Meeter, & other Poetical Writings, Leland forbears not to compare him to Dante and Petrarch; being sent Embassador from K. Henry to the Emperour Charles the Fifth, then in Spain; he died of the Pestilence in the West Country, before he could take shipping an. 1541.

Or perhaps, a decade later, he might somehow stumble across a copy of *Lives of the Most Famous Poets, or the Honour of Parnassus* of 1687, by William

Winstanley. The beginning of Winstanley's entry on Wyatt would have rung a bell if he had already read Phillips:

> This worthy Knight is termed by the Name of the Elder, to distinguish him from Sir Thomas Wiat the raiser of the Rebellion in the time of Queen Mary, and was born at Allington Castle in the County of Kent; which afterwards he repaired with most beautiful Buildings. He was a Person of great esteem and reputation in the Reign of King Henry the 8th. with whom, for his honesty and singular parts, he was in high favour. Which nevertheless he had like to have lost about the Business of Queen Anne Bullein; but by his Innocency, Industry and Prudence, he extricated himself.

Neither of these books takes poetry as the primary material: both are more interested in poets as persons. Winstanley sometimes quotes poetry, but Phillips almost never does. And like the encyclopedias they resemble, these books do not contain an overall narrative. They present a series of lives succeeding one another without causal connections. Winstanley's history is arranged chronologically, an improvement over the alphabetical morass of Phillips's book, but it is not evolutionary or genealogical. Winstanley's past has extension but no shape.

Mr. Harington might well have tossed Phillips aside once he came across Winstanley, since it would have been so much easier to stay oriented among material organized on a timeline and limited to poets writing in English. Winstanley also rendered Phillips's book obsolete in a different way, visible above: much of Winstanley's book is copied from Phillips, often while being extended a little.

In spite of Phillips's example, what Winstanley is doing is a new enough idea that his first task is to say why what he is doing is a good thing to do. He begins (in the Dedication) by quoting the "Judicious Philosopher *Philo-Judaeus*": "When God had made the whole world's mass, he created poets to celebrate and set out the Creator himself." This is the first turn in what turns out to be a curiously in-turning argument, highly reminiscent of the struggles in Tottel. Winstanley says his project is worth it because poets are really important; it is necessary because paradoxically poets are often forgotten, in spite of their participation in the project of history and their role in helping us remember the past. This is the beginning of his "Epistle to the Reader":

> As we account those Books best written which mix Profit and Delight, so, in my opinion, none more profitable or delightful than those Lives, especially them of

Poets, who have laid themselves out for the publick Good; and under the Notion of Fables, delivered unto us the highest Mysteries of Learning. These are
the Men who in their Heroick Poetry have made mens Fames live to eternity;
therefore it were a pity (saith *Plutarch*) that those who write to Eternity, should
not live so too.

Winstanley shares some of Tottel's worries over the worth of his project, and
especially the worry over the worth of poetry in English, and perhaps poetry
in general. "Mysteries of Learning," maybe: but the surest way for Winstanley
to find value in poetry, and hence in poets, is to associate them with the great
men and events chronicled in poems. Poetry provides a window onto the past
by recording men's "Fames."

This way of valuing poetry leaves poetry itself in a precarious place. Poetry
is in service to parts of the past that have already been remembered; poetry
is connected, as a sort of functionary, to the fame of people, to the existing
memory of great figures that is "fame." Winstanley drifts over from the fame of
the famous to the (yet unwritten) fame of the people who recorded the fame
of the famous. This kind of remembering is the only model Winstanley has on
hand, and its shortcomings as a conceptual foundation are painfully clear. He
can't escape the crack at the bottom: his poets are just like famous people except
for their lack of fame.

This model produces an understandable collection of small histories in the
lives of the poets. But since his "Lives" are most often actually about fame, repeating instead of creating fame, they are curiously short on poetry. In a plain
way, Winstanley is unsure whether he wants to (or should) remember poems
themselves, and so his entry on Wyatt contains none of Wyatt's poetry. It does
include, however, bits of poems that celebrated Wyatt's fame, poetry sneaking
in through the little logical door left open by Winstanley's plan. There is a bit of
a poem we know, by Henry Howard:

What holy Grave, what worthy Sepulcher,
To *Wiat's* Psalms shall Christians purchase then?

Like John Harington the Elder one hundred years before, Winstanley's instinct
is memorial: he celebrates Wyatt by quoting Surrey's celebration of Wyatt. This
leaves him caught. What makes poets worth remembering, their poetry, is
squeezed out of his history by his dependence on the notion of "fame" as his
rationale for remembering. So Winstanley's memorial for Wyatt can only be a
description of previous memorials. Those memorials establish that people found

Wyatt memorable in the past, and so by extension he is worth remembering. Winstanley does not want to remember new things; he wants to remember the already remembered.

For Winstanley, the narrative of history is guided and shaped by the size of the shadow people cast in their world. Surrey's section in the book (for instance) is much longer than Wyatt's because the Noble Earl seems to Winstanley to be a person of greater consequence than Wyatt. It did not matter to Winstanley that much of Surrey's fame did not derive from his poetry but from his place at the top of the Tudor world. The poems a poet writes may (help) create consequence, but they are in service to consequence.

Fame was not a dusty issue for Winstanley, or a question of books only. A rich and powerful man named Henry Howard, the Seventh Duke of Norfolk, was living in Winstanley's day. He was a direct (genealogical) descendant of Henry Howard, the Earl of Surrey, Wyatt's friend.

History as (ReTold) Story

How do you make history out of a life? In discussing the living, a nearly infinite number of facts compete for recognition and inclusion in the story. With the long dead, and the poorly recorded, the lack of data simplifies the task, but still the past does not arrive already told. Even the simplest histories must first be shaped out of the available facts.

Phillips's entry about Wyatt is a tiny Life Story, shaped by birth and death. He implies (but does not state) birth; Wyatt's work and character are depicted by a threat avoided through prudence; his paradoxically forgotten fame (why he is worth remembering) is attested to through a reference to John Leland, who published a memorial volume for Wyatt in 1542, and death provides the (natural) end.

Winstanley's account is longer, but the shape into which the meager but still chaotic material of the past is put is simply imported from Phillips. If he got his facts mostly from Phillips, he got his facts in the form of story. Winstanley adds Wyatt's son, beautiful buildings, and two more virtues but fits them into the same story. Narrative—the simple story into which Phillips fits the facts of Wyatt's life—makes unfolding order of the simultaneity of the past. Because narrative is such an important step toward controlling the past, it becomes fundamental, a fact in itself. Winstanley thinks to include Wyatt's birth, for instance, so the story is longer, but Phillips's story, simple as it is, has already become the shape of the past and the design into which further facts will be fit.

The Progress of Learning

Winstanley's book is full of errors of fact and errors of judgment, and by current standards it is directed by a foreign and flawed program of literary history. Who wants to reflect on the possible etymology of Shakespeare's name instead of reflecting on his plays? Why did he forget to put Herbert in? Why doesn't he say anything about Wyatt's poems?

Still, it is organized chronologically, and it contains entries for 168 poets, reaching back before Chaucer. If our Hypothetical Harington read this book, his work would jump ahead by years. What Phillips did for Winstanley, Winstanley could do for Harington. Occasionally Winstanley seems to be simply remembering a poem, or a play, and has included its author so that he can quote from it. He has no way of saying why he might do this or why anyone should read it. It looks as if he loved poetry, and every once in a while simply quotes bits he likes especially. Winstanley's love of poetry sits to the side of the project he can justify; but there it sits, and it may be the actual reason for the whole thing.

In the Wyatt entry, Winstanley doesn't quote any Wyatt, but he does quote Surrey. Where did he find the Surrey poem? Did he have a copy of Tottel? This snippet of Surrey is a sign of the forgotten life of books like the *Miscellany*. It was there, somewhere, but we can't see it.

And so learning progresses. Everything Phillips did Winstanley did not have to do; he could spend his time doing the next things. Here at the beginning each step is visible. Winstanley, carried along for a certain distance by Phillips, has the energy to go a little further, to make his story a little longer (but not different).

Reprinting and Its (Unsolvable) Problems

One Reason for Reprinting Old Poems: Money

In 1710 and 1711 a man named George Granville, sometime poet and politician, experienced a surge of good fortune. Having successfully bided his time in a less favorable political climate, he rose along with the Tories and was named Secretary at War; at the end of 1711 he received a title and became Lord Lansdowne. He also got married in 1711, to a young widow, Mary Thynne, who was born Lady Mary Villiers. Lady Mary was descended, directly if not memorably (that is: through people who were not first sons, or were women), from Henry Howard, the Earl of Surrey. Her grandmother was Lady Frances Howard; Lady Frances's grandfather was Henry Howard's son Thomas, the fourth Duke of Norfolk.

These events—the wedding, the title, and the Ministry—lead to the reappearance of "They Flee from Me" in the first decades of the eighteenth century.

When it appears, the poem is still sounding its bitter plangent note, its apparently intensely personal recall of love and alienation. And it is still sounding this note in an environment characterized by the exercise of despotic power in which good fortune, and especially money, flow down from the top. Wyatt, long dead, used his poems in charting his course through a much more dangerous and despotic world. When Wyatt's poems are republished, they are being used to further the ambitions of the publishers, in a dimmed and vaguely thought-out version of their original purpose.

People have emotions; they sometimes record them; they sometimes write poems; these poems are sometimes published. In each of these moments there is a mixture of feeling and finance, of spiritual and practical motives; but publication is, especially, a practical matter. In the background of the reprinting of "They Flee from Me" may have been a desire to make the ancient and sharply individual feelings spring back to life, but that desire is not visible or articulated by the publishers. Mostly, someone decided these old records of feeling could be profitably printed. That this happened is interesting, since it is inherently so unlikely.

It begins with Alexander Pope, that canny and ambitious literary business-man, in 1713, when he published a poem called *Windsor Forest* and dedicated it to George Granville. This poem contains (among much else) intent praise of Granville and of the policies of the current Tory administration. The possibilities presented by friendship with and favor from Granville were obvious. Less obvious, perhaps, was the faint air of ancient power descending through Granville's new wife; but Alexander Pope had a very sensitive nose for the scent of power. Some of the best-remembered poems by Surrey were associated with Windsor, and in the midst of *Windsor Forest* Pope praises Granville by comparing him to Surrey. This passage from Pope was cited, in turn, by a publisher named Edmund Curll as a Preface to his 1717 edition of the Surrey part of *Tottel's Miscellany* and was republished when the Wyatt poems were added in a reissue of 1728.

Curll uses Pope's appeal to power as part of his own appeal to power, though Curll appeals to Pope's power to determine taste in place of the more worldly power Granville represented. There is a quiet irony here: Granville suffered the setbacks of his administration in 1715 (with the accession of George II) and was virtually exiled by 1717. So Curll's gesture is not toward Granville but toward Pope, now deeply established at the heart of the English literary world. Pope's own appeals to power had already worked.

Reprinting an old book for which no publisher held copyright was not a big risk for Curll, and other publishers could imitate him, if they wished, with equally little risk. Shortly after Curll tried out Surrey's poems, a rival did him one better, adding the poems from Tottel that Curll had initially left out, including those of Wyatt. An appeal to power is also behind this book, but a new appeal, advertised in a dedication to "Thomas, Duke of Norfolk, Earl Marshal of *England*."

There is no indication that anyone associated with this edition (it was edited by a man named George Sewell) had any connection with the Duke, and there are no indications the Duke noticed the dedication or the book. It was worth a try, though. In 1717, the notice of the Great was still by far the safest route to good fortune. Ancient power was remembered in the Howard family, quite literally, having been transmitted (houses, lands, cash, consequence) from son to son.

Whatever appeal reading about Wyatt's old feelings might have, in the rationale of these books the poems themselves are less interesting than people (as in Winstanley). The dedication to the Duke of Norfolk is a simply associative enterprise. It associates the book with the current Howard family, a family constituted through the transmission of the past made possible by the disciplined, relentlessly conservative rules of inheritance. The past is *in* the Howard family. So a person might read the poems in order to be associated with this past, or the past of Britain; at least, Thomas, Duke of Norfolk, might read them and find himself gratified, his sense of his own consequence increased. He might send over a bag of money.

Reprinting Requires Imagining the Past

Richard Tottel issued at least seven editions of his miscellany *Songes and Sonettes*; there may have been more, now lost in time. In 1717, when Curll decided to try reprinting the Surrey section of Tottel's book, these editions were represented by (say) some tens of books spread around the Kingdom. Since there was as yet no public library, it is proper to say these books were all in private hands, though a few of them were in the semiprivate libraries of Cambridge and Oxford.

In broad form Tottel's various editions are identical, but if you are interested in reading the poems with even some degree of attention (the careful reading that lyric inspires and depends upon), these editions are rather different. Generally, the later editions (those after the two editions of 1557) have a fair degree of variation from the first two editions. These variations are almost all of the sort easily termed errors, and the errors generally increase in number as time goes on, until the last edition of 1587.

If different versions of a book come to us from the past, which should we reanimate in print? Which words should we remember, and which words should we forget? The immediate answer might be that we should forget the errors. This is Edmund Curll's first thought, which he describes in his "Advertisement to the Reader":

> In order to give the Publick as correct an Edition as I could of these valuable Poems, I procured among my Friends Three several *Editions*, printed in the years 1565, 1567, and 1569, all which I found very full of Typographical Errors, but the most correct, was that of 1567, from which this Edition is printed, and to which, the *Folio's* numbered by numeral Figures in the Margin refer. When I had made the edition of 1567 as correct as I could from the other Two; I heard of another Copy in the *Bodleian* Library in *Oxford*, among Mr. Selden's Books, wherein were many considerable Amendments, supposed to be made by that eminent Person: which I got collated by a learned Gentleman there. So that I hope it will appear I have given my Lord Surrey's *Poems* in their Antique Dress, in as careful and accurate a manner as possible.

"They Flee from Me," in its purported Antique Dress, appears in the reissue of 1728:

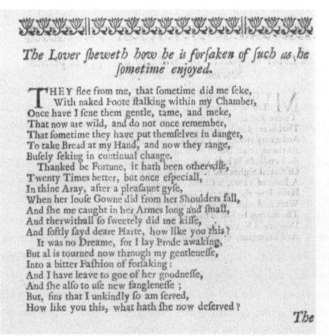

The Lover sheweth how he is forsaken of such as he sometime enjoyed.

THEY flee from me, that sometime did me seke,
      With naked Foote stalking within my Chamber,
Once have I sene them gentle, tame, and meke,
That now are wild, and do not once remember,
That sometime they have put themselves in danger,
To take Bread at my Hand, and now they range,
Busely seking in continual change.
      Thanked be Fortune, it hath been otherwise,
Twenty Times better, but once especiall,
In thine Aray, after a pleasaunt gyse,
When her loose Gowne did from her Shoulders fall,
And she me caught in her Armes long and small,
And therwithall so sweetely did me kisse,
And softly sayd deare Harte, how like you this?
      It was no Dreame, for I lay brode awaking,
But al is tourned now through my gentlenesse,
Into a bitter Fashion of forsaking:
And I have leave to goe of her goodnesse,
And she also to use new fanglenesse;
But, sins that I unkindly so am serued,
How like you this, what hath she now deserued?

The

Of course it is not any kind of stretch, from an everyday point of view, to think that there would be some "correct" version of a poem. Still, a totally correct version of the poem might not ever have existed in any physical form, and might never have appeared in a book. A typesetter might set the type incorrectly from the very start. Wyatt himself, or his secretary, could have misspelled or misplaced a word and then not noticed or not cared. So it is not certain that when tacking between various versions of the book Curll would be doing anything other than mixing and matching to produce a book with a purely imaginary relationship to the past. A "correct" text made in this way is very likely to be not a perfect representation of the actual past but rather a representation of the past as it *might* have been, if only people hadn't made all kinds of mistakes to start.

Correcting errors is usually perfectly simple in practice. Proofreading the writing materials of everyday life, we make such judgments all the time without any qualms. When things don't make sense, we can usually figure out what the (invisible) thought was that didn't get fleshed out. Reprinting old books, however, puts unusual pressure on these judgments. The losses of time make it dramatically harder to be certain. Curll can't be sure Wyatt used words in the same way he does, to start: Curll can't be sure of anything, really, because he is working with the barest remnant of the full life of the past.

Even the Smallest Decisions Are Impossible

Take, for instance, the word now spelled "been," which appears in the eighth line: "Thanked be fortune it hath been otherwise." This word appears in all printed versions of the poem in the same place, doing the same work. How might Curll spell it, given his search for the Correct, and his desire to print the poems in their Antique Dress? In Wyatt's book, it looks like this: *ben*

The terminal "n" is written with a flourish, but it is still an "n" in a plain way: "ben." In the first edition of Tottel's book (which Curll did not know about or have access to) it is printed this way: **bene**. The *Oxford English Dictionary* lists many older ways of spelling this word, among them "be," "bin," "bene," "beene," "byn" and "ben." The different editions of Tottel's book use a variety of these. Edmund Curll spells it "been" in the last sentence of his "Advertisement."

In short, Curll would not be able to tell if any of Tottel's typesetters made a mistake in setting up the type in this part of this line. There is something "correct" hovering behind the printed word, but it is not a physical thing, and in particular it is not *spelled*; it does not involve letters. It is a thought, a word, the past participle of the verb "to be." This abstract, unspelled thing is our common reference point as speakers of English, but it delivers only general guidance—delineating a kind of area—for the spelling. Curll would have to look at his copies of Tottel's book and make a decision about spelling. Describing one decision or another as "correct," though, simply does not make sense.

There might be comfort in the famously easygoing attitude toward spelling common in the sixteenth century. No Renaissance readers of Tottel's book would have thought of the variation in the spelling of "been" as an error. Because later practice is so different, however, reproducing Renaissance indifference might not work, in one way of thinking, since it might make these typesetters looks stupid when in fact they were not. Should the reprinter choose one of the old spellings, reproducing the word "correctly" in that sense, or should he print it in the modern way, and so communicate that Tottel had gotten it right (even though he, Tottel, had spelled it in a different way)? In the end, Curll's edition prints it been.

Of course if Curll did not insist he was giving us poems in their "Antique Dress," none of this would be a problem. He could spell it *correctly* by spelling it "been" and not worry about it. But he says that in his reprinting he wants to deliver Surrey's poems as they were, erasing the passage of time and the errors introduced by mortality: and so, in this small place, Curll would become lost, with no hope of deliverance. There is no way to make the past and the present match up. The past can be glimpsed, but only by looking through the present and using our imaginations.

The Bigger Decisions Are Even Worse

The title of Tottel's book, *Songes and Sonettes* . . . , does not refer to only one physical object. It names an array of books. Ignoring the physical differences that arise from leading different lives, none of the various editions is exactly the same as any other. Some editions are different intentionally; the addition of new poems in the second edition is not a "mistake." And the editions are different in the basic but not unstable or destructive way represented by the variation in the spelling of "been." These differences are variations but not errors.

Especially among the later editions, though, there are many errors that pose problems for the meaning of the poems. In the edition of June 1557, the first three lines of the second stanza of "They Flee from Me" look like this:

> **Thanked be fortune, it hath bene otherwise**
> **Twenty tymes better:but once especiall,**
> **In thinne aray,after a pleasant gyse,**

In the third edition of 1559, these lines appear this way:

> Thanked be fortune,it hath ben otherwise
> Twenty times better;but once especiall,
> In thinne aray,after a pleasant gise

In the edition of 1574, these lines are like this:

> **Thanked be fortune,it hath bene otherwise**
> **Twenty times better,but once especial**
> **In thinc aray,after a pleasant gyse**

The edition of 1585 looks like this:

> thanked be fortune,it hath beene otherwise
> **Twenty times** but once, especiall
> **In thine array,after a pleasant guise**

"Been" appears here in all its pleasant variety; but there are other variations as well. One, the disappearance of the word "better" in the edition of 1585, is the easiest of these variations to label as an error, since the line makes less sense in a simple snipped-off way, and there is even an evocative blank space left in the text. Somebody made a mistake.

More interesting is the variation in the last line, in the word spelled "thinne" in the two earlier editions (now spelled "thin") and "thine" in the later two. Here a typesetting variant, the dropping of one of the n's, produces a different word, "thine," which is at least not aggressively or egregiously incorrect in the context. Her array could be thin, but it could also be her own. This variation in spelling is important. A decision needs to be made. How to do it? In order to decide, the chronologically ordered material of the past must be fit into some narrative, and this narrative must be built from a set of values that will allow the story to sort the interesting and important from the uninteresting and unimportant.

In looking at the forward movement depicted by a chronological arrangement of the various editions of Tottel's book, "thinne" appears first and "thine" appears second. The (simple) story might be: a later typesetter, looking at "thinne" without reading the poem, mistakenly thought it was a misspelling of the word "thine," and so changed it, introducing an error. The reprinter, striving to reprint the correct words, should reprint "thinne." This is a (very) small story, but a story nonetheless. It is the familiar story of degradation and the losses of time. Another possible story, however, is one of antientropic improvement: the typesetter perceived that the word "thinne" was a mistake for the word "thine," and so corrected a previous error.

Other parts of the poem, especially the word "she," make the second-person address of "thine" problematic, especially since the address would then be switching to the third person in the very next line (from the 1585 text):

When her loose gowne Did from her shoulders fall

Anything, one supposes, is possible. It is possible that Thomas Wyatt himself did not notice or even liked the change in address, in which case the poem would have problems, but the reprinting of those problems would not be an error. Calibrating the difference between the story of degradation and the story of improvement calls up other stories, other ways of describing the past. Investing in one of these (tiny) stories means investing, in a quiet way, in larger stories about the past, about the practice of poetry, about Wyatt, about many things. A person's worldview might cause her to favor one story over another: improvement over degradation, say. One hundred and fifty years earlier, Tottel may have been thinking about a story of Wyatt's (in)competence when he "improved" the manuscript version of the poem, changing the length of the lines to make them more regular metrically.

The only way to decide about the validity of "thine" and to choose between Degradation or Improvement is to think about what the poem means, beyond this phrase, and use that larger sense of meaning as a way of calibrating, as best we can, whether "thine" fits. In a familiar editorial conundrum, however, the meaning of these specific lines creates, in part, the meaning of the poem as a whole. If the meaning of these lines is not clear, what then? We must know about the meaning of the whole poem in order to decide about the meaning of its parts, but we understand the meaning of the whole by thinking about the parts. This logical circle creates a small spot of uncertainty in the poem. There is a distressing tangle in the information delivered to Curll by the past.

Curll's reprinted poem has the word "thine." This isn't the best choice, of course, but he was facing a problem about which certainty is impossible. Besides, both the 1565 and the 1567 edition have "thine." And he may have not thought carefully about it at all. Our confidence in his editorial clarity is undermined, for instance, by his claim to have used an edition from 1569, since there is no known edition in 1569.

Even the Improvements Cause Problems

The second edition of Tottel's book has a "Table" of first lines; the first does not. Did the first edition forget to put it in? Is it a mistake, or a variation? In the first edition, Tottel's little preface, "The Printer to the Reader," is presented as a rectangle of text, and in the second edition it comes to an attractive point at the bottom. What sort of variation is this? Is it interesting?

A story depicting the absence of the "Table" as a printer's error would be convoluted and unconvincing, and so this variation is not easily described as a mistake, but that only makes it worse for the reprinter. This variation proves that the constellation of books with the title *Songes and Sonettes* includes more than one correct version. The notion of reprinting Tottel's book in its antique dress is an attractive project, but it seems like an inherently impossible one, and certainly, if one were to actually think about all the problems it brings up, an entirely exhausting one.

In the early eighteenth century the small but large problems involved in reprinting old books were new, grains of sand that might well render the whole editorial machine inoperable. People had just started thinking about them and were quite unsure how to proceed. They did not have a good sense of how they wanted to make decisions, in principle, and they were deeply hampered by their scattered knowledge of old books in general. So Curll, in spite of his claim to careful correcting, reprints "thine"; and Sewell's edition of 1717 begins this way:

THEY flee from me, that sometime did we seke,
    With naked fote stalking within my chamber,

In the end, Curll's book does not reduce the number of errors in the book, and Sewell's adds many more of its own, like "we" in the line above.

Not Deciding Is Deciding

It might be tempting to try to escape the curious and often essentially insoluble problems of reprinting an old book by somehow *not* making decisions. A re-printer could, for instance, print all the versions, or simply print exactly what is in one particular version. But these nondecisions present problems perhaps more troubling than the problems they are designed to avoid.

For one thing, these solutions do not acknowledge how important it is, gener-ally speaking, to distinguish between something that is right and something that is wrong. Not trying to distinguish right from wrong refuses to acknowledge the basic spirit behind the making of books, the creation of poems, the expression of the self. People have things to say; they have *specific* things to say. People try to get it right.

Second, nondecision threatens chaos at the moment when the task is to make sense and master the past. Entropy is an enemy. We need to make sense out of chaos in order to survive, in order to know ourselves and our world. This desire was one of Wyatt's motives when he made his poem, and might be one of the motives for reading old books.

Mastering the Past by Forgetting: Genealogy

Just beyond chronological sorting is genealogy; at the heart of genealogy is a disciplined kind of forgetting. In order to draw a genealogical line back into the organized space created by chronological marking, almost everything in that space has to be forgotten. Genealogies in the West, for instance, have almost always forgotten the lines drawn through women. In making genealogies, we forget lines marked by names different from ours, by uninteresting ethnicities, by poor people, by bad people. Genealogists sometimes forget all the lines not marked by eldest sons.

Such erasure deforms the material of the past, but something like it is also simply necessary. The math is simple. Even when we have gotten rid of all the irrelevant lines there are still too many to manage. Why sort if it doesn't help? The point is to find ways of forgetting that serve some larger purpose and provide a kind of control. That doesn't sound so good, but it is still true.

Genealogy produces an admirable if deeply reductive clarity. Such clarity is important: in the case of families like the Howards, for instance, it traces the handing forward of power from one generation to another. If the aim is a more generous depiction of the multiple causalities of the past, this scheme is deeply corrupt. Where are all the women, the other sons, the thousands and thousands of other lines leading to and away from the Heritable Howard? If the aim is to follow the descent of power, however, a genealogical history is highly practical. It tells the truth (about power).

Variation Measures Time: The Genealogy of Books

Without change, there is no time, there is no past. Physicists don't need time in their equations if nothing changes; evolutionary biologists chart the history of species by noting accumulating changes in DNA; and the ticks created by change (errors, mostly) also mark the passage of time in the world of old books.

A much later editor of Tottel's book named Hyder Rollins sorted out all the known editions and arranged them in genealogical order. It turns out to be a picture of very straightforward descent, with almost all editions having been set by using the previous edition. In some cases earlier editions or other sources were referred to during the printing, which creates multiple parents. Rollins determined this by tracing the appearance of change. For instance, the second edition in July 1557 contains lots of new things: the table of first lines was added, many poems were added, mistakes in the first edition were corrected. In our poem, the replacement of "thinne" by "thine" happens in 1565, and subsequent editions carry this mistake along through 1587.

Some changes can help track editions more carefully. For instance, Surrey wrote a lovely and pointed elegy for Wyatt, the first line of which begins "Wyatt resteth here." This poem appears near the end of the Surrey section in Tottel's book. In the first three editions this line is printed as "W. resteth here." In the two editions of 1559 it becomes "Wyat resteth," which happens to be the way this line appeared in its first printed appearance in 1542. In 1565 this line changes to "What resteth," and this unhappy mistake is carried along through 1587.

Curll's edition of 1717 contains "What resteth," which supports his claim of using the 1567 edition; Sewell's contains "Wyat," which strongly implies the use of one of the 1559 editions. But since Sewell's edition also uses "thine" instead of "thinne," the parentage of this book seems somewhat mixed. It was Hyder Rollins's opinion that Sewell used the second of the 1559 editions, but he also thought Sewell's edition to be a very bad one, with a wealth of additional mistakes (like "we" for "me"). So perhaps "thine" in Sewell is a *new* mistake, produced while trying to deal with the mistakes of the past.

Perceiving and giving direction to the flow of variations (finding them and marking them chronologically) allows the later reader to impose direction and coherence on the welter of information provided by the accumulation of editions. It does this by marking the passage of time and by assigning a direction to time's flow. Sewell doesn't say which edition he uses, but his book contains the DNA of its parent within it.

Curll, in his essential ignorance, cannot yet write out a genealogy for his edition, but, unlike Sewell, he can make a start, focusing on the 1567 edition, "correcting" it but also reproducing it. Lines begin with points. Using the 1567 edition allows Curll to forget the already overwhelming amount of information represented by the variation in the other editions. He needs to forget the other editions in order to understand what he will print: he masters the past through forgetting.

Reprinted, but Still Not Interesting

The genealogical line into the past becomes *important* by becoming relevant, by becoming part of the present. It becomes relevant by serving some purpose, like deciding who gets the money.

Sewell and Curll do not offer any reasons why anyone would want to read these poems other than their association with the illustrious. In the end, they demonstrate no particular interest in the poems themselves. The poems are the material that fills up the book; they are the past brought into the present in a lump. Sewell's edition is full of mistakes because he doesn't (seem to) care about the poems as individual events in the descent of the past into the present. In Sewell's book our poem begins, "They flee from me, that sometime did we seek," and there is nothing in the book to indicate that anyone has spent any time worrying about it. The individual poems are not being presented with any particular purpose in mind.

The Editor Takes Charge

Making Sense

Though they may look like one version or another of Dr. Dryasdust, the Editors of the eighteenth century are excitable, and they are in their way in the vanguard of our never-ending assault on the ravages of time. Thomas Percy's note on our page, "Surrey fo. 22," is a real, antientropic Event. Percy explains this note in another note, written near the front of the manuscript:

In this Volume such Poems are pointed out as have been Discovered to be already printed among "The "Songs & Sonnets of "the Earl of Surrey "& Others, 1557."

Separated since at least 1557, the paths of the handwritten and printed versions of our poem cross in the well-informed mind of Thomas Percy. After Percy wrote on the actual pages in the manuscript, the connection between these two texts became part of the life of Wyatt's book. This connection—this writing, this note—permanently changes the objecthood of the poem.

There is an interesting little bit: "*already* printed." A modern editor would not immediately progress from the discovery of this beautiful, initialed, astonishing temporal survivor to remarking, quietly, about the priority of print. But Percy distrusted handwriting, seeing it as the very mark of mortality. As he wrote this note, he was engaged in a forty-year-long effort to reprint Tottel, and this revelation from Wyatt's world did not deflect him from that task. As we will see, when he does reprint "They Flee from Me," the poem he prints will be unaffected by the version he found on the page in Wyatt's book.

Several amazing things have happened. First, somehow, out of all the millions of books in the world, Tottel's book, after its own long journey, has found its way back to its ancient source. Second, this astonishing event does not influence Percy's understanding of what "They Flee from Me" is. And third, Thomas Percy wrote this information in a book that did not belong to him and that is now a heavily protected national treasure.

This all needs explaining.

Thomas Piercy / Thomas Percy

Among the many illustrious and interesting people laboring to recover the British cultural past during the eighteenth century, Thomas Percy is among the most interesting and illustrious. He was endlessly busy with literary projects of various kinds, especially in the 1750s and '60s, and he was among the best connected of any scholar of the century: among his many strengths was a distinct talent for recommending himself to others. In 1765 he published the book that made him famous, *Reliques of Ancient Poetry*, which became one of the most read books of the later eighteenth century.

He was born in Bridgenorth, Worcestershire, in 1729, the son of a grocer; his name was then spelled "Thomas Piercy." He was a smart and ambitious young man, winning a scholarship to Christ Church, Oxford, in 1746. He was an early collector of books and had a library of more than two hundred volumes by the time he was seventeen. In 1753, following the orderly career path traced out by so many ambitious but socially obscure men of his time, he was awarded one of the livings at the disposal of Christ Church, in Easton-Maudit, northwest of London.

Two events of lifetime importance to Percy/Piercy happened during the summer of 1756. Through a mutual friend he was introduced to Samuel Johnson; and, after carrying out research in the Worcester city registers, he changed the spelling of his name from Piercy to "Percy," declaring this spelling to be the "most ancient and correct." He had discovered various spellings—Piercy, Pearcy, Piercey—and labeled others (which he could not bear to write out) as constructed "still more corruptly."

Samuel Johnson's dictionary (another of the century's great projects, published in 1755, the year before Percy changed his name) defines "corrupt" thus: "Vitious; tainted with wickedness; without integrity." It defines "correct" this way: "Revised or finished with exactness; free from faults." Percy evaluated his name by reference to the editor's ur-story of corruption and described the effort in a little pamphlet he wrote in the 1770s:

> My father had always written it thus, Piercy; and so had I myself until that time.
> But in the old Registers at Worcester it had been written Percy; and such of our
> Relations, as appeared to be best informed, had adhered to this orthography:
> while such of the others, as had inserted the i, had varied as to the place of its
> insertion; some writing their name Peircey, others Piercey, and some still more
> corruptly. I therefore determined to follow what appeared to me the most an-
> cient and correct Spelling; and I had my name accordingly written PERCY in

the Instruments of my Institution, Dispensation, etc. when I was presented by
the Earl of Sussex to the Rectory of Wilby in August 1756.

Percy's name changing plainly displays the full arbitrary glory of his notion of
editorial work. What about the spellings of the name that come before "Percy"?
And what would a "corrupted" name be, anyway? Why is it different from a
name that has simply changed? That is, it is easy to see the moral charge of the
story Percy tells about his name. All presents are the product of pasts; the present becomes "correct" or "corrupt" only through the creation of a (genealogical)
story that values some things more highly than others. The relevance of this
story, in this case, is that it tells Percy what to do as he corrects the present by
reference to the past.

This is the Editor's power. The scholar, the man who knows about the past
and who has looked into old books, can measure the shortcomings of the present
and then, guided by superior knowledge (of the past), can restore the present to
correctness. For Percy, the power of the Editor is not simply the ability to print
the right words in a book. It is the power to reorder and renew the world.

(Thomas Wyatt tells a very different story, about flighty creatures, "she" among
them, who came to his hand. Time begins when he is forsaken by "continual
change" and left with the memory of her arms. In Wyatt's story, time doesn't
end, and paradise is not restored. Time moves forward with bitter energy; the
story allows Wyatt to feel it but not to stop it. Mastering the past does not have
to mean declaring victory. Wyatt masters his past by declaring defeat.)

The (Corrupt?) Descent of Power

Another man had changed his name to "Percy" in recent times. The Percys
had been rich and on record for many generations: Thomas Wyatt knew Percys. The actual direct (male) Percy / Earls of Northumberland line, however,
had died out with the eleventh Earl in 1670. In the 1740s, political machina-
tions and time combined to create, by Special Act of Parliament, a new Earl
of Northumberland. The new Earl's daughter Betty was married to a man of
significant means but modest social pretensions named Sir Hugh Smithson. Sir
Hugh's grandfather had made a fortune in the hat business. When the (new)
first Earl died in 1750, his will stipulated that the title would descend to Sir
Hugh. Sir Hugh's wife, beginning as Betty Seymour, passing through Betty
Smithson, became the Countess of Northumberland. Hugh Smithson, upon
becoming Earl, changed his name to Percy. He was promoted to Duke in 1766.
His descendants own that name (and Alnwick castle) to this day.

Thomas Percy was deeply interested in genealogy. He traced his own descent through the ancient Northumberland family and insisted, in his intent way, on the interest and legitimacy of this ancestry. He wrote what amounts to a book about it, now in the British Library (Add. MS 32326). His little pamphlet describing the name change, quoted above, is stitched into this handmade book. The book is decorated with a version of the Percy Coat of Arms and is in certain ways carefully designed. But like any book Percy spent time with, it is covered with additions, notes, scribbles, and crossouts. It contains carefully drawn genealogical trees that connect him, the modest grocer's son, to the Earls of Northumberland, in the form of a "first Percy" who flees to Worcester after some unknown mixup in the North. This Percy "had been obliged to retire out of the North for some affair of honour."

Percy tells an evocative story. The First Percy arrives with jewels and a son, and hides among the tradesmen of Worcester; his descendants are forced by circumstances not into haberdashery but "cloathing manufacture." The whole of Percy's genealogy book demonstrates a pervasive anxiety about his own heritage (gentility concealed in grocers), and also a skittish awareness that others had noticed his attempts to make himself a Northumberland Percy. The interpolated smaller pamphlet finishes up this way: "[The name changing] was many years before I had the most distant hope of being ever known to the Duke and Duchess (then Earl and Countess) of Northumberland: the first time I had the honour to be introduced to either of them being in November 1764—All this is true." It is signed in a formal way: "Thomas Percy" (and dated 1776).

In his *Life of Johnson* of 1791, James Boswell, who liked Percy, slyly remarked that in 1778 Percy "was still holding himself the heir male of the ancient Percies"; and Percy was clearly fretting about what people might think. This little signed and dated pamphlet looks like a cross between a confession and an affidavit, designed to protect his honor from the (obviously true) accusation of ambition.

Henry VIII executed Henry Howard in part for improperly displaying part of his family's coat of arms (a gesture taken as a claim to the throne), but there is no record that the world was actually troubled by Percy's picture of his own past. The Earl/Duke and Countess/Duchess never seem to have bothered themselves about it, even though in principle Percy showed his claim to the Earldom to be genealogically superior to Hugh's own entirely arbitrary and manufactured claim.

They didn't bother themselves because there was no danger for the present in Percy's picture of the past. They didn't bother themselves because they knew, because the world always knows—Thomas Percy certainly knew—that beneath the placid factuality and apparently correct causality of genealogy lies simple power, the facts of the way the world actually goes and has gone. Most genealogies have crooks and turns in them, following paths not sanctioned by the strict rule of inheritance through eldest heirs male. The turns that matter are those along which power flows; power almost invariably trumps simple genetic causality. Hugh Smithson undoubtedly had infinitely less Percy in him than our quiet clergyman, but it didn't matter. An Act of Parliament made him the Earl, and power flowed down the new path.

Thomas Percy understood that power writes history in the deepest way. He was ambitious and successful, and ended up being called "my Lord" by his now-humbler friends. He did not use his knowledge of old books to claim the Earldom; but he did use it to catch the attention of the Countess.

Thanked Be Fortune

Having become the correct kind of Percy, Thomas Percy busied himself getting to know people and reading old books. This early phase of his career was capped by the publication, in 1765, of *Reliques of Ancient Poetry*, a collection of poetry reprinted from various old books and manuscripts (it includes, in fact, three poems from Tottel). The bulk of the poetry in the *Reliques* derived from a seventeenth-century manuscript in Percy's possession. Percy made the story of his discovery of this manuscript at his cousin Humphrey Pitt's house famous, and he also (typically) wrote the story on the first page of the manuscript itself: "I first saw it lying dirty on the floor underneath a bureau in the Parlour, being used by maids to light the fire." Percy "rescued it from destruction"; he asked Mr. Pitt for it and made his fortune from it. The *Reliques* became one of the most popular and influential books of the eighteenth century.

Percy dedicated the first edition of the *Reliques of Ancient Poetry* to the Countess of Northumberland. He had originally meant to dedicate it to William Shenstone, the sickly, poor, but well-connected poet and landscaper who had given Percy crucial help in meeting important people. Shenstone died shortly before publication, though, allowing Percy to inflect the project more precisely in the direction of his ambition. He had to take out some "indelicate" ballads before the new dedication would work, and he moved ballads featuring Percys to the front. The Countess liked his book and invited him over. In succession, Thomas Percy became tutor to her son, Chaplain to the family, historian of the Percys, Dean of Carlisle, and finally Bishop of Dromore.

Percy's Dedication to the Countess is a masterpiece of its kind. Samuel Johnson was visiting during the summer of 1764 and lent a hand in writing it. This is the third paragraph:

> No active or comprehensive mind can forbear some attention to the Reliques of
> antiquity: it is prompted by natural curiosity to survey the progress of life and
> manners, and to inquire by what gradations barbarity was civilized, grossness
> refined, and ignorance instructed: but this curiosity, Madam, must be stronger
> in those who, like your ladyship, can remark in every period the influence of
> some great Progenitor, and who still feel in their effects the transactions and
> events of distant centuries.

In *Reliques of Ancient Poetry*, poetry appears, once again, as part of a request for notice, a request for some portion of the consequence of the great. Percy was better at it than either Curll or Sewell. For one thing, he had written to the Countess beforehand and asked her permission.

A genealogical vision of the past is still fundamental here. As in Sewell's appeal to the Howards, the pleasure of the great in reading about members of their family and the affirmation of the importance of their genealogical, living history are (rhetorically speaking) reasons enough for publication. Percy's poems bring news from a past that is actually embodied in the living Percys (if you ignore the Act of Parliament). Beyond this simple, traditional flattery, and with Johnson's help, Percy has also added something new to the appeal of the petitioner. There is more "why" here. These poems, in their very past-ness and potential irrelevance, allow us to "survey the progress of life and manners."

Like genealogy, this way of describing the relevance of the past makes the present a destination instead of a simple way station on the path to the future. Looking at rude stuff from the past allows for a calibration of the polish of the present by measuring its distance from the past; looking over these old poems reveals the movement of time, and the end of time in the perfection of the present. This explanation for the relevance of the past becomes the basic rationale for the interest and importance of the eighteenth-century editorial enterprise. The seemingly innocuous and even unimportant activity of reading old books is described very plainly as nation building, as making possible a national project of triumphant self-perception (of perfection).

This story forms the heart of literary history as the eighteenth century saw it, and it contains a problem. Percy needs to convince his potential audience of the value of reading old poems if his book is to have any interest. But if the role of these old poems is to provide contrast to the perfections of the present, then in fact they need to be *bad* in some way, to provide room for improvement. In telling the Countess she perfects Time in her person, Percy has to insult the old poems, which he clearly loves just for themselves, and he needs to look away from the obvious goodness of the poems written (say) by Thomas Wyatt and Henry Howard.

Weaving the Web of Scholarship

The editing of the *Reliques* was a huge undertaking and required many years of effort. Percy reprinted poems from many different periods and many different sources, and also wrote extensive explanatory, editorial machinery. The *Reliques* is a very long way from the guesswork of William Winstanley. It contains notes to poems that explain authorship, delineate sources, draw parallels to other contemporary writing, and in general fill out the picture. In short, Percy knows exactly the kind of things that would have been so hidden and impossible for our Hypothetical Harington of the late seventeenth century.

By the time Thomas Percy began exploring older poetry, and *Tottel's Miscellany* in particular, half a century of busy interchange between people interested in such things had created the foundations of the human-technological web of learning so familiar and important to us today. People knew more facts, they developed ways of regularly telling others what facts they knew, and they developed shared expertise about the location of objects: books in particular. A few important people, on the order of ten or so, created conduits of access to the important libraries, among them the Library at the British Museum, opened in 1753. People like Percy understood better and better what books they were interested in and purchased them at sales whenever they could; they lent these books to their friends. Percy regularly obtained books he needed by borrowing from friends. The famous actor David Garrick, whom he may have met through Johnson, was an important and generous supplier, especially of old drama, sending whole crates of his books out to Percy's country parish.

Joining this network, for a man of mediocre status like Percy, began with a mixture of simple inquiry and canny self-promotion. He might just ask a question of someone, either in person (after a visit had been arranged—no small thing, if out of the way) or by letter, or through a mutual acquaintance. Connecting through mutual friends was perhaps the most important method, and often began at school or University—Oxford, in Percy's case. Percy met William Shenstone, his most valuable early resource, through a common Oxford friend, Robert Binnell.

Among many other connections Shenstone made possible was a connection to Shenstone's own patroness, the Countess of Hertford, who happened to be the mother of Betty Seymour/Smithson, later the Countess/Duchess of Northumberland, the very Target of the *Reliques* (which makes her displacement of Shenstone as the Dedicatee all the more naked and painful). Through Shenstone Percy met Richard Dodsley, the most important midcentury publisher of contemporary poetry, when Shenstone sent Dodsley a couple of Percy's own poems. Dodsley published two of these poems in his *Collection of Poems in Six Volumes* of 1758, which quietly put Percy's name before the whole of the London literary world. On Shenstone's suggestion, and perhaps mediated through Jacob Tonson, another London publisher, Percy met the capable though irascible Shakespeare scholar Edward Capell; through Capell, he met Richard Farmer, a Cambridge Don who would become his most trusted authority on Renaissance issues (he later fell out with Capell but kept Farmer). Through Farmer, Percy gained an entry to Cambridge, to its Libraries, and to Thomas Gray, a famous poet and a deeply learned scholar. He met Samuel Johnson, who provided friendship, a seasoned critical intelligence, and crucial connections to London publishers, through a friend named James Grainger. He had met Grainger through a friend from home in Bridgenorth.

Sometimes it was just plain spontaneous friendship, as in the case of Thomas Astle, whom Percy met by being near him at the British Museum Library, where Astle worked; many others met Astle there too. Astle gave Percy the 1559 edition of Tottel's book.

Percy introduced himself to Thomas Warton, Professor of Poetry at Oxford, a well-known authority on older poetry and the eventual author of the first systematic history of English poetry, through a letter, always the least reliable method, but Warton responded warmly and remained a stalwart helper through many years (as Percy was to him). Shenstone also smoothed this path; he knew Warton too.

Percy was good at this sort of solicitation, as the "Dedication" to the *Reliques* makes clear. Here is some of Percy's letter to Warton, from May 28, 1761:

Sir:

Though this letter comes from one, who has not the pleasure of being personally known to you, the subject of it will, I hope, serve as an Apology for the Abruptness of the address.

Spending a week some time ago with a very intimate friend of mine, who is also known to you, Mr. William Shenstone of the Leasowes; Our Conversation turned on your masterly piece of criticism on *The Fairy Queen*: we both of us joined in hoping for the Credit of the Public Taste, that a new edition would soon be called for: previous to which, I though you would excuse the Liberty, if I endevoured to send you information on one point (tho' a very trivial one) which wants to be set right.

Percy goes on, delicately, tactfully, to tell Warton about a mistake he (Warton) had made in his essay on Spenser. This helps Warton, and by the by demonstrates Percy's deep and rare knowledge of old books; he then tells Warton about his old manuscript of ballads, and the *Reliques*, on which he needs help. He drops Shenstone's name again later, and Johnson's.

Percy took great pains with this letter, writing out a full preparatory draft. He succeeded here as he did in so many other cases. Warton was no doubt encouraged to respond to Percy because of their connection through Shenstone and others. Affiliated enthusiasts' groups of this sort, then and now, are bound by a loose sense of Membership. If a member contacts you, you feel obliged to reply.

Initial entry into the interconnected web was often gained by the publication of some sort of poetry in one of the magazines or anthologies of the time. Through a poem or two a person could come the attention of established authors; Percy and many others did this. The publication of a major work like Percy's *Reliques* was a real benchmark, and his book served him as a sign and carrier of authority for the rest of his life.

The Court of Literature

Percy's career and his learning were served in precisely parallel ways by the same activities. His knowledge and his social/economic advancement both depended entirely on the creation of access to cultural capital. Percy was exceptionally good at opening doors for himself and very shrewd about exploiting the opportunities so created. He also saw his main chance very clearly: turning some of the enormous influence of the Northumberland household in his direction. He exploited this influence pointedly and thoroughly.

A picture of the web of connections Percy created and exploited in his manufacture of the *Reliques* and thus the rest of his very successful career would not look exactly like the picture of Henry's court, which depended so heavily on consanguinity. But navigation of both worlds depended upon a clear understanding of the consequences and advantages of finding a place within a finely articulated social network. A picture of Percy's world would have its Earls, like Samuel Johnson, and its baronets, like Thomas Astle.

Wyatt was a courtier in Henry's court; Percy was a courtier in the broader and somewhat more meritocratic court of mid-eighteenth-century literary London. Both Wyatt and Percy used poetry as a way to demonstrate their qualifications for their respective jobs. The courtier's work is to please those in power, and in pleasing them to also quietly convince them of the courtier's usefulness and the advisability of giving the courtier a place in the structures of power.

Among other things, Wyatt's poetry allowed him to demonstrate his mastery of various rules and values of court life. Percy's poetry, his own and that which he edited, allowed him to do exactly the same. The lyrics Dodsley published in his *Collection* of 1758 show a perfect absorption of midcentury lyric taste:

> A S O N G By T. P***cy.
>
> O Nancy, wilt thou go with me,
>   Nor figh to leave the flaunting town:
> Can filent glens have charms for thee,
>   The lowly cot and ruffet gown?
> No longer drefs'd in filken fheen,
>   No longer deck'd with jewels rare,
> Say can'ft thou quit each courtly fcene,
>   Where thou wert faireft of the fair?

The poem of which this is the first stanza was not meant, particularly, to do anything other than demonstrate a fluent understanding of contemporary literary taste. It is an expression of that understanding and an application for a modest management interest in national contemporary literary culture. Percy's application was accepted enthusiastically. He did not publish his own lyrics again after he became famous.

The Well-Compensated Minstrel

The role of the older poetry in the *Reliques* for Percy's advancement is perhaps less obvious than that of his charming, up-to-date lyrics. In the plainest way, through his editing of older material Percy demonstrated his learning, his attention to detail, and his ability to complete a project, talents attractive to a Countess (say) in the market for a tutor. But the *Reliques* also, as the "Dedication" makes clear, pointedly articulated Percy's commitment to the project of national ambition and Empire that was a central part of the lives of prominent families like that of the Earl and Countess of Northumberland. In the *Reliques* Percy fits older poetry into a programmatic narrative whose destination is the triumphant current moment. He says it this way in his "Preface" to the first edition of 1765:

> Such specimens of ancient poetry have been selected as either shew the gradation of our language, exhibit the progress of popular opinions, display the peculiar manners and customs of former ages, or throw light on our earlier classical poets.
>
> They are here distributed into THREE VOLUMES, each of which contains an independent series of poems, arranged for the most part, according to the order of time, and showing the gradual improvements of the English language and poetry from the earliest stages down to the present.

With a plain, beetle-browed seriousness that is alternately charming and hilarious, Percy associates himself with the improvement of the nation through a description of the role and nature of the ancient "Minstrels," whom he argues are the "authors" of most of the old ballads. His "Essay on the Ancient Minstrels in England" begins the business part of the *Reliques*, and in that essay his goal is to depict the ancient Minstrels as important persons and the source of the valuable old poems.

The detailed descriptions of Minstrels can almost always be read as (hopeful) self-descriptions of Thomas Percy, the ambitious reprinter of old poems and author of "O Nancy." Sometimes, given Percy's own situation, the transparency of the whole operation is rather breathtaking. This goofily autobiographical passage was added in a later edition, after Percy had done research in the archives of the Percy family:

> In all the establishments of the royal and noble households, we find an ample provision made for the Minstrels, and their situation to have been both honourable and lucrative. In proof of this it is sufficient to refer to the Household Book of the Earl of Northumberland, A.D. 1512. And the rewards they receive so frequently recur in the ancient writers, that it is unnecessary to crowd the page with them.

Percy's story of the development of poetry and the role of the Minstrels has only a moderate grounding in facts. One claim Percy makes for the Minstrels, which is not even mostly true, is that they created a pure and deeply English source for all of the important long poems of the past. For Percy, the singer of the national tune, the important thing is that the source of English poetry is not, God forbid, *France*.

Percy did his courtier's work very well. The plain details of the *Reliques* itself, which recovers the cultural past of the Nation, have a simple positive value. Percy flatters the great house of Percy through its past, a method at once highly traditional and effective. And through his picture of the Minstrel, he shows both where poetry fits into the national project and where he, Thomas Percy, can fit within the Northumberland household.

In short, Percy demonstrates that in mastering poetry, new and old, he has mastered and committed himself to the values of the imperial Britain that was busy imposing itself upon the globe. The Countess heard all that Percy was telling her in his book and invested in him in turn. She was right: Percy gave the family exceptional service. His devotion to any Percy cause whatsoever was absolute, and his very publicly articulated admiration of the Percy family was perfect and complete. Hugh Percy was made an overt imperial Power when he was made Lord Lieutenant of Ireland in 1763, and eventually he gave an Irish (Anglican) Bishopric to Thomas Percy. Percy made a fine and gravely responsible Bishop. For instance, when the abused and starving Irish rebelled under Wolfe Tone in 1798, Percy—now "Lord Thomas Dromore"—actively raised militias and helped put the rebellion down.

The Details, and Percy's Reprinting of "They Flee from Me"

The Secret Minstrel

It was unusual for a grocer's son to become a Bishop. Percy's success was earned through extraordinary hard work, shrewdly directed by his clear-sighted ambition. His methods were well suited to his world. Like all good courtiers everywhere, always, he adjusted himself to the shape of power he found.

The *Reliques* was the main lever by which Percy turned the world in his favor. What does that say for Percy's interest in poetry? It says first that poetry, in 1765, was still closely tied to elite culture and still, in many circumstances, functioned as a badge of membership in elite culture. Percy understood this very well (as did a lot of other people: Samuel Johnson, for instance). This was true when Wyatt bid for Henry's favor and the attention of his court, and it was still true when the grocer's son began his climb to "his Lordship."

Still, Thomas Percy was obviously smitten, in a plain way, by poetry. It was his good fortune that poetry could take him where he wanted to go. It was his good fortune that the poems he had fallen in love with as a teenager mentioned the Percy family in flattering terms. The poems he actually published show, at every turn, for better and for worse, the effects of his loving attention.

In his old manuscript Percy found a bit from a widely distributed old European ballad called "The Child of Ell." In the manuscript it was a small piece, some thirty-nine lines. Percy decided to finish it out himself, and the version in the *Reliques* has two hundred lines. He warned the reader in a coy way:

> THE CHILD OF ELLE, is given from a fragment in the Editor's Folio MS: which tho' extremely defective and mutilated, appeared to have so much merit, that it excited a strong desire to attempt a completion of the story. The Reader will easily discover the supplemental stanzas by their inferiority, and at the same time be inclined to pardon it, when he considers how difficult it must be to imitate the affecting simplicity and artless beauties of the original.

What was Percy thinking when he wrote 160 new lines as part of his presentation of the past? Partly he was carefully constructing a product that would sell. But he was also putting his old poetry to use with a purpose, making it his own as Mary Howard and her circle made Wyatt's poem their own. The editor of the old ballad has no author staring gloomily out at him from the shades. So Percy, "excited," imagines an author, and imagines the poem his imagined poet would write, or even did write, before time got hold of the text, and then he writes this imaginary poem out. Since in fact the difference between the original stanzas and Percy's own is not at all obvious, he secretly becomes the Minstrel, in his nearly overt way.

Percy was a bit duplicitous, and he was also cheating: one of the reasons the difference between his own stanzas and those from the manuscript is not obvious is that he changed the stanzas from the manuscript too. For instance, this stanza in the manuscript

> He leaned ore his saddle bow
> To kisse this Lady good
> The tears that went them 2 betweene
> Were blend water and blood

Became, in the *Reliques*,

> And thrice he clasped her to his breste,
> And kist her tenderlie;
> The tears that fell from her fair eyes
> Ranne like the fountayn free.

The carnal frankness of the ballad is quietly turned to tenderness, and the violent eroticism of these characters' union is turned to "free" feeling, felt by a sentimentalized Lady. The resulting poem has no factual integrity at all and is not part of any coherent or consistent history. It is imagined, and part of an imagined past, and its manufactured nature is concealed beneath a surface of pretended frank disclosure. But it is the genuine product of love, and excitement, and Percy's readers felt that part, and liked it, even though it made no sense.

More Corruption

The *Reliques* made Percy famous; eventually, because of changes like those he imposed on "The Child of Ell," his book also made him infamous. Even in an era when editors frequently changed a lot in the books they were reprinting, Percy was notable for how much he changed his texts. His changes are the natural consequence of his struggle with the problem lying at the foundation of the eighteenth-century editor's ambitions. As a servant of Empire, Percy invests heavily in the end point of the present, its polish and perfection. As an editor, however, he is a full inheritor of the editor's fundamental story: the textual fall into corruption that creates the need for the editor. His invaluable manuscript, for instance, saved from the fire, is for him full of corruption, the last material gasp of glorious old texts. He says in his "Preface": "And the Editor has endeavoured to be as faithful, as the imperfect state of his materials would admit: for these old popular rhimes have, as might be expected, been handed down to us with less care, than any other writings in the world." As fully as he voices his investment in the glorious imperial present, Percy is also very much the sadly, even tragically well informed antiquarian, who knows how far the present has declined from the past. The correctness of the present demonstrates the barbarity of the past and results from the narrative of progress. For the editor paging through the dirty and damaged manuscript, however, the present is also corrupted, eaten away by the fire of time, and hence in need of correction (by the knowledgeable scholar).

He can't have both of these, of course: or rather, when these two stories mix they produce simple incoherence, and that incoherence produces Percy's anxiously inconsistent editorial practice, the incoherence of "The Child of Ell."

The texts in his old manuscript demonstrate in a dramatic way the pastness of the past. They are written strangely, they are spelled strangely, their pages are ripped and torn. They tend toward brutality and carnality; they tend toward repetition and value vividness over polish. These qualities magnetized the next generation of poets (Wordsworth was born in 1770), but they were out of sync with the polished present, the present so beautifully defined by Thomas Gray and epitomized in Percy himself. Because they demonstrate the barbaric past so visibly, these poems are excellent material for telling the story of Progress. As evidence for that story, they are judged by the Imperial standard and found to be inferior: "rude." They show up the perfection of the present by being less good.

Percy loved these poems with a simple heartfelt antiquarian's devotion, for what they were in themselves and for their fascinating revelation of the lost past. He read them because they gripped his heart, and he would wish everyone to feel the same. He was introducing his charges to the public, however, and was anxious for approval. Percy distinguished himself from his fellow dusty scholars in his strikingly shrewd marketing, his careful understanding of contemporary taste: the Percy who published "O Nancy" in Dodsley. As a shrewd marketer, he faced that good question: Why, in the end, would people want to read poetry whose advertised attraction is that it is less good than contemporary poetry?

In fact, Percy knew they wouldn't. So, because he loved his poems and wanted others to love them, and because he wanted his book to sell, and because he wanted the Countess to give him a place, he changed his poems so people would like them better, and he placed them in a story that made sense of their shape. He was overcome by spiritual secular ecstasy. He felt himself in a miraculous state where all seemed to be tending toward the advancement of truth and Thomas Percy at once. In this way his book became a hit, and also nonsense as a presentation of the past. Most of his readers either did not notice or forgave him. Some noticed and did not forgive him: his archenemy will come on stage shortly.

The Problem of Classical (English) Poets

However flawed the fervor of eighteenth-century editors, their fervor fueled an intense and enormously productive period of learning. By the end of Percy's life, the basic facts that constitute the raw material for the history of poetry in English were known. A lot of work has been done since, but it has been mostly filling in.

Percy took up what was to be a fifty-year effort at editing *Tottel's Miscellany* in the early 1760s, right in the midst of his most productive years. He described his project to Thomas Warton in a letter of November 28, 1762: "I have some intentions myself of reprinting Surrey's poems in a neat 12mo form. We have no good modern edition of that ancient Miscellany, tho' most of its contents are of Classic Elegance. . . . " Percy's friend Johnson had defined "classic" this way, seven years previously: "Relating to antique authors; relating to literature."

Ballads, which make up most of what Percy published in the *Reliques*, were examples of poetry at large, circulating in the world and living by their ability to catch the memory of listeners. Because they had no recorded authors, Percy could do what he wanted with them. They were easily fit into the story Percy imagined for himself and for history, and the ambitions that produced this poetry could simply be made up: "Minstrels."

Partly because of what he and his fellow scholars had learned, however, the poems of Wyatt and Surrey were less amenable to Percy's storytelling. They had a firm identity as formerly living English people of consequence, a consequence identical in nature to that of Percy's Patroness. Wyatt and Surrey also already had a well-known presence in other, already told stories about the past that were not primarily about poetry. Their "classic elegance" made them like the authors of Rome and Greece.

Wyatt and Surrey themselves knew quite a lot about previous poetry and were working within a tradition they were creating and understood. They didn't need Percy to give them a place, and their poems could not easily be placed in the story of improvement. They were old, but they were accomplished, self-conscious, and elegant: the very opposite of "rude." Percy notices this problem in the "Preface" to the *Reliques*. Comparing his old ballads to the older lyric poems (like the three from Tottel) he has included in his book, he says: "The artless productions of these old rhapsodists, are occasionally confronted with specimens of the composition of contemporary poets of a higher class: of those who had all the advantages of learning in the times in which they lived, and who wrote for fame and posterity." This description is a plain disjoint moment and presents the kind of evidence that eventually renders the imperial history of improving poetry obviously partial and dysfunctional. Percy himself simply doesn't discuss the implications these poets have for the imperial story of poetry. Like so many master narratives of its type, the story of improvement obviously didn't work, but that didn't make it any less compelling to its tellers and consumers.

Percy knew a lot of facts about the poetry of the past, and he knew a lot about Tottel's book and its associated poets. A lot of sorting had been done, chronologies had been created, causality guessed at and determined. He and his fellow scholars had discovered the poetry of the past. "Literature" in Johnson's definition of "classical," however, was still a generous, inclusive term, gradually growing toward the value-based meaning of the word in our own time (as in "Are old ballads really literature?"). Johnson defined it simply: "learning; skill in letters." Percy's instinct was to associate Wyatt and Surrey with "classical" authors and hence writing that had already been periodized and sorted by value, which was being incorporated into the imperial story in this period. In this way the writing of Wyatt and Surrey was (said to be) "literature."

The storytelling stymie produced by the presence of consequential authors and their identity as makers of Literature was a profound impediment for Percy and was the source of the fifty years he spent on the project. He couldn't simply exercise his imagination, and he felt pressure to get it right in a plain detailed way. As we will see, his printed book is, quietly, as imaginary a representation of the past as the *Reliques* is, but he did not change any of the texts in Tottel the way he did the "Child of Ell."

Editing Tottel was harder because Percy couldn't make it all up.

Writing in the Old Book

Percy wrote copious notes in his copy of Tottel's book, a book now in the Houghton Library at Harvard. These notes depict, in miniature, the long labor of learning that constructed, during the eighteenth century, the history of literature and poetry we so deeply benefit from today. They do this through their simple existence and through their content.

These notes, most of them on the opening flyleaves of the book, record the labor of half of a lifetime. Much of Percy's great community of scholars is represented, and many of their accomplishments. He mentions copies of older editions he looked at (Curll); he mentions several scholars, both his friends and others (Capell, Farmer, Astle, John Aubrey). He mentions the "public" libraries of Cambridge and Oxford; he mentions private collections too (the Countess of Northumberland and Lord Holland). He refers to reference books, he describes what bibliography he has been able to assemble; he records his eventual discovery that his edition of 1559 was not the first (he learned about an edition of 1557 from Edward Capell). Percy's copy of Tottel is also full of annotation, the product of collations with other editions, amounting to instructions to the printer, written in red ink.

But why write *in* the book? Why not attach a note, or write it somewhere else? It might seem that an antiquarian of Percy's type, with his heartfelt reverence for old printed books, would be loath to deface this hardy survivor. But nothing could be more common than writing in such books. Percy and all his friends did it routinely. Why was the book not a more sacred object, in the way we think of such books?

There is a practical reason. The eighteenth century was, in particular, constructing the habits and technology of regular communication that would underwrite the various webs of interchange between people thinking about similar things and become the business of scholarship as we know it. This was most typically carried out by letter, especially as the century progressed. But scholarship is full of detail, and its real business, in fact, is in the smallest of details. Not many correspondents wanted or needed to get long lists of such small learning. Professional journals did not exist. The end result was that copies of old books owned and read by scholars in the seventeenth and eighteenth centuries are full of notes, many of them very elaborate.

Percy's notes sound, rhetorically, very much like typical "scholarly" writing of today. Who is Percy talking to? Us, for one thing; he is talking to the Future. He foresees an arc through time for the book now in his hands, and he sees himself in one spot along that arc. His book had past readers, and it will have future readers, and Percy is talking to them and providing his book with a coat of history to protect it as it goes along. These notes will keep it from falling out of the accumulation of facts so laboriously assembled by Percy in the course of forty years of thinking and peering into old libraries. Percy is imagining a community of people interested in this book and what it contains, but he is not imagining the continuing infrastructure of knowledge we take for granted. The book needs to carry its history with it because this history is not located anywhere else. Partly, Percy writes in the book because there is nowhere else to write.

Percy also does not fret about writing in his book because, in the end, this particular book is mostly just a damaged incarnation of an immaterial entity, *Songes and Sonettes*, the "book" Percy is editing. The physical book in his hands is not that object. Percy's book has many errors in it; his copy was (and still is) missing pages. It is part of the fallen (material) world, overwhelmed by time. The real book, the one Percy is editing and means to reprint, lives in a conceptual Elysium, beyond and above the book's fallen physical examples. So partly Percy writes in the book as a way of helping it be a *better* object, more complete, more like itself, more like the book that got so corrupted by entering into the mortal world.

Percy Overhears a Harington Puttering in His Library

Percy learned about the existence of the version of "They Flee from Me" in Wyatt's book because the (current) last of the Haringtons, named Henry, published some poems from it in a book called *Nugae Antiquae*, or, in English, *Old Stuff*. This book, published in 1769, with a second volume added in 1775, was one of many books appearing shortly after the publication of the *Reliques* that attempted to capitalize on the resulting craze for older poetry. Henry was in his teens at the time, and, in spite of his late date, this Henry Harington turns out to be the actual ignorant but hopeful Harington I imagined, standing in his library looking at his books.

Nugae Antiquae contains some poems by Wyatt: for instance, "My Lute Awake," misattributed to "Lord Rocheford" and given the seemingly random date of 1564. It also notes that this poem was "in Manuscript." Other poems are correctly attributed to Wyatt and come from either of the two manuscripts known to have been in the Harington family (Wyatt's book and the one John Harington the Elder made for himself, now known as the Arundel Harington manuscript).

Wyatt's book had remained within the purely domestic Harington world for almost two centuries, and wider knowledge of it had simply disappeared. It seems likely that Henry had just been fooling around in his family's library and, like Percy, was excited by what he found and by the idea of turning manuscripts into a book. In his note "to the Reader" in the 1775 volume, Harington, in an offhand, gentlemanly apology for the mixed nature of the stuff in his book, says: "Several [items] were accidentally met with on examining old Family-Books, whose contents were, as usual, truly Miscellaneous."

Henry was just another Harington in his library. He was making a book out of some old papers he had found. For instance, from damage to the two manuscripts, it seems that one of his methods was simply tearing out pages and sending them along as printer's copy. He did this, of course, because he wanted to, and he could do it because the books were his.

As goofy as it is, in all its gentlemanly, easy ignorance, the *Nugae* did do something important. It alerted Percy and others in the community of scholars to the existence of Wyatt's book. It was the first time after Tottel that the book had been used as a source for a printed text. Tottel began an era by printing poems from this book; the *Nugae* marks the end of the private world of Wyatt's book, the end of its life as a thing the Haringtons owned. It is not simply that people now knew about it, which had happened before. This time the information Wyatt's book contained had a place to go. It entered into a conceptual structure, the history of poetry, and would never lose its place again. It didn't just contain poems. Now it contained *literature*.

Henry refers in an offhand way to his library and to his manuscripts, but people like Percy were quite literally waiting for Henry's manuscript to show up, looking eagerly for things like it, so they knew already what it was when they heard about it. They were maintaining open files, trying hard to put things in. The creation of the larger shape of history showed them were to look. Like the old explorers' maps, the outline of history created blank spots that focused the energy of investigators. When Percy looked at Wyatt's book in the early 1790s (he borrowed it from Henry's modestly well-known father Henry Harington, MD; the younger Henry died young), he immediately saw *through* it to other facts and connections and to the larger, growing narrative of history. He recorded these connections in his cross-references to Tottel's book, penciling those jottings on the upper corners of our page.

After Percy looked at the poem on that page in Wyatt's book, beginning "They flee from me," and cross-referenced it to Tottel, the poem exchanged one kind of objecthood for another. Its life as an independent material object, as this particular poem and nothing else, came to an end. It became one of several versions of a poem by Thomas Wyatt the Elder, a poet and courtier in Henry VIII's court. It lost the integrity and sturdy isolated identity of the unique object, but it gained the stability and hardiness of a larger, less physically dependent object. It took its place in the flow of event and text that began, in this case, with the publication of Tottel's book two hundred years before.

Percy seemed to think the cross-reference was enough; or, in any case, it was all he did. He did not make any actual use of the manuscript text in reprinting the poem. Perhaps he was tired. Perhaps he didn't notice the differences. But mostly he distrusted handwriting, seeing it as the mortal preliminary to printing. As he says in the note he wrote at the beginning of Wyatt's book: some of these poems have *already* been printed.

Percy Also Wrote in the Haringtons' Book

Percy wrote in Wyatt's book, now the property of Henry Harington, MD, in many different places. He wrote notes, and he wrote a note at the beginning to describe why he wrote the other notes. He had borrowed the manuscript, keeping it for years before returning it, and so he also was writing in a book that was not his. He did this for the same reasons he wrote in his copy of Tottel.

There was, first, no other secure place to write down what he knew. Beyond that, the book was merely the physical incarnation of more abstract things, and in its fallen way was less valuable than those things. Percy wanted the information this manuscript contained, but he didn't seem to care much about what sort of integrity it might have as an object on its own. Even Henry Harington's ownership of the manuscript seems to be diluted by this way of thinking about it. It was not so much an object in itself as an indicator of the existence of other objects.

But it is striking that Wyatt's own book, now a treasure much more important than a copy of Tottel's book, should not have made Percy pause. Even the very paper Wyatt touched and wrote on took second place to the great, imaginary, immaterial story of time Percy and his friends were busy telling.

Percy's Tottel

Here is Percy's reprinted text of "They Flee from Me," in one of the surviving proof copies now at Yale's Beinecke Library (more on "surviving" in a moment):

The louer ſheweth how he is for-
faken of ſuch as he ſom-
tyme enioyed.

Hey flee from me, that ſometime did me ſeke
    With naked foote ſtalking within my chamber:
Once haue I ſene them gentle, tame, and meke,
That now are wilde, and do not once remember
That ſometime they haue put themſelues in danger
To take bread at my hand ; and now they range
    Buſely ſeking in continual change.
    Thanked be fortune, it hath ben otherwiſe
Twenty times better; but once eſpeciall,

In thynne aray, after a pleafant gife
When her loofe gowne did from her fhoulders fall,
And fhe me caught in her armes long and fmall,
And therwithall, fo fwetely did me kiffe,
And foftly faid; Deare hart, how like you this?
  It was no dreame; for I lay broade awaking:
But all is turnde now through my gentleneffe,
Into a bitter fafhion of forfaking:
And I haue leaue to go of her goodneffe;
And fhe alfo to vfe new-fangleneffe.
But fins that I vnkindly fo am ferued:
How like you this, what hath fhe now deferued?

Percy has changed some of the punctuation, changes visible in a spattering of red ink on this page in his 1559 copy of the original (the spelling is the same as this 1559 copy). He turns some colons into semicolons, a comma into a colon, and so on. The punctuation after "better" is a comma in his 1559 edition and a colon in Edward Capell's copy of the second 1557 edition, which Percy was using to "correct" the 1559 (just to keep things straight, the second edition consists of two separate printings; the second of these, which we know of through the copy owned by Edward Capell, is the source for all further editions). The change from a comma to a semicolon is, of course, a very small change, but it is nevertheless a change, and not authorized by any of the texts of the poem Percy had seen. Even just one is infinitely greater than zero, and these changes mark Percy's reprinted text as an imagined, improved text, and the improvement derives from something Percy is thinking, not something he has found in the world.

A more noticeable example of Percy's thinking can be found in his reprinting of Tottel's note "To the Reader":

¶ *To the Reader.*

THAT to have wel written in verfe, yea, and in fmal
  parcelles, deferueth great prayfe, the 'workes'
of diuers Latines, Italians, and other, doe proue

sufficiently. That our tong is able in that kinde to
doe as prayſe worthely as the reſt, the honorable ſtile
of the noble Earle of Surrey, and the weightineſſe
of the depe-witted ſir Thomas Wyat the elders
verſe, with ſeueral graces in ſundry good Englyſh
writers, do ſhew aboundantly. It reſteth now (gentle reader) that thou think it not euyll done, to pub-
liſhe to the honor of the Engliſhe tong, and for profite of the ſtudious of Engliſhe eloquence, thoſe
workes which the ungentle horders up of ſuch trea-
ſure have heretofore enuied thee. And for this point
(good reader) thine owne profite and pleaſure, in
theſe preſently, and in moe hereafter, ſhal anſwere
for my defence. If perhappes ſome miſlike the ſtate-
lyneſſe of ſtyle remoued from the rude ſkil of common eares ; I aſke helpe of the learned to de-
fende theyr learned frendes, the authors
of this woorke : And I exhort the unlearned, by reading to learne to
be more ſkilful, and to purge .
that ſwinelike groſſeneſſe,
that maketh the ſweete
maierome not to
ſmel to their
delight.

The dagger-point form of this text first appears in the second edition, Edward
Capel's copy. The presence of the reversed "P" before "To the Reader" proves,
by the by, that Percy had access to Capell's copy, since the reversed "P" appears
only in that text. The shape of the text might be incidental, to one way of thinking, and not related to the information contained in the words; or it might be
meaningful, as illustrating, perhaps, sixteenth-century printing styles. It might be
valuable simply as fact, as the actual way the old object appeared. Percy doesn't
say, but he retains it anyway, overwriting the semantic content of the prose with
its shape. This (momentary) interest in the physicality of the book is curious:
perhaps Percy just liked the way it looked, and love displaced theory.

Percy's fundamental distrust of the physical is here too: the "works" in the
second line is an editorial intervention by Percy, marked with inverted com-
mas in the same way he (sometimes) marked his interventions in the *Reliques*.
In Capell's copy this word is "woorkers." It is "workes" in Percy's 1559 copy;

so in this case Percy is going the other way and correcting the 1557 text by reference to the 1559. In correcting "woorkers" Percy is once again driven by his imagining of an ideal text, one that does not exist as an actual object in the world. He (easily) detects and corrects this error by thinking about the meaning of the sentence in which it appears; this process, in the normal way, guides him to print the word found in his 1559 text. Since (for instance) the 1559 text does not have the reverse "P," here again, in a small way, is the eighteenth-century editor's typical painful muddle. Percy is reprinting *neither* the 1557 text *nor* the 1559.

Percy knows about the past and wants to deliver it to the present, which can benefit from that past. He knows that the prose at the front of the book was (sometimes) printed as a tapered text. He also knows about the depredations to which mortal things are subject, and so, from his superior perspective, he remakes the past according to an ideal he can only imagine. The past he shows to the present, a past rescued (by Percy's remaking) from oblivion, is *better* than the past discoverable in any actual old stuff. His book, like the restored spelling of his name, represents the past as (he thinks) it would have wanted to be.

Fire, Time's Devourer

In a curious reversal of fortune, Percy's reprinting of Tottel is now considerably rarer than the original book it reprints. For fifty years he looked for various texts by Surrey to add to the book, in addition to the text from Tottel, and labored over his semicolons and other small details. Other things happened too. His publisher Jacob Tonson died in 1767, essentially halting work on the book. In 1783 Percy, now Thomas, Lord Dromore, had the sheets that had been completed transferred to the hands of the printer John Nichols, and work slowly began again. Percy seems to have put in some real work in the early '90s, when he looked at Henry Harington's manuscripts. The book slowly made its way toward publication during the first years of the new century, when Percy sent proofs to a few friends. John Nichols also had a copy at his house.

These proofs are all that now exist. John Nichols's warehouse went up in flames in 1808, and the entire edition was destroyed, except for these sets, along with most of Nichols's business. Neither Percy nor Nichols had the energy to start it again. Percy died in 1811.

On Beyond Percy

An Uncorrupted but Very Angry Antiquary

Among the few people who could see through Percy's imaginary past was Joseph Ritson, a scholar some twenty years younger than Percy. Ritson had announced his presence in 1782 when he published *Observations on the First Three Volumes of the History of English Poetry: a Familiar Letter to the Author*; the author referred to is Thomas Warton, whom we have met briefly already. Ritson's distinguishing mark, other than his minutely accurate scholarship, was the astonishing asperity of his tone, his tendency to both think and say the worst about any particular problem. Critique, for Ritson, meant attack. He assumed errors were the result of fraud. In his critiques of Warton, he rarely passes up an opportunity to include Percy in his attack. Here is a typical moment, when Ritson takes up Warton's description of Wyatt's translations of Petrarch; Ritson depends on his certainty that neither Warton nor Percy could read Italian.

> I had puzzled myself for a long time to find out how you could possibly become acquainted with the circumstance of Wyatt's obligation to Petrarch. . . . I have doubted whether you were not indebted to your illustrious friend the Bishop of Dromore: But alas! I know not that his lordship is much better acquainted with Petrarch than yourself. I might, indeed, have remained in perpetual ignorance; if I had not accidentally cast my eye upon the 15th page of the 10th volume of the last edition of Shakespeare; where I find the ingenious Dr. Farmer quoting this very sonnet, and referring to Wyatts translation with all the particularities you could have desired.

Because Ritson's scholarship was usually impeccable, those critiqued, however they felt about the tone, usually adopted his changes. His primary sin, the one people hated him for, was his refusal to honor the delicately articulated social network that made up the real technology of eighteenth-century scholarship. He neither politely ignored the errors of his colleagues nor wrote them kind solicitous letters, like the letter in which Percy introduced himself to Thomas Warton. He was radically passionate in all his reactions to everything; he was intensely agitated by errors other people made, and intensely agitated by criticism of his own errors.

A lawyer by profession—a desultory though apparently competent lawyer—Ritson was out of step with his colleagues in almost every way. He found the devotion to contemporary taste discoverable in a book like the *Reliques* repulsive.

He had not been educated at either Oxford or Cambridge; he was not socially ambitious; he insulted people in print and in conversation; he was a radical and angry vegetarian. He was a vocal and insistent Jacobin. He even objected to modern spelling habits and invented a system of his own, visible in the title of one of his later publications: *Ancient Engleish Metrical Romanceës*. So there is no surprise in his hatred of the imperial story given shape by Percy and fully applied by Thomas Warton in his history of poetry in English.

Corruption Exposed

Ritson began his direct attacks on Percy early, in material attached to his *Select Collection of English Songs*, published in 1783; he was still at it just before he died, with no diminishment of exuberance, in the "Dissertation" attached to *Ancient Engleish Metrical Romanceës* (1802). His critique in this Dissertation is thorough, taking Percy to task for bad scholarship as well as a toadying expression of Imperial Perfection.

To Percy's claim (in the 1794 edition of the *Reliques*) that the minstrels were "the genuine successors of the ancient BARDS, who, under different names, were admired and revered, from the earliest ages, among the people of Gaul, Britain, Ireland, and the ancient North," Ritson replies, in his "Dissertation": "It is a mere hypothesis, without the least support from fact or history, or anything, in a word, but a visionary or fanciful imagination." He is relentless in his critique of Percy's attempts to bring the origin of romance to Britain, which Percy does as the firm underpinning of his nationalist literary history. Ritson insists that all early English romances were translations from the French, and he pursues a spirited, consistently anti-History history of England. He calls the Saxons "a spiritless and cowardly race" and describes the Normans as imperial invaders, simply. He calls William the Conqueror "William, Duke of Normandy" or "William the bastard"; he insists King Richard (Ritson refuses him "Lionheart") was "never known to have uttered a single word of English."

His own description of the origin of romance is ferociously divorced from the imperial tale:

> After all, it seems highly probable that the origin of romance in every age or country is to be sought in the different systems of superstition which have from time to time prevailed, whether pagan or Christian. . . . There is this distinction, indeed, between the heathen deities and the Christian saints, that the fables of the former were indebted for their existence to the flowery imagination of the sublime poet, and the legends of the latter to the gloomy fanaticism of a lazy monk or stinking priest.

His direct references to Percy are full of sly energy: "the ingenious Doctor, or Bishop Percy"; "the ingenious Prelate"; "the Bishop of Dromore (as he now is)." He refers to Percy's doctored "minstrel" ballads thus: "such as may have been published with great inaccuracy and licentiousness by the Right Reverend the Lord Bishop of Dromore." Ritson's own descriptions of minstrels are brilliantly if viciously targeted at the carefully constructed picture into which the clergyman/scholar/poet Percy so perfectly inserted himself. Quoting Renaissance attacks on strolling singers, Ritson calls them "a parcel of drunken sockets and baudy parasites. . . . It is, at the same time, no small compliment to the minstrels of former ages that, as they were, doubtless, much more active and useful, they were infinitely better paid than the idle and good-for-nothing clergy." Sometimes Ritson is simply and fantastically abusive. Attacking Percy's justifications for his changes to a Scottish song, which Percy describes as "corrupted" in a printed version, Ritson lets fly: "This, however, is an INFAMOUS LYE; it being much more likely that he himself, who has practiced every kind of forgery and imposture, had some such end to alter this identical line, with much more violence, and, as he owns himself, actual 'CORRUPTION,' to give the quotation an air of antiquity, which it was not entitled to." And amid all the anger there is not a better, clearer description of Percy's methods than the following summary of his critique of Percy's presentation of the "The Marriage of Sir Gawaine":

> This mode of publishing ancient poetry displays, it must be confessed, considerable talent and genius, but savors strongly, at the same time, of unfairness and dishonesty. Here are numerous stanzas inserted which are not in the original, and others omitted which are there. The purchasers and perusers of such a collection are deceived and imposed upon; the pleasure they receive is derived from the idea of antiquity, which, in fact, is a perfect illusion.

Hatred

Though he professed otherwise, Percy was very sensitive to Ritson's attacks and made many changes in response for the fourth edition of the *Reliques* in 1794. This brief passage about his manuscript, for instance, which I quoted above from the 1765 edition of the "Preface,"—"For these old popular rhymes being many of them copied only from illiterate transcripts, or the imperfect recitation of itinerant ballad-singers, have, as might be expected, been handed down to us with less care than any writings in the world"—receives this nervously extended semijustification:

And the old copies, whether MS. or printed, were often so defective or corrupted, that a scrupulous adherence to their wretched readings would only have
exhibited unintelligible nonsense, or such poor meager stuff as neither came
from the bard nor was worthy of the press: when, by a few slight corrections
or additions, a most beautiful or interesting sense hath started forth, and this
so naturally and easily, that the Editor could seldom prevail upon himself to
indulge the vanity of making a formal claim to the improvement.

As with all of Percy's descriptions of his methods, this explanation, if anything,
makes his imaginary texts all the more troubling. His explanations also serve
as shrewdly effective methods of concealment: What better way to hide your
changes than to say you will mark them, and then not mark all of them?

In its strikingly perceptive if utterly contrary understanding of Percy's ambi-
tiously self- and nation-serving formulation of literary history, Ritson's critique of
Percy was, to Percy, simply intolerable, but since Ritson was mostly right, there
was no possible response he could make to the real content of Ritson's attacks.
Percy understood in his heart, if not elsewhere, that Ritson rendered the very
foundations of his life's project unstable. So he responded with hatred.

Joseph Ritson died in terrifying circumstances in the fall of 1803. We will see
him off in a moment. Percy, until his own death in 1811, busied himself in making sure that people knew the full circumstances of Ritson's sad end, contributing
some tasty tidbits he made up for the occasion. Writing on October 21, 1803,
shortly after Ritson's death, to Dr. Robert Anderson of Edinburgh, one of his
favorite correspondents of his later years, Percy says: "Wretched man!. . . . The
irritability and acerbity of his Temper, I have been told, was not more remarkable
than his immoderate pursuit of venereal indulgences, and it is the opinion of
some Philosophers that such a Regimen as his, promotes both more than a fat
fleshy diet, as it produces a keener Sensibility." The "regimen" Percy refers to is
Ritson's well-known vegetarianism. The last mention of Ritson's sins in Percy's
letters is June 1811, just a few months before Percy's own death.

(Vegetarians)
There is real, simple horror in Percy's focused nastiness about Ritson. His rel-
ish in imagining Ritson's way of life as leading to his terrible end was common at the time. Ritson was modestly well known. Only Walter Scott is on
record objecting to the retailing of nasty details about his death; Scott looked
past Ritson's flaws and saw a person of integrity (and good scholarship). The

fundamental source of Ritson's scary, verminous otherness can be summed up in one word: vegetarian.

Ritson wrote a book about vegetarianism, called *An Essay on the Abstinence from Animal Food, as a Moral Duty.* Then as now, eating theories had strong spiritual, political, and ecological valence. For Ritson being a vegetarian was thoroughly a way of life. Most of the people around him, and Thomas Percy certainly, would have felt it as a kind of un-English-ness, maybe even as Jacobinical French-ness:

> The barbarous and unfeeling sports (as they are call'd) of the Engleish—their horse-raceing, hunting, shooting, bul and bear-baiting, cock-fighting, prize fighting, and the like, all proceed from their immoderate addiction to animal food. Their natural temper is thereby corrupted, and they are in the habitual and hourly commission of crimes against nature, justice, and humanity, from which a feeling and reflective mind, unaccustomed to such a diet, would revolt, but in which they profess to take delight.

(People also would have noticed the curious spelling, the result of Ritson's spelling theories: another objection to the English way.) Contemporary vegetarians were sometimes Scottish doctors, sometimes murderous Jacobin military strategists, sometimes nudists and sexual free-thinkers, sometimes absolute Nutters. Sometimes they were Percy Shelley, who owned and heavily annotated a copy of Ritson's book. Sometimes they were interested in South Asian culture for its own sake and not as an object of plunder. If the Vegetarian way of thinking—presented as *moral duty*—were to be adopted universally, all kinds of things would have had to change. For Ritson, being a vegetarian was the same as regarding the slave trade as an "abominable violation of the rights of nature." Thomas Lord Dromore might think, might think correctly, that if vegetarians were in charge, he might have ended up at the end of the Irish rebels' rope instead of the other way around.

Another Fire

Joseph Ritson made an anthology himself. The first volumes were published in 1793, during a period when many anthologies were coming to market. In his "Advertisement" he makes typically high claims for his book, which he says is conducted "upon a plan hitherto unattempted"; he means his idea of presenting a very limited number of poems, comprising only the "best." In this idea, as in other of his ideas, Ritson looks more like us than his contemporaries do. The first poem in his collection is by Thomas Wyatt, but it is not our poem; it is "My Lute Awake." Ritson says that "no alteration (except in apparent mistakes) . . .

has been made either in the language or in the orthography," and indeed the poem he presents has some of the odder old spellings retained. But Ritson also makes some changes. He inserts punctuation, for instance.

There is a lesson in Ritson's small changes. It is one thing to show the corruption lurking within Percy's stories of the past: but it is another to entirely purge such corruption from one's own stories. The decisions a reprinter needs to make when reprinting poems from Tottel's book are not eased by refusing Percy's sort of imaginary work. The world *is* corrupt; to be in the world is to be mortal and subject to corruption. The several versions of Tottel's book demonstrate this truth if nothing else. Ritson can't reproduce the past exactly because, as the struggles of Edmund Curll demonstrate, the past does not exist in any exact way. One of the places to contact the famous unpleasantness of Ritson's personality is in his refusal to acknowledge the challenges inherent in *any* attempt to represent the past.

In the end, Ritson and Percy made perfect adversaries because they represented opposite approaches to the same project. It was a civil war. They were both in their own ways idealists, and they both felt that editing could erase corruption and change the world. Percy erased time by presenting an imagined past; Ritson erased time by insisting the past could be presented directly, without corruption. When these two deeply sympathetic but entirely opposed views encountered each other, an explosion was the inevitable result. They were, quite literally, incompatible.

Percy was born to operate in a corrupt world, being so good at understanding it and accommodating himself to it. Ritson had a predictably a much harder time. He expected the world to be free of corruption and so was continually disappointed.

Thomas Percy, Lord Dromore, died peacefully at the age of eighty-two. Joseph Ritson died a raving lunatic at the age of fifty. His last days in Lincoln's Inn, where he lived, were dramatic and terrifying. He raged at his neighbors with knives and daggers and threw his furniture from the windows. Eventually a keeper from a madhouse came to sit with him; he was then taken to the madhouse itself, where he soon died, in September of 1803. On the last unsupervised day of his life, his last act was to pile up his papers and manuscripts—a valuable collection, accumulated over a lifetime—and light them on fire.

Of Fire, More Generally

The great library of Sir Robert Cotton, a Renaissance collector of both books and manuscripts, formed the heart of the nascent Library at the British Museum, having been given to the nation by his descendants in 1702. As the Library struggled toward institutional reality, this collection, the physical stuff that was, for the moment, the Library's reason for being, wandered around London in search of a home, moving mostly because of a fear of fire. In 1731 it was located in Ashburnham House in Westminster, where, in fact, it caught on fire.

Several Cotton manuscripts represent true historical bottlenecks: texts known from no other copies. The alliterative poem *Sir Gawaine and the Green Knight*, for instance, one of the great poetic accomplishments in English, descends to us from its mysterious past in one single copy, a copy that was in Ashburnham House that night. The unique source for the poem we know as *Beowulf* was there too: it is charred around the edges. Many manuscripts were saved by being thrown out the windows, sometimes being pulled out of shelving that was already on fire. The arc from window to ground is just one part of the long path these poems traveled from the past to us.

It could easily have been otherwise, and no doubt really has been otherwise in many other cases. In the end, nothing can save us or our things: all will be consumed in fire. Perhaps Joseph Ritson was learning this truth in his last desperate days. For his whole life he had railed against the unnecessary contamination of a past that only needed showing to come to us intact. Corruption could be eradicated by doing the right thing. The darker truth about time and our relationship to it is in the flames Ritson tried to set in his pile of paper; these flames are kin to the flames that also consumed, with a sort of avenging appetite, Percy's reprinting of Tottel's book, and, with it, his reprinting of Wyatt's poem about the unforgiving progress of time.

Robert Anderson Makes the Point Moot

The conflict between Percy and Ritson is a life-and-death struggle over the editorial heart of the eighteenth century. Opposed but equally idealizing versions of the editor's task encounter each other and leave nothing but ashes behind. As it turned out, it didn't really matter. The world was moving along without them. The eighteenth century was over.

For instance, while Percy struggled over his edition of Tottel, the person to whom he sent his Ritson insults, the modest and highly energetic Robert Anderson, MD, of Edinburgh, assembled one of the first really representative anthologies of older poetry, putting together a remarkably full collection and publishing it in the mid-1790s. This edition marked if not made a sea change. In Anderson's volumes, whole tracts of older poetry could be held in the hand. William Wordsworth, for instance, a starveling poet in the 1790s, first read older poetry in Anderson's books. Wordsworth didn't need to know anyone famous or influential, in other words, in order to contact the past. Anderson included lives of the poets, with most of the text copied from Thomas Warton's history.

Anderson, with no apparent fuss, reprinted most of Tottel in his first volume. Here is our poem:

D SONETTES.   619

The lover sheweth how he is forsaken of such as he
sometime enjoyed.

THEY flee from me, that sometime did me seke,
With naked fote stalking within my chamber,
Once have I sene them gentle, tame, and meke,
That now are wyld, and do not once remember.
That sometime they have put themselves in dan-
        ger,
To take bread at my hand, and now they range,
Busely seking in continual change.
    Thanked be fortunc, it hath been otherwyse,
Twenty tymes better, but once especiall,
In thine aray, after a pleasaunt gyse,
When her loose gowne did from her shoulders
        fall,
And she me caught in her armes long and small;
And therwithall, so swetely did me kysse,
And softly sayd, dear hearte, how like you this?
    It was no dreame, for I lay brode awaking.
But all is turned now through my gentlenesse,
Into a bitter fashion of forsaking,
And I have leave to goe of her goodnesse;
And she also to use new fanglenesse,
But, syns that I unkendly so am served,
How like you this, what hath she now deserved?

This text clearly derives from a 1565 or later copy of Tottel, as the familiar "thine" shows; but it is not exactly like any of them. It might well derive from the much less rare edition issued by Curll in 1728. But above all it shows no sign of struggle. Reprinting was (comparatively) easy for Anderson because the whole of the eighteenth century lay behind him. He could correspond with Thomas Percy, he could read Percy's books and the books of Percy's friends and enemies, of both Warton and Ritson. He was without access to the great libraries of the south, and without access to the houses of the Great; but by and large poetry had escaped from those places anyway. He didn't need to invent history. He just needed to follow it, partly by reading Thomas Warton's book. He clearly didn't fret over the precise details of his texts. Above all, the poems in Anderson's book are *literature*. They are part of a highly detailed, continuously unfolding, chronologically ordered string of past events, narrated into history by their very order, and by the critical lives Anderson and Warton provide for each poet.

Anderson did care about his reasons for making his anthology, and he lists them out in generous profusion:

> To do justice to neglected merit; to extend the honour of our national poetry, as far as possible, both abroad and at home; to enlarge, however little, the boundaries of literary biography and elegant criticism; to strengthen and co-operate with the taste for poetical antiquities, which, for sometime past, has been considerably advancing; to hold out an incentive to the love of fame and the cultivation of the mind; to diversify the materials of common reading, and to open fresh sources of useful instruction and innocent amusement, are ends which, though to attain be beyond his powers, the honest ambition of the editor is something gratified by the attempt alone.

This is a good and ambitious list; but it does not include Percy's fundamental argument, repeated in Warton, that showing the past will demonstrate the perfection of time in the present. The imperial story, into which Wyatt cannot be inserted, is simply dropped. This is all the more noticeable because a lot of what Anderson says about Wyatt, for instance, is taken directly from Warton. No doubt Anderson forgets the imperial story partly because it makes no sense, but also partly because he doesn't need it. He is publishing a book, not looking for patronage. And there is also a quick vision of the future of "literature": "fresh sources of useful instruction."

Not Perfect, but Very Useful

How much does it matter that Anderson reprints "thine" in his version of the poem? From the point of view of a Ritson-like strict accuracy, not at all. This word is in more editions of Tottel's book than any other version of the word, and so to reprint it is not strictly speaking an error. It doesn't make good sense, however, and so from a Percy-ish point of view the word itself can be described as an error, and any reprinting partakes of that error. But does *that* matter? How much does it matter that the reprinted poem contains this little glitch? Would it matter to Wordsworth, for instance, as he read Wyatt's poems for the first time in Anderson's book?

No doubt it mattered more that Wordsworth could read the poem at all, in any version. Percy's fifty-year struggle did not make that possible and would have produced a book Wordsworth couldn't have afforded anyway. It is not hard to edit "thine" to "thin" as one reads. But even without this emendation, the blur in the meanings created by the poem is small. Almost all of the poem works anyway; the erotic suggestion erased by not getting that her array was "thin" is present elsewhere. The small patch of corruption will not, generally speaking, overspread and somehow destroy the poem. Like our bodies, the being of the poem is still whole even when some parts are damaged.

The Progress of Learning, and the End
of the Century of the Editor

In writing his *History of English Poetry*, published in 1774–81, Thomas Warton acted as a kind of Recording Secretary for the far-flung network of scholars to which he contributed and from which he benefited. He wrote out, as a quasi-public service, the content of many books and letters written by himself, his friends, and their predecessors. This accounts for the quite pervasively plagiarized nature of the book, which weaves the work of many people together with Warton's own. Warton's *History* plainly records the tightly knit social network that underlies eighteenth-century learning. Since this network is precisely the world Joseph Ritson felt so alienated from, no wonder he hated Warton's history (and Warton himself) so much, and no wonder he reacted with such complete social deafness to the many borrowed passages in the book. Here is Ritson attacking Warton's usual practice, in his "Observations" of 1782: "Pray, Mr. Warton, will you do me the favor to inform me how came by these notes?— Few people can write better language than yourself; what necessity, therefore, could induce you to pilfer from a dead man? I say, PILFER; for each of THESE

NOTES, as you know, is STOLEN VERBATIM from the late Mr. Fawkeses Imitation of Douglas." Indeed, Warton's section on Wyatt—rather shorter than the section on Surrey—begins familiarly: "Wyat was of Allington Castle in Kent, which he magnificently repaired, and educated at both our Universities. But his chief and most splendid accomplishments were derived from his travels into various part of Europe, which he frequently visited in the quality of an envoy. He was endeared to King Henry the Eighth, who did not always act from caprice, for his fidelity and success in the execution of public business, his skill in arms, literature, familiarity with languages, and lively conversation." Warton knows more than Phillips and Winstanley did, a century before: almost infinitely more. Yet the shape of the story persists, as it was first sketched out in Phillips's book, growing as knowledge is added to it but not changing in any fundamental way. Wyatt is given more virtues; his life has more details, his context grows fuller; but it is the same story. Warton spends much more time on Surrey—Wyatt and Surrey come together in histories from this point forward—and much of that ruminating on biographical detail, feeling out the consequence and worldly fame of the "noble" one of the pair.

Warton, however, is now able and willing to quote poetry—quite a bit of it, leading off in the Wyatt section with "My Lute Awake," which had appeared in the *Nugae*, but which Warton knew was also in Tottel. He goes on to print several other poems, all from Tottel. "They Flee from Me" does not appear.

What is entirely new is something that looks like a critical discussion of poetry. Poetry is quoted, not simply as illustration of Wyatt's poems or his fame, but as material in an ongoing evaluation of poetic accomplishment in English. Wyatt gets a medium endorsement, paling in comparison to Surrey, in Warton's view:

> Wyat co-operated with Surrey in having corrected the roughness of our poets. Wyat, although sufficiently distinguished from the common versifiers of his age, is confessedly inferior to Surrey in harmony of numbers, perspicuity of expression, and facility of phraseology. Nor is he equal to Surrey in elegance of sentiment, in nature and sensibility. His feelings are disguised by affectation and obscured by conceit. His declarations of passion are embarrassed by wit and fancy, and his style is not intelligible, in proportion as it is careless and unadorned.

This is a confident evaluation. Behind it lies a confident sense of both "taste" and "literature." Warton's taste is that of 1780, marked by the slogan of the day, "sensibility." More important is the placement of Wyatt in (literary) history. Wyatt is indebted to Petrarch; he corrects the roughness of previous poets; he writes in a couple of different genres (lyric, satire); he is better than the common versifiers of his age; he is less good than Surrey. He is not only artificial but *too* artificial, more artificial than he should be as measured by an applied standard. He fits within an historical period Warton takes for granted the reader already knows about and understands (from somewhere else, other books).

A certain part of the spirit of these objections is like the objections of the people who silently smoothed "They Flee from Me" as they put it into their books: Mary Howard, and Tottel himself. Two and a half centuries later, Wyatt's verse is still rough; Warton calls Wyatt's versification "negligent." Warton conceives of his *History* as above all a sorting of good from less good from bad. It is "history" in a most basic sense, a disciplined sort of forgetting (and remembering). Who are those common versifiers of Wyatt's era? Never mind: Wyatt is better than them, and besides, Surrey is better than Wyatt.

The story of improvement, of forward and positive motion, is Warton's template, as befits the recording secretary of the eighteenth century. It is not visible everywhere, but there is a glimpse of it in his description of Wyatt and in Surrey's correction of previous poets. Warton really believes this story. He is capable of complimenting Surrey by saying, "Some of the following stanzas . . . have almost the ease and gallantry of Waller." Warton begins his *History* by rearticulating his friend Percy's Imperial Present, adapting Percy's "Dedication" to the *Reliques* and giving this story as pure an expression as it finds in the whole of the century. These are the first two paragraphs of his "Preface":

> In an age advanced to the highest degree of refinement, that species of curiosity commences, which is busied in contemplating the progress of social life, in displaying the gradations of science, and in tracing the transitions from barbarism to civility.
>
> That these speculations should become the favorite pursuits and fashionable topics of such a period is extremely natural. We look back on the savage condition of our ancestors, with the triumph of superiority; we are pleased to mark the steps by which we have been raised from rudeness to elegance: and our reflections are accompanied with a conscious pride, arising in great measure from a tacit comparison of the infinite disproportion between the feeble efforts of remote ages, and our present improvements in knowledge.

This imperial anti-Fall is the story underlying the *History*; it is the conceptual apparatus that allows Warton to write it all out with a shape beyond the chrono-logical list. It makes (problematic) sense of the past.

Joseph Ritson hated Warton, and he hated Percy; he was a Jacobin and a radical vegetarian and stood in angry opposition to their imperial re-vision of the past. Toward the end of his life he published a plain, tidy book called the *Bibliographia Poetica* (1802), in which he wrote small lives for the poets he knew about of the twelfth through the sixteenth centuries. This is a useful book; it is full of information, plus entertaining digs at Warton. But while its organization is chronological in main, the different centuries are organized alphabetically by author, essentially the same way Winstanley organized his book more than a century before.

Ritson hates the story Warton tells, but his equivalent book tells no story at all. Unwilling to contaminate himself with the stain of mortality, imagining there is an alternative, Ritson has no story to tell.

PART III

More Learning, the British Library, and the Song of the Professor

George Frederick Nott, a Nearly Perfect Editor

Collections like that of Robert Anderson begin to pour out of the presses after about 1790, a stream flowing unabated into our own times. The stupendous accumulations of these multivolume double-column anthologies transform reprinting old poetry from deep cultural discovery into book-derived book-making. "They Flee from Me" thus appears many times in the course of the nineteenth century, always in the same Tottel form, with no recognition of the note Percy made in the upper-right-hand corner of our page (which re-animated the larger, multiversion object the poem had been in the sixteenth century). Each Reprinter just uses another recent reprinting.

There is a single, remarkable, clear-sighted exception:

O D E S.   23

The Lover sheweth how he is forsaken of Fortune who sometime favoured him.

THEY flee from me that sometime did me seek,
    With naked foot stalking in my chamber.
I have seen them gentle, tame, and meek,
    That now are wild, and do not remember,
    That sometime they put themself in danger
To take bread at my hand ; and now they range,
Busily seeking with a continual change.

    Thanked be Fortune, it hath been otherwise,
        Twenty times better ; but once in special,
    In thin array, after a pleasant guise,
        When her loose gown from her shoulders did fall ;
        And she me caught in her arms long and small,
Therewithal sweetly she did me kiss,
And softly said : " Dear heart, how like you this ?"

It was no dream, I lay broad waking ———
But all is turned, thorough my gentleness,
Into a strange fashion of forsaking ;
And I have leave to go of her goodness,
And she also to use new fangleness :
But since that I so kindly am served,
I would fain know what she hath deserved.

Here the sullen resentment of the last lines of the poem in Wyatt's book, and their expressive dead rhythm, the lines Wyatt approved in the margin, appear in print for the first time. In the previous 250 years, the number of people who read these lines could probably be counted on two hands: maybe one. A full array of modern punctuation has been added, offering a much more detailed set of reading instructions than that provided by Wyatt's manuscript. Spelling is modernized.

This version of "They Flee from Me" is produced by a preternaturally gifted cleric, scholar, and editor named George Frederick Nott, who published an edition of the collected poems of Surrey and Wyatt in 1815 and 1816, not so long after the ashes of Percy's fire (and Percy himself) had cooled. In his methods Nott was so idiosyncratically far ahead of his time that it would be the end of the century before anyone recognized the magnitude of what he accomplished.

Nott's achievements are astonishing. He understood what is in the Harington manuscripts, and he also found out about and understood what was in Mary Howard's book. He was very well connected (he was, for instance, a tutor to the Royal Family), and the exercise of these connections allowed him (like Percy) to borrow the important manuscripts relating to Wyatt's poetry. He got the Wyatt/Harington family book from the cheerful and generous Dr. Henry Harington, and he borrowed Mary Howard's book from the Duke of Devonshire, in whose family it had come to rest after posthumous travels of its own. He knew enough to recognize most of the various handwriting in these books. He knew Wyatt's book intimately, and he knew it contained poems in Wyatt's hand. He knew that Wyatt had initialed poems in this book and that it contained working drafts of poems in Wyatt's hand; he knew that the details of the poems in this book were often different from the details of the poems in Mary Howard's book *and* in Tottel's book. He knew that the manuscripts predated Tottel and assigned them priority on the basis of the history of the individual texts they contained. What is more, Nott was immensely erudite. When Wyatt translated Petrarch, or someone more obscure, Nott knew, and could read the original. He effortlessly refers to centuries of poetry in Greek, Latin, Italian, French, Spanish, and English (not German, as far as I can tell). He is like a whole University compressed into one man.

Nott also thought carefully about his editorial methods and about the nature of literary history. In comparison, editors like Percy and Ritson look willful and parochial; Nott worked from carefully articulated principles. For instance, Nott didn't just modernize the spelling in the poems he published; he also took time in his prefaces to say why he did so.

Handwriting and the Scene of Making (Poems)

In reprinting the version found handwritten in Wyatt's book, Nott simply discards the priority of the printed text and so, also, the way all editors before him thought. It is a dramatic shift and indicates the presence of a highly independent spirit. What Wyatt wanted his poem to be like at the moment of writing it down matters to Nott. He is highly skeptical of the work of previous scholars, and says so at the beginning of his "Memoirs of the Life of Henry Howard, Earl of Surrey," part of the prefatory material in the Surrey volume. After archly rehearsing a time-worn version of Surrey's life, Nott vigorously declares his refusal to simply retell the inherited stories:

> We love to hear, and to repeat what is wonderful. To this propensity the above romantic story owes the credit which it has obtained. Almost every part of it is fiction; and the fiction might have been easily at any time disproved. But the received account was one which caught the imagination; and the reader being satisfied, there was nothing to induce the writer to enter on the thankless task of critical inquiry.

When Nott writes the life of Wyatt, the sentences from Phillips's book on which Winstanley and Warton and everyone else rang their changes finally disappear. Nott writes it all afresh. He does laborious, inventive primary scholarship. For instance, instead of taking at face value the evocative story of the fever that killed Wyatt, Nott traveled to Sherborne Abbey in Dorset and read the parish records of Wyatt's untimely interment.

Nott's great and clear faith in documentary fact changes the status of the manuscripts. Percy regarded manuscripts with a sort of (fascinated, enraptured) horror, as bespotted and begrimed relics left behind in the progress of time. For

Nott this grime is a sign of closeness to the making of the poems, the very sign of the Real. The scene of poetry making, represented in the manuscripts by the working drafts (one of which Nott re-creates in printed form), is for Nott the vital center of attention. The closer one gets to the scene of making, the closer one gets to the real thing, the poem in its fact-ness and historical reality: the "original." The Original is the form of the poetic object that generates, has generated, all the other forms, including the printed forms. In his "Preface" to the Wyatt volume, after reviewing the contents of Wyatt's book, the Harington family manuscript, Nott sums it up simply: "Nothing need be said to enhance its value; or prove the high importance it is of [sic] towards settling the real state of Wyatt's text."

For Nott, in perfect opposition to Percy's practice, Tottel's book is a derived, subservient object. The messy primal energy of handwriting, generated in an endlessly attractive, almost-lost past moment, is primary for Nott. It is a pathway to Wyatt's lost inner life. Deciding that writing supersedes print signals a profound shift in editorial practice, powered by a shift in the picture of where the "correct" poem is located.

If the task in editing Wyatt is one of adjusting the texts to correspond to versions that appear to be the way Wyatt himself wanted them to be (at some point), Nott nearly finished, at one go, the physical task of editing Wyatt's poetry.

Why Nott Reprinted Old Poems

G. F. Nott had many responsibilities other than looking into old books. He was (eventually, by the time he was working on the Surrey and Wyatt editions) Prebendary of Winchester and Salisbury Cathedrals, and in this role supervised extensive renovations and repairs to those great buildings. He had responsibilities deriving from his connection to the royal family. In the ancillary materials to his poetry editions he speaks often of the many cares and sorrows of his personal life. Like Thomas Percy, Lord Bishop Dromore, Nott was not a Professor. He was not paid, specifically, to fool around with old poems. So why did he do it?

Nott himself felt the interest of this question and frequently says why Surrey and Wyatt should be the target of such energy. Nott's reasoning derives from an early description of Wyatt and Surrey's poetic accomplishment, made by George Puttenham in his *Arte of English Poesy*, published in 1589, already (briefly) mentioned. Puttenham called Wyatt and Surrey "the first reformers of our English meter and style." Nott cites this as the fundamental reason Surrey, and Wyatt, whom he sees as a kind of Elder Helper to Surrey, are worthy of the labor he expends upon them.

Nott sings their accomplishments continually, but especially in the "Disser-tation" attached to the Surrey volume, as well as the "Essay on Wyatt's Poems" prefatory to the Wyatt volume. Nott's story of the "improvement" produced by Surrey and Wyatt is a close relative of the great imperial story Percy told and Ritson reviled. It has the same blandly happy ending, with the state of the language "finally settled." Like Percy, Nott enlists the story of improvement to celebrate his own project. Is the "he" in the following extract (from the Surrey Dissertation) Surrey, or Wyatt, or G. F. Nott?

> There is no subject of inquiry connected with human learning, that can be presented to the mind more interesting than what concerns the progress of improvement in language. . . . He who labors to improve, enlarge and fix the language of any country; he who adding to its graces and its harmony adapts it to the purposes of poetry; and by giving it strength and precision, makes it adequate to the higher purposes of science, is entitled to public gratitude, as well as commendation.

Nott's praise of Wyatt and Surrey is quite a lot like saying they wrote good poems, but not exactly the same. Nott's Wyatt and Surrey are like Nott himself: earnest craftsmen with a high-minded cultural project in mind.

In the "Dissertation" Nott spends a great deal of time describing the metrical systems of poets previous to Wyatt and Surrey. He says this poetry was regulated by ear instead of by rule, and his description of why this was a problem sounds in both poetic and moral registers: "The defects of that system were evident. It opened the door to great license, it encouraged carelessness and irregularity in composition; and kept the pronunciation of the language in an unsettled state." The simple solution, it turns out, was to count syllables and restrict meter to iambic progressions; Nott refers to this idea as the bringing of "law" to poetry. Wyatt and Surrey are the key workers, and in Nott's exciting story they apply themselves to the problem of "rudeness and deformity" with a sort bricklayer's plain sense of purpose. Wyatt begins the project; Surrey, his noble successor, (almost) completes it. From the "Essay": "Had not an untimely death taken Wyatt away just as his taste and judgment were matured; and had not the unrelenting jealousy of political intrigue cut Surrey off in the vigor of his youth, there seems no reason to doubt but that they would have perfected their undertaking." A man who thinks language can be "perfected" is thinking very abstractly about the daily mess of poems and people, and this conceptual notion of the work of poetry not only deepens as Nott goes on but becomes a kind of value and a form of compliment. Beginning the sixteenth chapter of his "Dissertation," Nott rises to a grand claim: Surrey is the first true poet because he is "universal." "Poetry is the language of the universal man; the language of the heart in all ages, and in all countries, unmodified by the particularities of fashion. Poetry therefore should borrow no aid from any thing dependent upon casual opinions: it should select and dwell upon those points of feeling which are not the result of a particular state of manners, but exist in human nature generally." Surrey's general diction and sentiments place him "beyond the injury of time." Wyatt, the writer of "They Flee from Me," which depicts the bitter losses of time's progress, would have been impressed.

So: Nott reprints Surrey and Wyatt because they are the key laborers in another story of Progress. Nott's story is different from Percy's: for one thing, it has worked out a place for the classical poets. But it remains a story in which an escape from entropic scattering is the great end and goal, and the Editor remains a key actor in making this happen.

Mad, Bad, and Dangerous to Know

This serene picture of (reprinted) old poetry defeating Time develops urgency, for Nott, through the vapors from a nearby Boiling Pot: the Reprinter has a desperately important task on hand. At the end of his preface to the Wyatt volume, after advocating for the role of the clergy, people like himself and Thomas Percy, in "the concerns of our national literature," Nott's rhetoric intensifies and rises in pitch and volume. It turns out old poetry can be a bulwark against a rising tide:

> For what has been the cause which of late years has so much relaxed the ties of moral and religious obligation, and disposed men fearlessly to engage in skeptical inquiries, and licentious indulgence? What! But the prevailing influence of a corrupt Literature moulded to meet the taste, and suit the dark designs of a set of men, who . . . had prostituted Poetry and Polite Letters to the base purposes of vice, by undermining moral principle, and by encouraging the most seductive, and therefore the most dangerous propensities of human frailty.

Nott's diatribe is given a date: "May 1816." In April of 1816, after months of public scandal, and after his affair with his half sister had become public knowledge, George Gordon, Lord Byron, aristocratic author and enactor of racy works of poetry and personal passion, left England, never to return (his poems, however, returned regularly). He went to join the infamous atheist and vegetarian Percy

Shelley, already in Europe with his companion Mary Godwin; Shelley had left his first wife Harriet and their children behind.

Nott really means it, and all of the prose attached to his two volumes (the two prefaces, the "Memoirs" of Surrey and Wyatt, the "Dissertation" in the Surrey volume, and the "Essay" in the Wyatt volume) rises, usually at the end, to this subject, at this level of upset and this level of generality. The "Memoir" of Wyatt ends with a description of what these poets can do—or did, in the past?—to help us resist the corruption of bad literature. They are, or were, poets "who . . . have ennobled learning, and rendered Poetry and polite attainments honourable, by making them subservient to the cause of Virtue and Religion." If this is what reading old poetry can show us, then the reprinter of old poetry is an important person and the reprinting is a service to the world.

But is "They Flee from Me" subservient to the cause of Virtue and Religion? Does it encourage or discourage the most dangerous propensities of human frailty?

The Details, Once Again
Spelling Matters

In the "Preface" to the two editions, which begins the Surrey volume, Nott explains very carefully why he has inserted punctuation and modernized the spelling in his reprinting of Wyatt and Surrey's poems. It is a nice example of his surprising capacity for clear-sighted self-conscious thinking about his methods. With particular reference to spelling, Nott says using older spelling "gives er- roneous impressions . . . of the language itself as of the taste and character of the writer." He uses in illustration a letter written by the Duchess of Norfolk to the Earl of Essex; it contains words like "My ffary gode lord her I sand you . . . " Nott modernizes: "My very good Lord; here I send you . . . " Nott's justification for modernizing is pointed, and unprecedented in the history of editing: "Here the idiom peculiar to the times is preserved, without any appearance either of vul- garity or ignorance. The writer appears, as she was, a liberal and well-educated gentlewoman of the sixteenth century." The tangle that caught Edmund Curll one hundred years previously is straightened out. In order to show the past as it actually was, Nott is clear that he needs to change it.

The theoretical confidence behind Nott's substitution is so fundamental it hides behind his work. Nott believes his learning has allowed him to make the past continuous with the present, and consequently believes he can accu- rately judge the relationship between the present and the past. For instance, in modernizing the spelling of the poem Nott replaces the word *[kiss]* with **kiss**. Nott insists he knows what *[kiss]* means, and he is certain it can be more accurately represented (in 1816) by **kiss**. Percy printed "kisse"; Anderson printed "kysse." Printing "kiss" is like substituting "very" for the Duchess's "ffary": but of course "kiss" is a more interesting word.

The smooth surface of Nott's reprinted page conceals his labor and also the enormous weight of learning he could have brought to bear if asked about it. It looks as if nothing has happened. In his "Preface" Nott admits his method would not serve the antiquarian's traditional fascination with old things. Nott's revolutionary purpose is to serve "general interest" and readers without specific training. Retaining old orthography "deters those from reading our early writers, who would otherwise study them with pleasure."

Nott's conception of his role is another unprecedented development, and another part of Nott's practice that closely resembles our own. He puts his learning in service of culture broadly conceived, and he assumes there are "general" readers who will want to read what he has produced. His job is to enable this reading, and he does so by erasing the signs of the long trip "kiss" has made on its way from the Secretary Hand to the printed present.

As we have seen, choosing even one word to print in a re-presentation of the past is impossibly encumbered by inescapable paradoxes and problems. And so, of course, Nott does not escape.

The Scholar's Chaste Kiss

Nott included copious notes with his edition of these poems, at the back of the book. The endnote or footnote as the location of a supplemental, intimate, and even anxious authorial voice is one of the developments of the eighteenth century, and Nott practices this method with great enthusiasm. The apparent calm of his smooth editorial surface can be maintained, it turns out, only by bleeding off anxiety and energy in the endnotes. As far as I know this is the first time since Tottel's tinkering that our poem has been singled out and received specific, detailed, and sustained attention; it is the first time a compliment has been paid in print. Nott says it is of "no inconsiderable merit" and "original and full of feeling."

Nott first retells the drama that the poem so intently enacts, cushioning the eroticism with an insistence that it is all "figure" and metaphor. If Wyatt's poems are going to help readers resist the dangerous example of Byron, they can't be soliciting us to think about actual arms and kisses and pettish postcoital grumblings.

He also discusses the word "stalking," initiating what will be a centuries-long scholarly puzzling over what, exactly, is doing the stalking; and then he goes on at anxious learned length about "kiss."

The weight of Nott's learning, invisible on the surface of the printed poem, reappears to smother any inappropriate feelings the word "kiss" might create: "The propriety of this image depends in great measure on a circumstance which grew out of the days of chivalry, which is now forgotten." Drawing on his vast store of remembered poems and other writings, Nott uses quotations and references from Erasmus and "*Troilus and Cressida*," among others, to prove that in spite of the appearance Nott himself has so carefully created, the word "kiss" is a *different* word from the one the General Reader is thinking of. As Nott tells it the kiss is a "formal" cultural exchange, a gesture of chivalry, and the reason the reader is thinking anything else is that chivalry has been "forgotten."

Having helped the poem escape its captivity to time and old books, and, especially, having traced the finger-touched ink of the very people who made, modified, and enjoyed this poem so long ago, Nott then panics and tries to stuff it into a flameproof box of High Church propriety and antiquarian hobby-horsical learning.

Nott could have stuck with *kysse*, which the General Reader probably couldn't even read in the first place. He could have used one of the versions in Tottel, kiſſe, as Percy did, which at least looks slightly odd and thus could conceivably be the different word Nott wants to convince us of. By insisting on kiss Nott opened the door for readers to think their own everyday thoughts about men and women and kissing. And so Nott's anxiety in the note is his own fault. If reading old poems did not have to support Virtue and Religion, he could just print "kiss" and let the reader read it as she would. Of course, he would also have no reason to reprint the old poem in the first place.

The Right Answer

From a documentary point of view, Nott's note about chivalry and the kiss, and the theory he proposes about the meaning of the word (and the poem), are either right or wrong. Saying the poem is not an erotic poem is not reconcilable with saying it is an erotic poem. Nott offers himself as an expert and as a person who could decide such a question. He would be able to say to someone reading "kiss" in a different way: you are wrong. You are making a mistake.

Part of the air of futility surrounding Nott's ambitious, large-scale project derives from this finger-shaking. There isn't really anyone to argue with him about

"They Flee from Me." Dr. Nott wants to say—you are wrong, this isn't about a woman—but there isn't anyone there; the "student" of English Literature, who is accountable to the censorious Teacher, has not yet been invented. Nott can't give his General Reader a test, and so the General Reader doesn't have to listen to him.

Unsurprisingly, This Big Story Doesn't Work Either

Nott's forward-looking scholarly discourse, already knotted up by his morally driven reprinting agenda, also gets disrupted by the sudden eruption of the feelings of G. F. Nott, who was a person as well as a Cultural Servant. After winding up the argument in the "Dissertation" about the "general" nature of Surrey's poetry, its mobilization of the language of the Universal Man, Nott suddenly turns aside and starts talking about himself, a nonuniversal person who was once a boy who loved reading and imagining. He says that "generalizing" destroys "that air of antiquity which sometimes sheds a peculiar charm over the poems of our early writers." This makes him sad, because "I have found now and then a quaint expression, or a period of an antiquated structure, will bring before my eyes, as it were by magic, the place, the time, and all the forms and modes of life which were present to the antient bard himself whose strains I am perusing." Perhaps Surrey did reform and generalize English poetry; perhaps the reason to read Surrey (or rather, to edit and publish Surrey [and Wyatt also]) is to counteract the baneful influence of Byron and Shelley; perhaps all reading should be supportive of the causes of Virtue and Religion. But sometimes Nott just likes thinking about the deep past, and sometimes an old sentence, a curious construction like "long and small," say, carries him away, partly because it is ungeneralized and personal. The inscrutable past can be a source of *magic*.

Nott's charming detonation of his argument about universals and generality helps us notice that under the influence of this conjuring of the "antient bard" Nott also left a small old thing in his reprinted poem: the word "themself," in the first stanza. This spelling, according to the OED, had died out by the late seventeenth century. Nott also includes a title for the poem, which is *almost* the title in Tottel: "The Lover sheweth how he is forsaken of Fortune who sometime favoured him" (enacting the worries of his note, Nott has gotten rid of the word "enjoyed" in Tottel's title). The poem in the Harington family manuscript doesn't have a title, and so using one runs against his carefully articulated editorial principles. But like "themself," Nott's title sheds an air of antiquity over his modernized poem, restoring some of the magic his own modernizing has erased.

Cultural Status, Classical Learning,
    Classic English Poets (and Magic)

Nott's excursion into unsystematic feeling and the melodic, magical call of the past is almost perfectly implosive of his larger theoretical claims about the universal, timeless worth of older poetry. It takes on its own energy and rises to a kind of ecstasy in a section ending with a quotation from Horace:

> While I listen [to the old poets], I almost persuade myself that the artless expressions of passion to be found in the pages of our early poets have a character of greater truth and more genuine feeling than is to be discovered in our own more polished protestations;

> Auditis! An me ludit amabalis

>   Insania!

In David Ferry's translation (Ode 4 in Book 3), Horace's lines are rendered thus:

> Companions, do you hear her too, or does
> Some pleasant day dream play with me?

> ("Her" is Calliope, the muse, whom Horace summons, or requests, in this Ode, to come down and play a lingering melody.)

This quotation from Horace is evocative and illustrative, and it is also socially cozy, since it asks the reader to participate in knowledge held in common by a well-defined set: men trained in the Romanophilic, Imperial methods of British public schools and Oxford and Cambridge. It is meant to echo the call from Nott's ecstatic soul as he ponders the misty, backlit "antient" world. By quoting Horace, and by leaving the lines untranslated, Nott quickly, fluently, and familiarly opens the culturally prestigious space in which he hopes to place Surrey and Wyatt. He also identifies *himself* as cultured and as an occupant of that space. He demonstrates his own taste, and the value of his work, by marking it with an unchallengeable tag of cultural value.

If Nott's reader could translate these lines, that reader might also remember (along with Nott) his school days and the schoolroom and the Latin lessons, wearisome, perhaps, almost certainly accompanied by punishments corporeal and psychological, but in retrospect golden times of youth. The memory of school days thus summoned is mellowed like Nott's idealized and profoundly incorrect depiction of the brutal, corrupt, murderous, and libidinous world of Henry VIII and his courtiers. The exclamation marks have been inserted by Nott, implying or creating an imperative mood: not "Do you hear?" but rather "Listen!" This change expresses the mood Nott has fallen into as he listens to the language of the Past, its "magic richness" drifting through him like incense in one of his cathedrals.

Erudition

Nott's immense, eye-opening erudition is not the same kind of knowledge Wyatt had as he adapted several European traditions in his poems. It is what Wyatt knew run backwards. Wyatt would have learned "chivalry" as he learned other everyday things, like rhyming and horsemanship and the names of streets in London. Wyatt would not have had to read Erasmus to know what "kiss" meant. Wyatt read Petrarch and remembered poems he liked; he had no responsibility to remember any particular poem. Like all of us, Wyatt knew just what he knew.

That is, what any single person knows is, for others, an obscure pattern only "research" will unlock. The passage of time makes this worse. It was not an exercise of what the scholar would call "learning," necessarily, when Wyatt chose out a poem from Petrarch to imitate or translate. If we read a book and that book shows up in our writing, there is nothing obscure about this process to the rememberer. But if we are looking over the border of the self and back into the dark of past time, it is difficult to locate the very poem Wyatt imitated from out of all the poems in the world. From the point of view of the future, the simple choices of personal life become a nearly undetectable pattern in the vast field of facts that is the past. Wyatt knew what kind of kiss he was describing, and it was not difficult for him to know, but it might well be hard for us to know.

The erudite scholar maps out the whole landscape of the cultural past so as to track the poet as he makes his way through it, but the poet had only to walk forward to go where he wanted. For Wyatt the pattern created by his knowledge was just himself: taste and love and accident and ambition and places he had been, the forward movement of life choices. For the scholar, Wyatt's choices are hidden among infinitely many other possible choices. In following the patterns the scholar is more likely to be lost than found. Nott needs to know everything about Petrarch because he cannot know Wyatt's particular way of knowing. He has to bait all the trails and wait for Wyatt to show up.

Of course, we don't have to care what Wyatt knew or meant. "Kiss" means something now, no matter what Wyatt was up to so long ago. What the kiss in "They Flee from Me" means is bound by what Wyatt wanted it to mean only if we want it to be bound in that way. Nott has strong, pressing reasons why a reader of Wyatt should try to know what he, Nott, knows; but we don't, his readers didn't, have to agree.

The Inevitable Mistakes

Along with "themself" and the presence (and modification) of Tottel's title, there is also an extra word ("she") in the thirteenth line of Nott's reprinted poem: "Therewithal sweetly she did me kiss." This is Nott's alone. No other reprinting of the poem, from the first edition of Tottel forward, includes this particular emendation. Mary Howard's book changes this line, but in a different way.

This was either an idea on Nott's part or a simple transcribing error on someone's part. Either way it is a mistake, since Nott's theories wouldn't support the idea of this addition. Gifted as he was, Nott makes mistakes of both the simple and complex kind: lots of them, and he knew he would. He knew he already had, and apologizes plangently and profusely for them. He has been sick; he has experienced "domestic sorrow." Besides, it is just hard, detailed, careful work: "It will often cost the labor of weeks to ascertain a single date." People are dogged by the limitations inherent in physical being. From the preface to the Surrey volume: "Where is the man whose memory has always at command even what he knows, when he wishes to apply it? Or who may not be liable to mistakes in referring to authors read many years ago in the vacant intervals of youthful studies, and long since laid aside for pursuits of a graver cast?" Mistakes mark our humanity; mistakes derive from the deep entropic forces at work at the heart of the universe and in our lives. This, of course, is part of what "They Flee from Me" is about.

Schooling, Exams, Textbooks, Professors

In his disciplined approach to fact and textual scholarship, Nott foreshadows the attitudes common to the (academic) business of scholarship about literature in English; in his voluble excitability and susceptibility to Antique Charms he resembles his forebears, the Antiquaries, with their idiosyncratic motivations and hobbyhorses. Perhaps because he was thus both ahead of and slightly behind his time, the novelty of Nott's work was not appreciated until the end of the century. In the meantime, in the course of the century, the practice of scholarship continued to mature, and in a related but not identical development English Literature appeared as a school subject and expanded its presence slowly and steadily.

By the later nineteenth century many notable things have happened to the conceptual space "They Flee from Me" occupies or might occupy. The exam system appears as a way of creating and monitoring access to the British Civil Service and the Indian Foreign Service. These exams included English language and literature as subjects from the beginning. The presence of English as an exam subject exerted pressure downwards, causing secondary schools to teach English literature before it was taught as a separate subject in British Universities. Change came relatively late at Oxford and Cambridge, but in American Colleges and Universities, as well as British Universities other than Oxford and Cambridge, English literature increasingly becomes a staple of curriculums after 1860 or so.

The business of schooling, like any other business, has its practical needs, and so the appearance of English as a subject in schools drives the appearance of the printed apparatus of the schoolroom and of school and student libraries: anthologies, textbooks, guides, dictionaries, encyclopedias. The appearance of English as a school subject also drives the need for a new type of academic professional: the Professor/Lecturer/Instructor/Teacher of English. This person, unlike George Frederic Nott, is paid to fool around with poems (and other kinds of writing). This person also needs to be trained to do his or her job, a need that dawned only slowly on the developing business. In America, toward the end of the century, many scholars later prominent as College and University Professors went to Germany, earned PhDs, and then returned to start similar programs in the United States. This process was less common in Britain, and places like Kings College at the University of London began issuing degrees in English on home ground.

The burgeoning School market was populated by a version of the "general" reader G. F. Nott imagined, and so created commercial viability for reprints of old poetry. Our poem tags along in several reprintings of Tottel's miscellany, as well as a few editions of the poems of Thomas Wyatt. These books resemble the editions from the eighteenth century more than they resemble Nott's books. They habitually steal Nott's facts, especially in their biographical material, but they do not repeat his textual care or even his interest in individual texts. The reprintings of the nineteenth century instead continue the old practice of importing poetry wholesale from previous editions, and as in the eighteenth century "They Flee from Me" is simply caught in the draft, appearing in print many times, coyly concealed in the crowd of its fellow poems. These books retail Poetry, not individual poems. They are interested in Poets but demonstrate no particular interest in the existence of poems as individual objects in the world. At least, their editors appear incapable of or simply not interested in the work required to deal with poems as individual objects with a history.

Indeed, there is a cooling of the momentary warm if odd glow of Nott's attentions. He noticed "They Flee from Me," and all the other poems, and put all that attention into his thick books. He (mostly) published the poem Wyatt's secretary wrote into his book all those centuries before, which to the World of Print should have been a revelation; but in all the reprinting in the nineteenth century—until the 1890s—"They Flee from Me" appears only in its previously printed, Tottel guise. In principle the reprinters *could* have known otherwise, but generally speaking they just didn't notice. They looked into Nott's book, but mostly blindly.

Henry Howard, the Earl of Surrey, and,
Also, by the Way, Thomas Wyatt

Nott's detailed attention to Wyatt, the first of its kind, did not change the received truth that Surrey was the greater and more important poet of the two, partly because Nott himself would have ranked them in this way. In Chambers's *Cyclopaedia of English Literature*, a basic reference anthology first published in the 1840s and still being republished and reedited in the early twentieth century, Howard's entry comes atemporally first and contains sentences like these, which can stand in for all the hundreds of other nineteenth-century anthologies and histories: "The poetry of Surrey is remarkable for a flowing melody, correctness of style, and purity of expression; he was the first to introduce the sonnet and blank verse into English poetry." Wyatt helps Surrey in his poetic task by writing poems that aren't so bad: "Surrey had a fellow-labourer in Sir Thomas Wyatt (1503–1541), another distinguished figure in the court of Henry VIII. . . . The songs and sonnets of this author, in praise of his mistress, and expressive of the various feelings he experienced while under the influence of the tender passion, though conceited, are not without refinement, and some share of poetical feeling." Chambers prints "Blame not my Lute," and three other poems, but not "They Flee from Me."

An Exception: An Attentive Reader of Nott, and a Spark of Life

William Minto, a person who taught English and Logic at the University of Aberdeen, was a product of the vital Scottish system of higher education and also an important laborer in that system. Scottish writers and academics of the eighteenth and nineteenth centuries were enormously influential in the development of both American and British higher education, and especially in the nascent business of teaching English. Minto died comparatively young (aged forty-eight, in 1893), and the memorials included in the posthumous, memorial edition of his *Literature of the Georgian Era* show him to have been an especially devoted and beloved teacher.

In 1874 Minto published a book called *Characteristics of English Poets from Chaucer to Shirley*, and in this interesting, lively, and unpretentious book he discusses Wyatt and Surrey at some length. Minto has read his Nott with attention, and with Nott in hand can write about Wyatt more accurately than Nott could. Minto, for instance, objects to the view illustrated by Chambers, above, that Surrey was the leader and Wyatt the follower. His evidence for Wyatt's priority is humorously simple and entirely convincing: he notes, among other things, that Surrey was ten years old when Wyatt wrote his first sonnets in English, and that Surrey's own writings describe Wyatt as his teacher. Minto is the first writer to describe Wyatt's irregular metrics positively, saying they derive from Wyatt's "fine ear for varied melodies." Minto has also paid close attention to individual poems. Instead of focusing on Wyatt's "conceits" and his adaptation of the Petrarchan manner, Minto notices the poems that are different. "Wyatt's poems are full of melancholy, dispersed sometimes by a firmer and more confident mood, but frequently deepening into bitterness."

Minto reads Wyatt's poems as a developing confessional stream, and we find "They Flee from Me" and other poems literally taken up in Minto's own stream as he tells Wyatt's poetic story: "He complains sadly that he has been deceived and forsaken: 'they flee from me that sometime did me seek.' He reminds himself bitterly of better days; tortures himself with rapturous memories of her visits to him in his chamber. Then he makes an effort, and addresses her with resolution to know the worst—'Madame, withouten many words. . . . '" Minto notices features of Wyatt's verse and biography that have lain exposed and ready for view for centuries, like the simple fact that Wyatt was older than Surrey, or that poems like "They Flee from Me" are not Petrarchan and are different from all lyrics written previously to them in English. Why could Minto see these things when his predecessors could not?

Surely part of it, most of it, is the increasingly detailed conceptual field in which "Wyatt's poetry" is now located. Minto is able to think about Wyatt in a more accurate way because of all the thinking that came before him, all the voyages of the scholarly Ship of Fools and their discoveries, misguided and otherwise. Nott's mistakes, often deriving from the conflict in his soul, are often goofy enough to be highly visible: visible, that is, once Nott has made them, and once Nott has written out all the amazingly accurate things he also noticed, which provide a foil for the mistakes. Minto needed Nott's mistakes as much as he needed Nott's accuracies. When the scholar's fingers catch on a snag in the cloth of previous argument, off he goes: but without the accumulating labor that made the thread, which wove the cloth, he might never have noticed.

What Holy Grave, What Worthy Sepulture?

The Continuing Journey of Wyatt's Book

George Nott had Wyatt's book—or Henry Harington's book—rebound, an improvement that was also a profound interference with the physical structure of the object. He also added pictures to it, one a copy of an engraving he had made to put in his published Wyatt book, another an image from John Leland's 1542 book, from which his engraving was adapted.

The addition of pictures intensifies the bookification created by the cut pages and the rich binding. In doing this Nott repeats, in careful, late-era form, what John Harington the Elder did when he copied Surrey's "The Great Macedon" into Wyatt's book as a title-moment to the translations of the Penitential Psalms, topping it with Surrey's coronet-like initials. The object resulting from Nott's decoration and transformation of the physical being of Wyatt's book is like the Ark that Surrey says Alexander made for Old Dan Homer's works. Nott's new book is a memorial, but a memorial incorporating into itself a piece of the person and poems being memorialized, like a reliquary containing the writing hand of a Saint. Or: the images Nott inserted look like carvings on a headstone, and the new book looks like the headstone itself, standing in the graveyard of culture.

There is also a fine-spun highly attenuated thread of life in this new, old book, stretching all the way back to the moment Wyatt's secretary took the pages from Wyatt and started entering the poems. Nott loved Wyatt; he clearly felt himself to still be within the force field of Thomas Wyatt, Knight, whom he served. The book was handed to Nott out of the expiring past, as it had been to John Harington the Elder, and Nott accepted it out of responsibility to the faint vibration of Wyatt's touch. To change the book so it better memorializes Wyatt was for Nott the fulfillment of his place in the handing forward of Wyatt's deep-witted spirit: Nott's place as a Clergyman, as a knower of old things, as an inheritor of the Antiquarian tradition, and as a self-appointed keeper of the (pure, restorative) Flame of Culture.

Life and Death in the Holy Grave of the British Library

In early 1889 the British Library purchased Wyatt's now-bookified manuscript using a fund established in 1829 by the Earl of Bridgewater, Francis Egerton, and so it acquired its modern title: BL MS Egerton 2711. This purchase, which amounted to a change in state, brought to a point the slowly wrought change in the status of English-language poems in English-speaking culture, the slowly rising status of English literature generally, and all the accumulating knowledge that allowed for the discovery of its existence and the estimation of its value.

Until 1889 Wyatt's manuscript had been in private hands. After finding its way to the apparently extraordinary safety of the Harington family library, and serving that family for so long in various ways, Wyatt's book was lent to Thomas Percy, and then to G. F. Nott. As we have seen, Nott took the Antiquarian's high hand with this precious relic, though he didn't write in it, as Percy had. And then he did, or didn't do, an astonishing thing: he *kept* it. He also kept Mary Howard's book, borrowed from the Duke of Devonshire, which from a social faux pas point of view is even more astonishing. When Nott died his huge collections of old stuff—books, paintings, coins, manuscripts, bronzes, and so on—were sold, in early 1842. The library alone took two weeks to auction off. Among the books sold were the two manuscripts, now bound in similar modern ways, "books" in the contemporary sense of the term.

The interregnum between the safety of stable family libraries and the impregnable confines of the British Library is an exposed time for these manuscripts, and it is lucky they survived as they did, rebound and all. Mary Howard's book, similarly bookified by Nott, was purchased by the British Library in the 1840s. The Harington family book disappeared for a while and then surfaced in a sale of the books of a person named James Bowker; Bernard Quaritch, a dealer working for the library, purchased it. Bowker was an attorney, apparently not connected to any scholarly networks, antiquarian, professorial, or otherwise, and so scholars had not been able to see Wyatt's book for most of the century.

National Treasure

Like the people into whose hands Wyatt's book fell over the years, the library immediately marked up the manuscript, this time with vigorous declarations of ownership. The library had, after all, paid for it. It is stamped in five places with marks referring to the Egerton bequest (this Continuing Thanks could easily have been required by the deed of gift), and a librarian also wrote in the book, tidily, discreetly, but quite in keeping with the practice of previous custodians of the book:

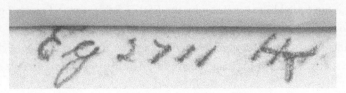

This note marks its place in a filing system of other old books: MS Egerton 2711.

The Nation, in the form of the British Library, hadn't just adopted the book, as most previous participants in its life had. The British Library *owned* Wyatt's book. A person who once lived, Thomas Wyatt, owned things: a castle, a pile of papers that may or may not have been bound as a "book." The King sometimes took Wyatt's things, because he could, and sometimes gave them back or gave him new things. Wyatt's son then had this book, naturally, we might say, and then the Johns Harington had it for centuries. Did they own it? Yes, certainly, but they didn't sell it, and they didn't buy it. Henry Harington lent or sent it happily: he didn't sell it either. George Nott didn't sell it. His heirs did, though, and eventually the book's time in the marketplace allowed it to escape from the informal world of the personal library and enter on a new sort of life, the life of a national treasure owned by the State.

The British Library, behaving just like an Owner of Things, put its marks upon the book and made rules about how it would be used and where it would be kept. Not everyone would be allowed to touch it, but people with the right credentials could, then and now (though those credentials keep creeping Upward). Professors, for instance, not rich and not members of any English social elite but rather members of a new profession and a new kind of elite, gained access to it and adapted its contents for consumption by the growing business of professional literary scholarship.

Glowing Coal, or Ashy Cinder?

Nott's alterations erase traces of the past but also include the book in the present and are in that way signs of continuing if somewhat chaotic vitality. In its first moments of ownership the British Library, with its stamps and jottings, participates in this life too, but these alterations have a new purpose. The library's marks are like the wrappings of the Mummies in the British Museum next door; they clothe the book in preparation for its entry into the eternity of a brightly lit, accessible, and well-kept Crypt. They are (meant to be) the last marks. After being stamped, the book is meant to be stable forever more. No one will be allowed to mark or write in it again. When it is read, a white-gloved functionary of the library will stand by, watching, to make sure no reader takes the book's animation of their feelings or reanimation of Wyatt's old feelings too personally. The British Library means to be the *last* owner of the book.

Like the Museum's stuffed animals, Wyatt's book has been killed so that it may live (in a museum). If "killed" seems too strong, call it Cryogenically frozen. The library's aim is to stop the book from moving through history and thus turn it into a motionless witness from the past, which is a different thing. It is now a resident of the Eternal Past that the Museum and the Library present within their walls. No doubt some of the many people who will thereby gain the opportunity to see the book will want to take it in their hands, trace the old writing with their fingers, tuck it into a bag, and then do something with it expressing their susceptibility to its ancient charm, something that would ruin and reanimate it. Since the book is now loudly, aggressively the Nation's property, to do so would, of course, be a crime.

The More Things Change . . .

Surrey's poem "The Great Macedon" presents Wyatt's psalms as a national treasure, in parallel with Homer's place in Greek nationhood. Surrey was, in some people's eyes, the Nation in himself, which eventually got him in trouble. When Harington inscribes Surrey's Quasi-Coronet in front of Wyatt's psalms he is saying something about Surrey, Wyatt, and nationhood. Percy, writing in the manuscript, was working out the Nation's literary heritage and fixing the manuscript's location in that heritage by cross-referencing it to Tottel. Nott, a step on from Percy and using Wyatt (and Surrey) in a project of national restoration, follows Surrey in making Thomas Wyatt into Old Dan Wyatt, displayed in his fancy book/Ark. The library at the British Museum, as it was known then, is motivated in the same way, and the library also, in some ways, is itself the Nation, like Henry Howard; so it makes sense that the Library aggressively stamps the manuscript into a National conceptual space. The nature of this space has changed over the centuries, and so the Library means it in a more final way than previous holders of the book. There it will stay, until something drastic happens.

Something Drastic always does happen, of course. She who kissed him left; Wyatt died suddenly, Surrey got his head chopped off, as did Thomas Wyatt the Younger; Queen Mary perished, suddenly; Percy's manuscript went up in flames. Ritson went mad; George Frederic Nott fell off a scaffold, hit his head, and was never the same. Someday, England will be only a memory. Where will the book be? Who will remember the poem?

The Professors Read Wyatt's Book (in the Library)

Ewald Flügel, a German English Professor

If the Scots were primary influences in the teaching of English, German Professors were, as the nineteenth century drew to a close, the strongest influence on the practice of scholarship directed at English literature. This influence, which was by its nature comparative and cross-cultural, led to the prominence of philology, language study, and detailed textual criticism in scholarly practice—and some other things, like the creation or articulation of an Anglo-Saxon heritage and the resurrection of *Beowulf* as an "epic" progenitor of literature in English. German scholars trained rising scholars, especially Americans, and they talked to each other in journals that dealt entirely with literature in English; one of these was the journal *Anglia*, founded in 1878. It is still publishing today. In the early years one of its editors was Ewald Flügel, who, being disappointed in his desire for a position at the University of Leipzig, where he was trained, took advantage of the growing international market for his skills and became one of the founders of the Department of English at the then brand-new Stanford University.

In 1893 Flügel published what amounts to a carefully edited, highly attentive edition of Wyatt's poetry in a series of two articles in *Anglia*. He begins by lamenting the obscurity into which Nott's textual accomplishments have fallen, saying publishers have "ransacked Nott's treasure chest": "All of the fine, pioneering work that Nott did in this area is in danger, I think, of not being updated."

Here is Flügel's reprinting of "They Flee from Me":

39.

[26ᵇ; 46]   1 ent.

> They fle from me | that sometyme did me seke
> with naked fote stalking in my chambre
> I have sene theim gentill tame and meke
> that, nowe are wyld and do not remembrᵉ
> that sometyme they put theimself in daunger
> to take bred at my hand & nowe they raunge
> 7] besely seking with a continuell chaunge.
>
> Thancked be fortune it hath ben othrewise
> twenty tymes better but ons in speciall
> in thyn arraye after a pleasaunt gyse
> when her lose gowne from her shoulders did fall
> and she me caught in her armes long & small
> therewithall swetely did me kysse
> 14] and softely saide dere hert howe like you this
>
> It was no dreme I lay brode waking
> but all is torned thorough my gentilnes

into a straunge fasshion of forsaking
and I have leve to goo of her goodenes
and she also to vse newfangilnes

but synes that I so kyndely ame s^er^ued
21] I would fain knowe what she hath des^er^ued.

Am rande von v. 7: Tho.
Nicht in A, D. In T (40: The louer sheweth how he is forsaken
of such as he somtime enioyed) mit den varianten: 2. stalkyng within
my chamber. — 3. Once haue I seen them. — 4. do not once remember.
— 5. they haue put them selues. — 7. sekyng in continuall. — 9. once
especiall. — 10. thinne. — 11. gowne did from her shoulders fall. — 13. And
therwithall so swetely. — 15. dreame: for I lay broade awakyng. —
16. turnde now through. — 17. into a bitter fashion. — 20. I vnkyndly
so am serued. — 21. How like you this, what hath she now deserued?
Nott p. 23 (liest daselbst v. 13: she did), 546.

This is international professorial academic culture and convention in its
fully mature form, as created in the nineteenth century and as it is still practiced and represented today. Informed by the study of the various printed
and manuscript poems, the work pioneered by Nott, Flügel's reprinting,
with elaborate effort, puts the labor and learning that have produced it right
on the surface of the page, with reading priority communicated by font
size. It uses a full set of printed conventions that allow for a great density
of information to be presented very economically. In the top left are the
page numbers of Wyatt's book, including Percy's "46." The other number
("26b") refers to the physical leaf of the book, in the British Library's way
of counting: "26 verso."

"1 ent.," top center, is a transcription of the first attempt at creating a conceptual field in which to locate individual poems, written by someone, sometime,
at the top of the page in Wyatt's book. Flügel shows us how the words are
spelled by Wyatt's secretary, though not how they are written; he represents
the secretary's single mark of punctuation, the virgule in line 1, by a straight
printed line, a convention well established by this time. Other scholars would
have known what the line meant. All of the variations from Tottel's text are
listed below the printed poem, their position below the poem communicating
their subordinate status. As for Nott, for Flügel the poem as entered by Wyatt's
secretary and initialed by Wyatt is the important version. Flügel also notes the

page in Nott's book on which the poem appears, and the page on which Nott's note to the poem appears.

Flügel compresses his debt to the labor of centuries into a dense but readable and remarkably informative (if slightly idiosyncratic) text. It is, in this history, a new kind of object. It is made possible by the existence of the British Library, where a scholar like Ewald Flügel can go and ask to see a three-hundred-year-old book, even if he doesn't know any old families with old libraries. He just has to fill out a slip of paper, and someone brings it right to him. They also check to make sure he gives it back.

Even So, Another Mistake

Flügel represents only selected information from the page of Wyatt's book. He does not represent the math on the left side, nor does he reproduce Percy's note in the upper right. Leaving off the math is simple: it floats on an upper temporal layer rendered transparent by Flügel's learning, and so he doesn't even see it. Setting the book into the conceptual field of "Wyatt's poetry" has dissolved away some of these longtime companions of the poem. They are not important for creating this new object. The invisibility of Percy's note is a little aggressive, though understandable. Percy's cross-reference to Tottel's book has been superseded. It is no longer needed. Percy's great accomplishment, the correlation between old handwriting and old print, is now just a bit of unnecessary distraction. Of course, Flügel does retain the "1 ent" at the top, another note made by someone other than Flügel trying to make sense of what is on the page, which is arguably irrelevant in the same way. Flügel was, simply put, more interested in the (older) note.

Flügel also makes a mistake: "Nicht in A, D." That is, he says that "They Flee from Me" is not found in two other manuscripts, the so-called "Arundel Harington" and Mary Howard's book, the "Devonshire" manuscript. Our poem isn't in the Arundel Harington, true enough; but it is in the Devonshire. The centuries of conceptual weaponry Flügel had in his hand didn't prevent him from just missing the poem in Mary Howard's book, which he had looked through carefully. Perhaps an ill-timed yawn, induced by the task of reading old handwriting in a language not his own; perhaps a hunger pang, perhaps a twinge of distracting sadness or exhilaration: but, as G. F. Nott said: "Where is the man whose memory has always at command even what he knows, when he wishes to apply it?"

The Progress of Learning

No matter. Flügel's mistake is corrected some twenty years later by an English scholar named Agnes Foxwell, the product of training at the University of London. The first woman to record her thinking about our poem since the 1530s, Foxwell advances the documentary project one more step and also evolves the new object. She doesn't mention Flügel's articles in her book *The Poems of Sir Thomas Wiat*, published in 1913. One hopes she read them, since it would have saved her a lot of work:

THE POEMS OF SIR THOMAS WIAT

II

(1)

They fle from me, that sometyme did me seke
With naked fote, stalking in my chambr.
I have sene theim gentill, tame, and meke,
That now are wyld, and do not remembr
That sometyme they put theimself in daunger   5
To take bred at my hand; and nowe they raunge
Besely seking with a continuell chaunge.   7

(2)

Thancked be fortune it hath ben othrewise
Twenty tymes better; but ons, in speciall,
In thyn arraye, after a pleasaunt gyse,
When her lose gowne from her shoulders did fall,
And she me caught in her armes long and small,   12
Therewith all swetely did me kysse
And softely saide : "Dere hert howe like you this?"   14

2 stalking in] T. *stalking within.*
3 gentill] D. *both gentill,* the line scans with initial strong accent. T, *Once have I seen them.*
4 remembr] T. *once remember.*
5 they put theimself] T. *they have put them selves.*
7 with a] T. *in;* D. omits.
9 in speciall] D. *in especiall.* T. *especiall.*
11 from . . . did] T. *did from.*
13 Therewithall . . . did] D. *but therewithall . . . she did.* T. *And therewith-all so swetely did me kysse.*

86

MISCELLANEOUS POEMS

(8)

It was no dreme : I lay brode waking
But all is torned, thorough my gentilnes,
Into a straunge fasshion of forsaking ;
And I have leve to goo of her goodenes :
And she also to use new fangilnes ;   19
But syns that I so kyndely am served,
I wold fain knowe what she hath deserved.   21

(Signed "Tho.")

15 I lay] D, T. *for I lay.*
16 torned] T. *torned now.*
17 straunge] T. *bitter.*
18 to goo] D. *to parte.*
19 also] D. *likewise.*
20 so kyndely am served] D. *so gentelly am servid.* T. *vnkyndly so am serued.*
21 I wold . . . deserved] D. *What think you by this that she hath deserved.*
T. *How like you this, what hath she now deserved ?*

Foxwell's version of the professorial poem is different from Flügel's but very closely related in spirit. She corrects Flügel's error—perhaps she didn't know he had made it, but in any case she gets it right—and adds the details of the poem in Mary Howard's book. As Flügel did, Foxwell ignores Tottel's title; she also shows us how Wyatt's secretary spelled the words (though again, not how he wrote them). By using old spelling Foxwell shows us the labor of her transcription on the surface of the poem, as Flügel did, and as Nott did not. But like Nott, Foxwell has added a full complement of modern punctuation. To mix old spelling and new punctuation in this way is not coherent from a conceptual point of view, but it makes for a pleasing object. We can read it relatively easily, and the spelling brings with it the incense of the Antient that G. F. Nott loved so. We presume "Miss Foxwell," as she is invariably called by other scholars, was, like Nott, subject to these charms; her spelling of Wyatt's name in her title, for instance ("Wiat"), is also charmingly Antient.

The Professorial Poem

Poems are a resonant mixture of the material and the immaterial, and so reincarnation always produces a new thing. This was true of the first version in Wyatt's book, written down by the Secretary and initialed by Wyatt as all correct, ready for some purpose now lost in time. Nott's reprinting was aware of the difference between the poem in Wyatt's book and the poem in Tottel—and perhaps in Mary Howard's book—but it did not try to incorporate those differences into the reprinted object.

Flügel and Foxwell print the poem in a way it has not been printed before, and their reasons are of a different kind than previous reasons. For them, the material identity of "They Flee from Me" is an ever-growing number of very closely related versions. The name for this multiple object is "They Flee from Me."

The professorial reprinting of the poem, which Foxwell and Flügel are working out for the first time, is driven by an attempt to represent this group of poems all at once. Unspooled time is raveled up and present all at once, as it was for the old Haringtons in their library, but the surface of the page is now a conceptual space on which time can be arrayed and displayed. Like the library, the Professors want to take the poem out of time so that the passage of time can be better seen. Professorial printing conventions have been developed, partly, to help accomplish this project. Foxwell has a clear idea of what the new reading version should be like, of course, and this is the poem printed in larger typeface. The roots of her version, trailing down through time, are represented in smaller typeface and in a subordinate position, underneath the fresh new sprout.

This professorial machinery draws specific attention to the reprinter's labor, and is clearly meant to diminish worry about the reprinter's decisions. It allows the reader to examine some of these decisions and perhaps to make different ones. This method also allows for an unprecedented level of responsibility to documentary fact. We are used to it; we hardly notice it; but watching the method appear in this way helps show just how much went into preparing the paper to receive it. Foxwell's version is more "accurate" than previous versions, since it involves less forgetting.

When Foxwell calls Wyatt "Wiat" in her title, however, she is acting like an eighteenth-century builder constructing a Ruin. She does not want to simply reanimate the past, since the charm of the past is created for her (in some way) by its past-ness. Inside the new life that her reanimation creates is an intentional, even delicious admixture of Death. In the professorial poem the past-ness of the poem competes equally with its present-ness. The past is returned to us by the knowledgeable and responsible Professor, but this also, paradoxically, emphasizes just how past the past really is.

The professorial "They Flee from Me" is partly just a poem, a compelling, present-tense description of a tangled personal experience and the resulting psychological state: and it is partly an old thing on display in a Museum. The Professor has taken the poem from Wyatt and turned it into a fact. It is not what Wyatt wrote; he wouldn't have wanted to write it, and he couldn't have written it anyway.

In being represented more accurately as historical fact, "They Flee from Me" has come to life and also died. The source of this paradox is already in the poem. When Wyatt made his poem both general and specific, he created a way for the inner state the poem describes to return to life, again and again, as if this state was and is *always* happening "now." The poem was then carried away on the stream of time in the same way he, Wyatt (says he), was carried away from her and from happiness. Wyatt and his poem are both objects in the stream of time; but the poem is a capable swimmer. Foxwell is happy about the present-ness of her version, and melancholy, maybe even sad, about the past-ness of Wyatt and his life. In that way she is a natural audience for the present and past song that "They Flee from Me" sings, and sang, now, and then.

Of Course—

Foxwell says she has taken BL MS Egerton 2711 as her absolute authority, but Wyatt's secretary did not write "therewith all" in the thirteenth line of the poem. He wrote "therewithall," as did the writer in Mary Howard's book, something learnable from Foxwell's own note. Tottel printed "therewithall" in his black letter. Well: we can imagine a future edition that would feel compelled to include Foxwell's version in the notes. Perhaps "therewithall" didn't look ancient enough to Agnes Foxwell; perhaps she knew something no one else does or did. We can't ask her. Reprinting is reincarnation—printed words are a made of matter, like we are—and matter is ruled by entropy.

The Oxford Book of English Verse
Flower, Flowers, Nosegay, Bouquet, Garden, Anthology

While Flügel and Foxwell were busy pulling "They Flee from Me" from Wyatt's attenuated grasp, the poem was also awakening to vigorous new life in a spate of smaller, highly selective anthologies. In the later nineteenth century makers of selected collections of lyric poetry had the whole of literary history spread before them in the great reference collections. How to choose just a few poems? The editors of these volumes often discuss their methods in prefaces and introductions like the note Richard Tottel wrote to the Reader of his miscellany, a very distant ancestor. A (common) goal is that the select anthology should contain only the "best" of all that is already written, a goal truly more easily said than accomplished. The most popular and influential select anthology of this period is Francis Turner Palgrave's *The Golden Treasury*, first published in 1861. The "Preface" begins by just saying it: "This little Collection differs, it is believed, from others in the attempt made to include in it all the best original Lyrical pieces and Songs in our language, by writers not living,—and none beside the best."

Palgrave's calls it a "little collection." The rationalizations, justifications, defenses, and celebrations of select anthology prefaces often adopt a rhetoric of self-depre-cating smallness, frequently with reference to the origin of the word "anthology" in the Greek word for a bouquet of flowers. They also often describe reading lyrics as a very important activity. Sometimes these two opposing moods happen in the same preface. Palgrave's dance through the simultaneous smallness and importance of his lyric garden is both adept and representative. In his dedication to Tennyson (who helped make it), Palgrave says he hopes his book "may be found by many a lifelong fountain of innocent and exalted pleasure; a source of animation to friends when they meet; and able to sweeten solitude itself with best society,—with the companionship of the wise and the good, with the beauty which the eye cannot see, and the music only heard in silence." Palgrave is a softened cleric in the newborn church (or school) of literature; his reasons are like those of Nott, but made smaller and less alarming. Nott's exacting service to Virtue and Religion is replaced by "in-nocent" pleasure and companionship, with poems now "wise" and "good," friends to beguile the weariness of the sickbed, or to distract us after a long day. Palgrave also feels no guilt about being fully invested in the floating incense of the voices from the past, now made a Keatsian unheard melody.

Palgrave's rhetoric intensifies, however, at the end of his preface, as often happened at similar moments in Nott's prose: "Like the fabled fountain of the Azores, but with a more various power, the magic of this Art can confer on each period of life its appropriate blessing: on early years Experience, on maturity Calm, on age Youthfulness. Poetry gives treasures 'more golden than gold,' lead-ing us in higher and healthier ways than those of the world, and interpreting to us the lessons of Nature." Leading us in higher and healthier ways seems like an important, even Nott-ish mission. For Palgrave and his many descendants, down to our own time, the mixture of big mission with small pleasures does not produce obvious conflict (as it did in Nott) because it turns out smallness is the very quality people need. The benefit of poetry, as enabled by the select anthology, is like that of a garden: a small, select and hence improving refuge, supported by expert selection, exclusion, and weeding.

Palgrave doesn't include "They Flee from Me." It did get his attention, though, and (like a Renaissance reader) he left a note next to the poem in the reprint of Tottel he was sorting through: "Natural—a little too natural." Like Mary Howard, like Tottel, like Nott, Palgrave was both impressed and bothered by the personal, bitter scent of Wyatt's vigorous flower. "They Flee from Me" is not noticeably "good," and really not at all "innocent." Natural, yes, but prickly, pointy, fibrous. He declares "They Flee from Me" a weed and doesn't transplant it into his garden.

The (Re)Invention of Lyric

Palgrave avoids long poems, and he most especially avoids poems that are topical, or distractingly pointed in the weedy way of "They Flee from Me." This preference makes plain sense, especially for older poetry, since poems that are disturbing or in need of a lot of explaining don't work very well in a book that means to allow readers to progress from one poem to the next without catching on difficulties or struggling to understand. Palgrave wants his poems to be quiet companions. The select anthologist favors lightly rooted poems that can easily be moved into the anthological garden, with other lightly rooted poems for company.

The paradoxical work Palgrave gives to lyric poetry, to be Small and Big at the same time, drives his algorithm for choosing the poems in his anthology, and so also determines the dominant aesthetic of the poetry that appears there, and in the subsequent anthologies in its long shadow. Through the popularity of Palgrave's anthology and its descendants, the kind of poetry included in *The Golden Treasury* becomes the very definition of "lyric." The idea of the companionable, mildly improving poem is another modification of Nott's notions, as when Nott insists Surrey's poetry is valuable precisely because it "dwell[s] upon those points of feeling which are not the result of a particular state of manners, but exist in human nature generally."

What's more, *parts* of poems that are too obscure or too personal or too dated are sometimes excised by anthology editors also. If a poem isn't the Best, but almost, the editor rewrites it. Manufacturing "lyrics" by clipping bits from Shakespeare plays, a very common feature of anthologies of this type, is a variation on this method.

In *The Golden Treasury* the "best" of all lyrics in English become by default short poems with tight dramatic or emotional focus that can be read with comparatively little effort. The inheritance of this method is visible in *The Oxford Book of English Verse*, published in 1901, edited by Arthur Quiller-Couch, later the first Professor of English Literature at Cambridge. Oxford's anthology inherits the mantle of *The Golden Treasury*, selling hundreds of thousands of copies in its first decade and creating the franchise still publishing today; Quiller-Couch celebrates his debt to Palgrave in his preface. The Oxford anthology offers many examples of poems and plays modified to make them fit for inclusion in Anthological Space, a practice Quiller-Couch thoroughly owns up to in his preface. Since this book has been the source for many digitized versions appearing on the Web, many of the modifications imposed in it persist today.

Fame

Queen Victoria died in this same year, 1901, which might be the companion of another change: *The Oxford Book of English Verse* includes "They Flee from Me." In this reprinting, our poem, after centuries of waiting, circulates throughout the former, present, and expiring Empire and becomes famous. It becomes *the* Wyatt poem the "general" reader knows:

---

37.   *Vixi Puellis Nuper Idoneus . . .*

THEY flee from me that sometime did me seek,
   With naked foot stalking within my chamber:
Once have I seen them gentle, tame, and meek,
   That now are wild, and do not once remember
   That sometime they have put themselves in danger
To take bread at my hand; and now they range,
Busily seeking in continual change.

Thanked be fortune, it hath been otherwise
   Twenty times better; but once especial—
In thin array: after a pleasant guise,
   When her loose gown did from her shoulders fall,
   And she me caught in her arms long and small,
And therewithal so sweetly did me kiss,
And softly said, '*Dear heart, how like you this?*'

It was no dream; for I lay broad awaking:
   But all is turn'd now, through my gentleness,
Into a bitter fashion of forsaking;
   And I have leave to go of her goodness;
   And she also to use new-fangleness.
But since that I unkindly so am servèd,
'*How like you this?*'—what hath she now deservèd?

Q, Breeder of Gentlemen

Arthur Quiller-Couch (pronounced "Cooch"), universally known as "Q," was a famous person in his time. Q was a scholarship student at Trinity College Oxford, to whose President, Fellows, and Scholars he dedicates his anthology: "A House of Learning Ancient Liberal Humane and my Most Kindly Nurse." He spent his early career as a journalist writing about literature, and he was also a modestly popular author of adventure fiction, much of it set in Cornwall, where Q grew up. In 1895, before he edited the Oxford anthology, he published a more chronologically limited anthology of Renaissance poetry called *The Golden Pomp*. This anthology includes Q's first reprinting of "They Flee from Me," with the same title. In 1913 he became the King Edward VII Professor of English Literature at Cambridge. Since the initial incumbent of this Chair had died shortly after assuming office, Q was really the first. He was an important force behind the creation of the Cambridge Tripos in English Literature, begun in 1918, and also something of a phenomenon at Cambridge. His lectures, especially early on, were very popular (later he would sometimes, alas, not show up for them). He published his lectures every once in a while, and the resulting books were quite popular. Q identified very thoroughly with Cornwall, and lived there for much of the year. His arrivals and departures from Jesus College at (what his colleagues hoped would be) the beginnings and ends of term were events at which the Master and his staff would preside personally.

Q was a dedicated enemy of Flügellian textual scholars, Philologists and their ilk; he was an enemy of all things German and Anglo-Saxon, especially after his son died just after the war ended in 1918. His printed lectures are continuous in their insistence on the importance of reading current and older literature, and every lecture, in some way, claims that reading literature is fundamental to creating healthy individual moral character and robust national spiritual health. Q also, in addition to talking about the importance of education, worked hard on its delivery. For instance, he spent decades overseeing the local school systems in Cornwall.

His inaugural lecture as a Professor at Cambridge, delivered in 1913 and published later in a book called *The Art of Writing*, is typical in its ambitions and its rhetoric. His aim in this lecture is to describe what the new English school at Cambridge will be like—studying English literature "on literary and critical rather than on philological and linguistic lines." There is a whiff of Nott and Palgrave's magic incense: "We should lay our minds open to what [the author, "he"] wishes to tell, and if what he has to tell be noble and high and beautiful, we should surrender and let soak our minds in it." An educational scheme that does this will produce "gracefully-minded youth": "The man we are proud to send forth from our schools will be remarkable less for something he can take out of his wallet and exhibit for knowledge, than for *being* something, and that 'something' a man of unmistakable intellectual breeding, whose trained judgment we can trust to choose the better and reject the worse." Thomas Wyatt really was bred to his service at Henry's court: genetically, spiritually, intellectually, personally. This "breeding" was a way of life. At birth Wyatt was already (assumed to be) the "best," a *natural* member of the elite. His literary interests and skills were pronounced, but the kind of knowledge of literature Wyatt possessed was an inherent part of his upbringing. To read and write poetry was expected to be among the (natural) accomplishments of a Gentleman. The word "Gentleman," for people like Wyatt, was not a description of character only but also a description of his place in the world, something like a job and a calling at once—a profession, complete with duties.

(In his lectures Q always referred to members of the audience as "Gentlemen." This was a running joke for him and his audience, apparently, since most of them, sometimes *all* of them, were women, who could not take degrees but could attend lectures. This gesture is a little hard to read from our distance, but Q seems to have been broadly speaking a supporter of women's access to education.)

The whole long growth of education for people other than the hereditary elite in Britain can be summarized as an attempt to substitute some reproducible, systematized process of learning for Wyatt's breeding. Q insists that (the best) literature should have a central place in this process, because it is the very essence of culture; an ambitious person can find out about literature by attending Cambridge, where learning about poetry substitutes "intellectual breeding" for Wyatt's kind of Breeding.

Q's kind of elitism has two sides. Q was a scholarship boy, and from that side to be able to learn the things needed for entry into the Elite is primary and reclaims the Elite from charges of simple exclusion. From the other side—the side of the many people still excluded by Q's version of meritocracy—this way of thinking only adapts older notions of Breeding so they may survive in a new era. Q accepts the idea of an Elite and also embraces what qualities the Elite should have. He just wants to produce the Elite in a different way.

Horace, Again

Q derives his reprinting from the 1557 Tottel text. He has also given the poem a new title, made out of the first line of the twenty-sixth poem in the third

Book of Horace's Odes, plus an ellipsis. This Ode was well known in Oxford/
Cambridge/Public School circles, mostly remembered through the tag of its
first line. It is occasionally adapted for comic purposes in the eighteenth and
nineteenth centuries, sometimes being identified as an adaptation of Horace
by being titled with the first Latin line and an ellipsis, just as Q does in his title.
This same tag is sometimes used just by itself—as Q is using it—to summon the
general subject of middle-aged wise (sexual?) weariness. This is the first part of
the poem in David Ferry's translation:

> Experienced in your wars
> Not long ago I was
> A not inglorious soldier,
> But now upon this wall,
> Beside the effigy of
> Venus, goddess of love,
> Born from the glittering sea,
>
> I place these weapons and
> This lyre no longer fit
> For use in the wars of love.

Leaving the work being done by the title aside for the moment, generally speaking Q has been modestly clever here, since Horace's poem and Wyatt's poem
have a passing similarity. The general plot of slightly dissatisfied retirement
from Love's wars is an easygoing parallel to that of "They Flee from Me," and
Horace's Ode even ends with a potentially parallel flick of a lash at a former
lover, a slight suggestion of bitterness. The Latin words describing the lashing—
"sublimi flagello tange"—make up the other tag associated with this poem. The
end of the poem is thus just a little bit naughty, and its naughtiness is one of
the things being summoned by Q's ellipsis: "You know how the rest goes . . . ",
with the implied Wink.

The phrase is left untranslated and unattributed, and so Q the editor is making
the general reader feel that he *should* know this tag from Horace, and so be able
to enjoy the (gentle) knowing elbow about the eroticism in Wyatt's poem. Q also
used this technique in the lecture hall, as an educator of the Elite. It amounts to
a pedagogical method. Q wants us to feel a need to know; he wants us to want
to belong to the Elite, and he wants us to strive for Intellectual Breeding. When
Q cocks his eyebrow at us, at the end of the title, during the three dots, before

the poem, he wants us to feel like scurrying off to see what he means, what a person of Intellectual Breeding means when he does something like this. The performance of cultural knowing is one of the basic moves in Q's lectures. The idea is that the student will want to be like him.

Q is using the ellipsis at the end of his quotation or title to summon a whole world of reference and culture, the learning and breeding Horace both represents and exemplifies. Wyatt's poem is placed, artfully and discreetly, in the same cultural spot as Horace's poem. This is in line with Q's eventual work at Cambridge, the creation of the English Tripos, which put the study of English literature on par with the study of the classics. In other words, Q's summoning of Horace is just exactly what George Nott did when he summoned Horace, only now the whole operation has a carefully articulated conceptual environment and an audience to receive it.

Q was appalled by the rise of text-focused, Germanic-influenced English studies and took any opportunity he could to insist that the true source of literature in English lay in "Mediterranean springs." And so, in applying the tag from Horace to "They Flee from Me," Q is paying the poem the highest kind of complement he can. His reprinting calmly and even slyly insists that Wyatt's poem is of classical quality, descended from high parentage and worthy of inclusion in the center of British imperial culture. Like Q's putative students, the poem is one of the Best. Reading it should be part of learning how to exercise the kind of judgment Q himself has exercised in making the anthology, part of becoming "a man of unmistakable intellectual breeding, whose trained judgment we can trust to choose the better and reject the worse." It is not obvious that a capacity to tell the difference between a better poem and a worse one is the same kind of judgment a Cabinet Minister, for instance, needs to exercise, but Q clearly thinks so. He really means it.

Sticking with the Rewrite

Q stays close to Tottel's text, adding and changing punctuation but not changing any words. His is the first ostensibly modernizing reprinting to actually, entirely resist the charm of some quaintly spelled word. He was not a scholar at heart and would not have been very interested in Nott or Egerton MS 2711. He says in his preface—again echoing Palgrave—that he felt he was justified to "prefer the more beautiful reading" in the case of competing texts. Given the fundamentally instrumental nature of his conception of reading poetry, Q has made the right choice. Tottel's smoothed and less cranky poem better suits his needs.

His manipulation of the last line is a new touch and notably directive. It is as much as an editor can do short of wholesale alteration. By italicizing and inserting quotation marks around "How like you this?" Q attributes voice in a way the poem as written by Wyatt's Secretary did not. Q's poem insists that she says, "How like you this?" in what might be supposed to be a light, mocking tone. The speaker of the poem is now quoting these words as an example of the behavior that has made him wonder, in a light, mocking way, what she deserved. It is as if Q is reading it to us, complete with the elbow and the wink.

Instead of sullenly bitter, Q's version of "They Flee from Me" is lightly mocking, maybe not bitter at all; it touches on possible bitterness in an urbane and cultured way, as the University Gentleman might do if he quoted Horace's urbane poem about loss in the course of a conversation or a witty bit of writing. In Q's poem the losses the speaker has experienced are attributed, lightly, to the game of love, the tit for tat. The speaker in Q's poem might ask Venus to give her a little flick of the lash, maybe for the sting of it, or maybe so she would think fondly of him again. Q's modification further abstracts the poem away from the (overly) personal interiority of the poem Wyatt's secretary wrote down, the quality Palgrave calls "too natural." If this is the language of Nott's Universal Man, the Universal Man does not get (unpleasantly) invested in his own feelings.

How, Exactly, Does Poetry Help?

Q knew and admired William Minto, who mentioned "They Flee from Me" in his book *Characteristics of English Poets*, and he contributed a short essay to Minto's memorial volume, issued in 1894. It is easy to imagine that "They Flee from Me" was brought to Q's attention by Minto's writing, which Q might have reread as he composed his memorial essay after Minto died in 1893, the same year Q was constructing *The Golden Pomp*, his first anthology, in which "They Flee from Me" also appears.

Minto's approach is broadly biographical. He is interested in poetry as something an individual person might write for particular reasons, and he likes to ferret out those reasons. In the passage I quoted above, Minto uses the first line of "They Flee from Me" as part of a dramatization of Wyatt's emotional history, deploying the first line of the poem as if it were Wyatt talking about his own feelings. This is neither a bold nor an unreasonable approach, but it does not easily lead to a justification for using the poem in training members of the Elite. How, exactly, could this intimate, "too natural" picture of Wyatt's inner life be construed, for instance, as "noble and high and beautiful"? What exactly could "They Flee from me" do for someone reading it at this (very) late date?

Minto doesn't have to answer this question. He is a historian, trying to say true things about the past, and mostly leaves it at that. He only has to claim it is interesting to think about Wyatt's poem. In spite of his ambitious rhetoric, Q clearly, obviously, thoroughly felt this way too: his lectures often amount to simple celebrations of the joy of reading and knowing about literature. But Q insists on the programmatic importance of reading old poems, and he helps establish the English Tripos, so he does have to say why reading poetry might be a key part of intellectual breeding. Or at least we might expect he *could* say why.

In 1958 E. M. W. Tillyard, a younger colleague of Q's and one of the first generation to teach in the English school at Cambridge, published a history of the school called *The Muse Unchained*. Tillyard shared Q's admiration for Wyatt and published an edition of Wyatt's poems in 1929. He also liked and admired Q himself, and *The Muse Unchained* contains what feels like a relatively unbiased account of Q's pros and cons. Tillyard thought Q was especially good at getting people to be interested in English: he had a gift in the "art of initiation . . . a virtue unequalled in its kind by any member of the English staff as long as the Cambridge English school has existed." He admired Q's lectures, and also found them a bit "thin":

> Q had the art of making you think in the course of a lecture that he was about to reveal a very profound truth about the subject of his discourse, that there was a *something* to which all the time he was leading. Actually the something never enjoyed embodiment, but you clung to the hope that, perhaps at the very end of the lecture, perhaps in the next, it actually would.

In his inaugural lecture Q offers "principles" by which he will be guided. They are all a little difficult to get hold of. The first is that he and his students will study literature "absolutely," with "minds intent on discovering just what the author's mind intended." The second is "eschewing, for the present at any rate, all general definitions and theories, through the sieve of which the particular achievement of genius is apt to slip." The third is to treat "the English tongue" as "alive," current and growing (like the British Empire), and to teach students to "strive, each in his own way, to adorn it." Very solid, so far, but perhaps a little short of the ambition implied by creating Intellectual Breeding. At the end of the lecture, Q goes on, kind of: "But here at the close of my hour, the double argument, that Literature is an Art and English a living tongue, has led me right up to a fourth principle, the plunge into which (though I foresaw it from the first) all the coward in me rejoices at having to defer to another lecture." As far as I know, this fourth principle, which sounds very important, falls into Tillyard's trap and never appears. Perhaps the fourth principle would have explained what is inherently important about short, designed descriptions of personal feelings like "They Flee from Me," the quality that makes them worthy of a school. The easiest way of putting it, that they can be used as the basis for tests and schoolwork, is not as impressive as Q wanted his lectures to be. Perhaps that is why he simply didn't say it.

Questions and Answers: That's How

Teachers (and students) might have a variety of ambitions for schooling and what it will do for people and the world more generally; some of these ambitions might refer to the soul and the spirit. As fuzzy as they are, these are the referents of Q's ambitions. Almost all versions of schooling, however, and certainly the version at Cambridge in 1920 or so, end, at some point, in the practical business of Questions and Answers. The student needs a task, and the sponsoring institution/system needs a way to find out if the student has performed the task satisfactorily. There are a lot of school questions with answers essentially no one will dispute: What is two plus two? When did Lincoln issue the Emancipation Proclamation? In what year did Thomas Wyatt die? How many lines does "They Flee from Me" have?

The Teutonic way of studying literature tended to produce questions like that last one. The kinds of questions deriving from Q's approach, however, are potentially more difficult to ascribe Right or Wrong answers to. Take this question on the first Tripos in English at Cambridge in 1918: "With the substitution of which of the three characters Rosalind, Celia and Miranda for Desdemona as the wife of Othello would the play have been least likely to culminate in a tragedy?" Does this question have a Teutonic-style right answer? If it doesn't, what sense would it make as a question by which Cambridge will sort and evaluate its students?

For the purposes of evaluation, the important thing is to establish a sense of general agreement about the subject matter, so students and their evaluators know what to do. What is Rosalind really like, anyway? Most specifically, this is the job of individual teachers, who help students learn the answers to questions they will (eventually) be asked. They, teachers, have been taught what the questions will be. More broadly, the "subjects" teachers teach need to be shaped by some kind of overall clarity or definition, a set of boundaries fencing in the relevant and the interesting and fencing out the irrelevant and uninteresting.

For the study of literature in English, this kind of definition appears slowly but steadily, through constant tending by people like Percy and Nott and Minto. The equally slow but steady transformation of antiquarianism into academic culture comes along at the same time, and eventually it all coalesces into a self-policing and self-perpetuating system. The right answers to the questions are the answers academic culture agrees upon.

This is true of all academic disciplines, but the dependence of rightness on agreement is and always has been especially visible in the study of literature in English. Take this apparently simple question: is "They Flee from Me" one of Thomas Wyatt's best poems? For more than a hundred years after people began to want to ask such a question, the answer was a definitive No. After Q's intervention, by 1930 or so, the answer is a definitive Yes. This kind of reversal happens all the time in the (still short) history of the discipline of English and has made English the target of much derisive doubting.

English teachers are always to some degree taking on the traditional teaching of Language Arts, so no doubt Q and his colleagues, in grading exams, would have looked for consistently argued and clearly written answers to the above question, essays that did not defeat themselves with internal problems. They would also have looked for answers demonstrating knowledge of the important features of these characters and their plays, and "important" is the nub of it. Not "Rosalind has dark hair" but (something like) "Rosalind is strong-minded while also capable of change." Distinguishing the important from the unimportant or the interesting from the uninteresting is an exercise of judgment. As Q would say, it is the capacity to distinguish Better from Worse.

So the right answer is, can only be, an answer Q would like, and that is how the teaching of English is put in service of reproducing in its students the values of its teachers: which *might* be the same as the way the study of English can induce the qualities required by the Nation in its Elite.

Retrospect and Summary

With "They Flee from Me" chosen out by Q as one of the Best, and with the new Court of Professors and their students assembled around it, our poem is poised for a miraculous second life. Before I follow it there, a little pause.

Mature academic culture substitutes schooling for breeding. Generally speaking, with respect to lyric poetry, this also means that *studying* poetry has been substituted for *writing* poetry as the task through which elite culture is accessed. Reading and writing were always mixed, since Wyatt's day, as Mary Howard's book demonstrates so vividly, and so this is not a clean distinction. But when Q says the students and graduates of Cambridge's English School will "adorn the language," he is fudging it. He doesn't mean they will all be writing poetry. He means they will be culturally capable, that they will know about literature and they will take the right kind of joy and lessons from it. He also means the plainer part: that they will be capable speakers and writers of the language in their everyday lives.

Q's evocative conflation of Horace and Wyatt in his reprinting of "They Flee from Me" represents his methods and his ambitions perfectly and also provides a specific example of how lyric is, through this period, being taken up by the project of breeding through schooling. Poetry in English, and the history of poetry in English, are increasingly a central part of the shared culture being purposefully created and imposed in Universities. To be able to talk fluently about a poem like "They Flee from Me" is now a way of demonstrating intellectual breeding. Q fervently insists, continually insists, that judging poems is either the same as or good training for other kinds of judgment.

The world of the school, and especially the University, bears a strong resemblance to the world presided over by Samuel Johnson in eighteenth-century London, to which Thomas Percy gained access by writing (light, easy) poetry. Johnson's world in turn had a resemblance to the world of Henry's court. The school is different, being much more programmatic, much more tightly organized, and characterized by specific evaluative exercises through which cultural fluency is judged. These exercises foreground certain kinds of judgment. They show in small and large if the student can distinguish the Better from the Worse. Student fluency is now judged by paid professionals with increasingly specific training carried out in an increasingly consistent and programmatic way. The fitness of Professors for their jobs is judged by their mastery of a body of knowledge shared—and agreed upon—by an increasingly well-organized profession.

The Professor is a new kind of cultural courtier. Especially in Q's charismatic version, the Professor self-consciously performs the history of culture, revoicing the long dead and their feelings. The Professor models and exercises Judgment by choosing the Best for the lecture or the syllabus. The School insists its students will learn what the Professor has to say and evaluates their success through testing. The World validates the whole package by accepting the University Degree as a ticket of entry.

The Old Poet, and maybe also the New Poet, rise along with the Professor. That is: if lyrics are going to be convincing as targets of the machinery of the school, they need to be *really good*. As individual poems receive increasingly specific attention, the skills and intentional capacity attributed to the poet need to increase also, so as to produce a convincing picture of the poet who can load in all the good stuff the Professor later extracts. For the work of Professors of English Literature to be believable, the objects they work on have to have material in them worth all the work. In the court of the School, the Professor and the Poet need each other.

The idea of the supercapable Poet who can create objects worthy of processing by the machinery of professorial culture takes shape during this period, assuming definitive form soon, especially in the textbooks and critical writings of the 1920s. Agnes Foxwell's praise of her Poet in the introduction to her 1913 edition of Wyatt's poems is a preview: "Wiat's life and work is a song of harmony. The 'music of the spheres' is here. It is a vindication of what man can become with lofty aim and purpose."

We are used to it, of course, but with the step back provided by history it is clear how curious this arrangement is. The Professor becomes a kind of Maker himself, equal in his way to the Poet, especially the dead and old Poet; the Professor does this by saying noble and high things about the noble and high things the poets put in their poems. After this kind of schooling is systematized as a way of gaining access to the Elite, students *want* to take tests showing what they have learned about literature. Too late for G. F. Nott—but these are the people he wanted to talk to.

There are three specific illustrations before us. The first is Foxwell's reprinting of "They Flee from Me," which is not an object Wyatt wanted to make or could have made. It is the Song of the Professor. The second is Q's reprinting of the poem, differently but as thoroughly processed as Foxwell's reprinting. The poem comes to us out of Q's hand, singing Q's values, in an atemporal environment curated by Q. And so the third is *The Oxford Book of English Verse* itself, with its valorization of the short, relatively abstract poem as the definitive example of "verse." The aesthetic of the Oxford anthology is imposed by its purpose. All of the history of poetry in English is meant to be in it, and the general reader is supposed to read it. Poems that function well in this environment are the poems that make it in, which also stamps them as the Best. The Professor, being now a Maker himself, either extracts these poems out of the past or handily snips them out of the involved and foreign fabric of actual old poetry.

Professors are now in charge of old poetry, but they still haven't answered the big question about the small thing: what, specifically, does reading "They

Flee from Me" teach that is so valuable? Such a poem can be used in the daily business of schooling, but that is a different matter, just as the daily business the poem helped Wyatt with, long ago, was different from any actual feelings he might have had on any particular day. Q says we should listen to the Noble and High and Beautiful, and that sounds good, even very good. "They Flee from Me" might be beautiful; its narrative might be compelling—but it isn't very Noble or very High, and certainly it is not offering the behavior in the poem as a model, even if that behavior is interesting, to use Minto's word. What exactly could reading it do, that it should be wakened from its long sleep?

PART IV

Coming to America, and Making It Big

Cleanth Brooks and the Rise of the (Old) Poet

Cleanth Brooks, who would go on to become a major influence on higher education in America, and in particular on the place of English literature in higher education, arrived in Oxford in 1929 to begin his association with Exeter College as a Rhodes Scholar. He also published a poem that November, in the *New Republic*:

Geometry of Sunset

Geometricians, you who plot the curves
And angles of the earth, and who lay bare
Beauty in her nakedness, your nerves
Projecting their own fabric on the air,
Graph the one consummate, perfect line
With which the day meets night, the splendid arc
That bends, yet does not seem to bend, so fine
And delicate is its gesture toward the dark.

Unloose these clouds; sheer off this purple crest
Of hills; cleave through this twilight; leave only
The tenuous line described· upon the sea
Of nothing by earth's poles—emancipate
From the body of this death—this dying west,
The living Beauty, stark and ultimate.

CLEANTH BROOKS, JR.

While not the most memorable poem, as demonstrated by its not being remembered, this is a modestly accomplished poem. It is a sonnet, and hence a little difficult to execute, and this difficulty is also a mild sort of statement, in its summoning of old poetry and the parallel, implied insistence on the worth of knowing about old poetry. The pointed, mildly ambivalent challenge to the abstract(ing) work of Geometricians has a similar, mildly progressive, mildly conservative, book-learned air (like the *New Republic* itself). The poem's thinking is also a little bit difficult, requiring sturdy cognitive effort and the management of abstraction. It has no thin arrays or bewitching beloveds. It is a poem of ideas, or perhaps one idea: and a bit of a Head Scratcher, to be read with (mildly) furrowed brow.

In these qualities, especially in the head-scratching and the idea-driven movement, it is very much like the poems of Brooks's friends and mentors, especially John Crowe Ransom and Allen Tate, whom he had met as an undergraduate at Vanderbilt, and very much like a lot of poetry being published in magazines like the *New Republic*. Brooks may have had a deep love for writing poetry, but his later career does not show any particular sign of it. His career shows, instead, a deep love for studying poetry and writing about poetry, as well as a remarkable aptitude for knowing influential people and a capacity for turning his interest in literature into fame and fortune as an English Professor, a kind of national public intellectual, and even a sort of diplomat.

Cleanth Brooks bears, in other words, a strong resemblance to others in this long story: Thomas Wyatt, for instance, but especially Thomas Percy, who published a few poems when he first arrived in Samuel Johnson's London in the mid-eighteenth century. Like Percy's much less brow-furrowing poems, Brooks's poem demonstrates his mastery of a specific form of literacy and also his interest in and approval of the world marked out by this literacy. Brooks's poem is an application for membership in this world, mixed with a contribution to its making. In short, "Geometry of Sunset" is a competent performance of shared notions of what poetry should be like, and as such shows anyone who cares to read that Cleanth Brooks has learned and also values these notions. Since he shares the values, perhaps he belongs, and if he belongs, perhaps some of the power and money resident there can flow in his direction.

"They Flee from Me" Comes to America

As he published his poem Brooks was already in the midst of a remarkable social and economic rise that would end at Yale University and a perch at the very top of the American academic hierarchy. His father was a Methodist minister in the rural South, and Cleanth's youth was subject to the constant relocation and rural isolation that was the routine for Methodist ministers of that era. He began his entry into the wider world at Vanderbilt University in Nashville, Tennessee. Vanderbilt was then in the midst of its own rise, and in particular was the home of John Crowe Ransom, a poet and critic who presided over a club of intellectuals who called themselves the "Fugitives." The Fugitives were mostly poets and students of culture of one sort or another, and they had been publishing their poems and other writings in a magazine called the *Fugitive*. They included people who would go on to have an outsized influence on American literary culture—Robert Penn Warren, for instance, Brooks himself, Ransom, and Allen Tate.

Cleanth had been admitted to the Fugitives, and he was beginning to thrive as an academic, partly as a result of the devotion the Fugitives had to each other and to their cause of (southern) cultural revival. And, again like Thomas Percy, Brooks had a talent for acquaintance, for getting to know people who could be useful to him. The Chair of the Committee that chose him for his Rhodes Scholarship, Charles Pipkin, was also a graduate of Vanderbilt. After he returned home, Brooks got a job in the English Department at Louisiana State University, another institution in the midst of a remarkable if fitful rise in status and quality (as a result of the patronage of Huey Long). The Dean who brought him there was this same Charles Pipkin, who also brought Brooks's friend and fellow Fugitive Robert Penn Warren. Warren had also been a Rhodes Scholar, a year ahead of Brooks: Warren's scholarship was also awarded by a committee chaired by Charles Pipkin.

While at Oxford Cleanth worked closely with David Nichol Smith, one of the great detail-oriented scholars of the twentieth century. Smith was a product of Edinburgh University and, like William Minto, was a strong inheritor of the rich scholarly and pedagogical traditions in the study of English literature resident in Scotland. He had come to Oxford in 1908, at the behest of the curiously named Sir Walter Raleigh. Raleigh's role at Oxford was like that of Q at Cambridge—he founded the English School, and bringing Smith was part of that project. Like Q, Raleigh was a good writer and a good lecturer but not a scholar: Raleigh was a "Gas Man," as he said about himself, and hence Smith's role was to provide some scholarly rigor. Smith was especially an expert in the eighteenth century.

Among Smith's many scholarly projects was the editing of the correspondence of Thomas Percy, and Brooks cheerfully enlisted in that project, working in particular on Percy's correspondence with Richard Farmer, a Cambridge don who was an important part of the web of scholars and antiquaries Percy created and exploited in his work. Brooks eventually published the Percy-Farmer volume through LSU in 1946. Richard Farmer had been especially helpful in Percy's work on Tottel's miscellany and the poetry of Surrey and Wyatt, and the correspondence is full of references to that work and to Tottel's book. For his volume of 1946 Brooks wrote an excellent essay about Percy's editing of Tottel.

"They Flee from Me" had appeared in the *Oxford Book of English Verse*, of course, and certainly Cleanth Brooks, like any student of poetry in the period, would have seen it there. His work on the Percy letters would have led Brooks deep into the heart of the story of "They Flee from Me."

And so Wyatt's intricate, centuries-old set of patterns and grievance could have climbed into Brooks's briefcase while he sat in the Bodleian meditating on Thomas Percy, another rural kid made good, to come back with him when he returned to America and to LSU. Thomas Percy's personal example might have climbed in along with the poem: in particular Percy's remarkable talent for cultivating acquaintances like Richard Farmer and cannily turning that acquaintance into personal prosperity.

Schooling: The Poem Put to Work

Cleanth Brooks is one of the most important figures behind the creation of the mostly not-for-profit, troubled but thriving modern American industry of the study of English. In particular, his textbooks, which he wrote with his friend Robert Penn ("Red") Warren, formed a deep foundation for the actual details of what happened in classrooms throughout the United States. Brooks and Warren's textbooks, more than any others, articulated reasons why it might be worth looking at old poems and helped teachers see how they might make that study happen in the everyday classroom, where poems had to be both a subject of interest and also the sponsors of tasks to which students might be set, and on which they might be graded.

In 1935, being deeply dissatisfied with the textbooks they had available for use in class, Brooks, Warren, and a graduate student made their own, which carries the practical title of "Sophomore Poetry Manual." This workaday book is kept in an evocatively tattered state in the Yale University library, among many other bits of Cleanth Brooks's mortal remains. Out of the millions of poems written in English, Brooks and his two friends have chosen sixty or so as objects on which their students might labor. "They Flee from Me" is one of them:

lmer, all were thine.   I consecrate to thee.

III THEY FLEE FROM ME
Sir Thomas Wyatt(1503-1542)

They flee from me that sometime did me seek,
  With naked foot stalking within my chamber:
Once have I seen them gentle, tame, and meek,
  That now are wild, and do not once remember
  That sometime they have put themselves in danger
To take bread at my hand; and now they range,
Busily seeking in continual change.

Thanked be fortune, it hath been otherwise
  Twenty times better; but once especial—
In thin array; after a pleasant guise,
  When her loose gown did from her shoulders fall,
  And she me caught in her arms long and small,
And therewithal so sweetly did me kiss,
And softly said, 'Dear heart, how like you this?'

It was no dream; for I lay broad awaking;
  But all is turn'd now, through my gentleness,
Into a bitter fashion of forsaking;
  And I have leave to go of her goodness;
  And she also to use new-fangleness.
But since that I unkindly so am served,
  'How like you this?'—what hath she now deserved ?

IV ON THE LATE MASSACRE IN PIEDMONT
John Milton (1608- 1674)

This is a version of Q's version of the Tottel text, with punctuation performing the emphasis Q produced through italics. It has a manuscript-like
air, since the typewriter communicates something of the Hand that Typed, in
the varying darkness of the letters, the raised "W," and because the book in
which it is contained is now extraordinarily rare. I do not know of another
copy in existence.

By the fall of 1936 the "Sophomore Poetry Manual" had grown into a full-
fledged, multigenre anthology and textbook, published by LSU as *An Approach*

to Literature. This book was picked up by a commercial press soon after, and "They Flee from Me" appears in this book also:

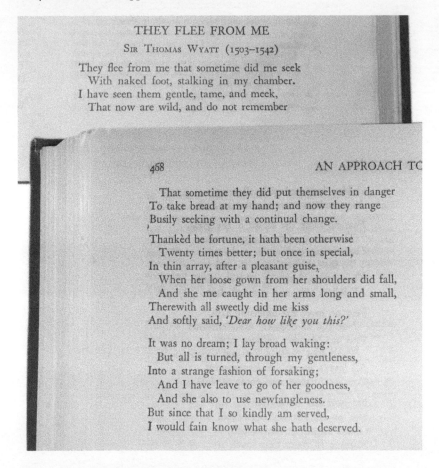

THEY FLEE FROM ME

Sir Thomas Wyatt (1503–1542)

They flee from me that sometime did me seek
  With naked foot, stalking in my chamber.
I have seen them gentle, tame, and meek,
That now are wild, and do not remember

468   AN APPROACH TO

    That sometime they did put themselves in danger
    To take bread at my hand; and now they range
    Busily seeking with a continual change.

    Thankèd be fortune, it hath been otherwise
      Twenty times better; but once in special,
    In thin array, after a pleasant guise,
      When her loose gown from her shoulders did fall,
      And she me caught in her arms long and small,
    Therewith all sweetly did me kiss
    And softly said, *'Dear how like you this?'*

    It was no dream; I lay broad waking:
      But all is turned, through my gentleness,
    Into a strange fashion of forsaking;
      And I have leave to go of her goodness,
      And she also to use newfangleness.
    But since that I so kindly am served,
    I would fain know what she hath deserved.

Wyatt's poem continues into later editions; in the third, 1952, it picks up a small task-oriented tail, five questions addressed to the Reader, of which more later.

Something has been learned, or decided, since 1935, since this version is based on the poem in Wyatt's book instead of Tottel's. It is a little curious as a reprinting: it is almost entirely Wyatt's version, but Brooks has adopted Q's italics, and his quotation marks have been retained for good measure. There is also, of course, an error: in the last line of the second stanza the word "heart" has been left out. This error calmly persists decades into the life of this textbook.

Q plucked "They Flee from Me" out from the vast welter of all that has been written; and then in *An Approach to Literature* the poem is centrally located in

American academic culture and sinks its roots into the deep, life-giving soil of the classroom, with its stream of students, instructors, and their respective Tasks. The poem's academic career will be a distinguished one. By the early 1960s many Professors will have published essays about it, and will regularly refer to it as Wyatt's greatest poem. Almost perfectly neglected for the 370 years before Q noticed it, by the middle of the twentieth century "They Flee from Me" is called a "universal favorite."

Practical Criticism: Getting It Wrong

Relatively late in life, when Brooks and Warren were famous men, they recorded a long conversation between them about literature and their careers. These recordings now sit near the copy of "Sophomore Poetry Manual" at Yale's Beinecke Library. The two old friends speak with the easy authority of men whose words have been thought worth paying attention to by decades of students and colleagues. They also speak with strong, twangy Kentucky accents, like actors playing people who grew up on Kentucky farms. On the seventh tape, a good ways in, they are recalling the days when they invented their textbook. Brooks begins by describing their unhappiness with the textbooks they had available for use in class, and then Warren interrupts. It began before that, he says, with animation. It began when we were both at Oxford, when we were thinking hard about the writings and attitude of I. A. Richards.

Richards spoke at Exeter while Brooks was there. Brooks was already reading and interested in Richards before he went to England, but later in life he remembers the importance of hearing Richards's voice and seeing his face.

Richards was a colleague of Q's at Cambridge (and a colleague of, say, Ludwig Wittgenstein), a member of the English School, though as a student of culture he was profoundly different from Q. Richards, in the 1920s, was, like Q, an extremely popular lecturer: after the hall was filled, people would stand outside just to overhear. He was a polymath and participated in a number of what are now crisply defined disciplines—Psychology, Philosophy, Linguistics, English, Sociology, Composition. He wrote in-between books that mix all of these plus some other stuff, with titles like *The Meaning of Meaning*. Brooks was interested in all of it, but he was clearly deeply interested in and especially influenced by a book called *Practical Criticism*, published in 1929. From *Practical Criticism* Brooks learned ways of saying why thinking about "poetry" could be important, and he absorbed Richards's deeply practical attitude toward education and the study of literature. *Practical Criticism* presents a kind of Program, and Brooks, while he quibbled with Richards's ideas for decades, looks like a believer in the program.

Like the sort-of experimental psychologist he was, Richards used his students to gather data about how people read poetry. Over a period of years he handed out poems without any contextual information or author's names and asked his students to write down what they thought of them. He called these written responses "protocols," and he called the effort and time his students spent in making the protocols a "reading." The protocols, in anonymous form, were used as the central subject matter in his lectures and then the book itself.

Richards quotes extensively from his students' writing, and what these responses show, fundamentally, is that his students, who were University students and hence among the most literate people in Britain, were having a hard time understanding poetry. Richards explores why his students misunderstand poems with a searching, categorizing, sort-of-scientific spirit. He enumerates the Four Kinds of Meaning; he counts and explains the Ten Difficulties his students demonstrate. In short, though, the issue is that more often than not his students were simply getting it wrong.

The pervasive confusion and incompetence demonstrated by his students makes Richards unhappy, and he broods upon it as Professors always have. But unlike so many such Brooders, Richards is full of hope. He is, as his title indicates, a practical man. He believes people can get better at reading poetry through "training." People could, for instance, be trained in handling ambiguity of meaning, or what he sometimes calls "multiple meaning" or "multiple definition":

> We receive no systematic training in multiple definition, and so the required attitude towards words is hardly ever developed. . . . We succumb easily to the temptation of supposing our "adversary" to be in obvious error when, in fact, he may merely be using words for the moment in another sense from our own. To the eye of an intelligence perfectly emancipated from words, most of our discussions would appear like the manoeuvres of three dimensional beings who for some reason believed themselves to exist only in two dimensions.

Richards often describes education as a progress toward mastery and often parallels the possibilities of progress in cultural and psychological study to the progress so evident, in the 1920s, in physical science: theoretical physics, for instance. The study of poetry is thus being enlisted in a process aimed, quite plainly, at perfecting human intelligence and thus human life. In fact, figuring out what poems are about is being given a *central* role in this progress toward a godlike exercise of power. By studying poetry, we might become "an intelligence perfectly emancipated from words," looking benevolently but sadly down on the beings below, caught, with their adversaries, in a web of (poorly understood) language.

Like generations of professors before and after him, Richards also takes his students' misunderstanding as a sign of a general decline. His descriptions of contemporary culture are invariably gloomy: for instance, in his summary, he says that machine-driven modern life is "disturbing throughout the world the whole order of human mentality." Misunderstanding poetry is not just a problem, it is a Serious Problem. Still, as an inspired and inspiring teacher, Richards is ready to roll up his sleeves and get to work. As he moves to conclusion, his voice rises in a way deeply reminiscent of our previous nostalgic, alarmed, morally motivated writer and proto-Professor G. F. Nott:

> If we are neither to swim blindly in schools under the suggestion of fashion, nor to shudder into paralysis before the inconceivable complexity of existence, we must find means of exercising our power of choice. The critical reading of poetry is an arduous discipline; few exercises reveal to us more clearly the limitation, under which, from moment to moment, we suffer. But, equally, the immense extension of our capacities that follows a summoning of our resources is made plain.

Like G. F. Nott, Richards believes studying poetry will save us from an encroaching and debilitating modern world. Richards's vision is much broader, his tastes are much more catholic, his instincts are much more generous; but still, "good poetry" will save us. Since professional academic culture and its associated school have now appeared, Richards has people in front of him, listening, and therefore he has hope. He is excited.

> . . . if there be any means by which we may artificially strengthen our minds' capacity to order themselves, we must avail ourselves of them. And of all possible means, Poetry, the unique linguistic instrument by which our minds have ordered their thoughts, emotions, desires . . . [sic] in the past, seems to be the most serviceable. It may well be a matter of some urgency for us, in the interests of the standard of civilization, to make this highest form of language more accessible.

What is this "Poetry" Richards refers to? The human constraints of classwork—the limited time and attention of the University student—force Richards to use poems of the type created and celebrated by the great lyric anthologists like Palgrave and Q: short, compressed, structured in some mild way, expressive of (some kind of) inner state or a single thought. Some poems are longer than others, but the poetry Richards features in his book must be suitable as the target of the student's cognitive effort and time, which produces the page or so of the protocol. Only the select anthologist's kind of poem will work.

There is, however, an urgent, almost desperate appeal to something greater resident in the Capital "P." Poetry is the "highest form of language," which one supposes it needs to be if studying it is to be so important, if an improved capacity to construe what a poem says is to save us from ourselves. This way of referring to poems as "Poetry" appears later in the nineteenth century and reaches a kind of excited peak in the 1920s. "Poetry" has an On Beyond Zebra quality, like the big points Q never put words to.

Richards is an evangelist, trying to bring the good news of Poetry to the people. It is Richards's sense of the urgency of the study of poetry that reappears so thoroughly in Cleanth Brooks, and especially in Brooks and Warren's textbooks—along with the correlate insistence on the consequences of getting Poetry wrong.

A New Approach to Literature

Much of *An Approach to Literature* reads as if Brooks and Warren had decided simply to implement the program either described or implied in *Practical Criticism*. It was meant as a vigorous intervention and was taken as such by teachers across the United States. A textbook they were competing directly with, *The College Omnibus*, edited by J. D McCallum, talks this way about poetry, in its 1936 version: "The wish to spread the contagion of beauty, whether it be the play of the fancy or the emanation of truth, is the deepest reason for poetry." *An Approach to Literature* talks this way instead, a little way into the "General Introduction": "The question of the value of literature is, as a matter of fact, not very hard to answer provided one understands what literature essentially is: that is, what sort of information it gives, and how it is related to, and how it differs from, scientific information. And these points can perhaps be best made by examining a concrete case." Earlier in the introduction, the high-sounding invitation to elitism of people like Q and Palgrave has been swept away with brisk, practical questions and gestures: "We shall not try to quibble or side-step the real question, or retreat into some vague statement that literature is 'cultural' and that all the 'best people' have always enjoyed it." The "concrete case" Brooks and Warren "examine" in their introduction turns out to be an elaborately choreographed drama of explication using a bunch of made-up documents plus one genuine item, Browning's poem "Porphyria's Lover." Browning's poem describes the unsettling murder of a young woman by her lover, who strangles her with her own hair and then meditates happily beside the body. Brooks and Warren make up several different versions of this story, imitating various types of descriptive modes, intended to demonstrate by contrast what is different and distinctive about the poem itself (which is serving as an example of "literature").

Brooks and Warren concoct a "coroner's report" and an "indictment" against the speaker, whom they call "John Doe"; they make up a newspaper article. Referring to these made-up factual approaches, Brooks and Warren say: "All three of these accounts are concerned with facts, and *only* with facts. . . . The primary purpose of each of these accounts is to give information. But they are not literature." What is "literature"? In a delightful downright way Brooks and Warren declare that it is "not a mysterious or strange sort of thing" but rather something most people are interested in, even if they "never actually read a poem."

The Sob Sister and the Sin of Sentiment

The last mode Brooks and Warren imitate is called "the sob sister's story." "Sob Sister" is a phrase from the period used to describe the (female) writers of sensational news stories. The (imaginary) sob sister does a lot of bad things, and the editors go after her relentlessly. "Her" account is "general" and hence "crude"; her arrangement is "haphazard," and because of this—because writing drives thinking—she "does not have a firm grasp on the nature of the murderer." Therefore she has to "resort to description that is designed to pull the heartstrings of her readers." This, in turn, means she has committed the worst crime in Brooks and Warren's affective universe: "The effect of the sob story is *sentimental*."

Being "sentimental" is a highly gendered affliction that derives from not being mature: "The really grown-up reader grasps the fact (though he may not state it to himself in so many words) that the sob sister has tried to stir his emotions without knowing exactly why they should be stirred *and* without showing exactly what emotions should be stirred." The effect of the poem—which is standing in for literature, even though, the editors let slip, it is "not a great poem"—is different. It is, it seems, something like Manly. Because "he" has a "real grasp on the situation," the poet can "afford to suggest rather than demand that we react in a certain way. The feeling of experience as a result of the poem is based on understanding; it is not detached from understanding and judgment. Therefore, it is not sentimental, for as we have observed, sentimentality is the enjoyment of emotion for emotion's own sake, separate from intelligence." Brooks and Warren are interested in, and have sympathy for, the person who is struggling to resist this effeminate interest in emotions for their "own sake." This person is now announced to be the "student," and the idea is that this person is aspirational and wants to leave feminized emoting behind by training his understanding and judgment: "The issue then is not whether the student is content to do without literature; it is whether he will be content with bad literature rather than good." Like the would-be gentleman-by-training wishing he knew what Q meant by winking and whispering "Vixi puellis nuper idoneus . . . ," this "student" is meant to feely mildly on-the-spot and hence discontented. The student may not have known he was ill, but his teacher is there to tell him he is sick and to offer the cure at the same moment. The "student," in fact, is defined quite specifically as a person who suffers from a debilitating attraction to badness but who has come to know it and wishes to learn to resist. How can he learn to love the Good? *An Approach to Literature* tries to say exactly what the student should do when reading a poem. He can "analyze its content and effects." He should think carefully, use his understanding, and try to say exactly what is going on (in the poem).

Anthology, Textbook

The twin focus on the dangers of the Bad and the remedy of schooling produces the hectoring air of so many old textbooks—but *An Approach to Literature* outdoes them all. It is relentless in its pursuit of the right way of reading, relentless in its pursuit of literary malefactors (like Percy Shelley), and relentless in its prodding and elbowing of the struggling student, through the medium of the "readings" of poems it offers every few pages, and through the "exercise" attached to many of the examples.

Textbooks appear in their modern form in the middle of the nineteenth century. Their direct ancestors are rhetoric and grammar books. Grammar books, in particular, contain the mixture of explanation, rule, example, and exercises that characterizes the literature textbook. The old grammar book is designed to be a classroom helper, but it has the feel of a kind of virtual or dramatized classroom. It often begins with addresses to the teacher—and then to the student—and then it takes off on a programmed path, a minicurriculum that builds on itself and moves to a destination. The harder bits are at the end; the beginning has a pleasant let's-get-started air, with easy entryway examples and exercises.

The old grammar books, like their cousins, the rhetoric books, contain and attempt to domesticate a central conflict: between *listening* to what people are saying or writing and *telling* them what to say or write. The source of grammar is what people fluent in the language say and write; grammar, plainly speaking, is a description of the already said, the already written, and so the inner pain of the Grammarian is that in some fundamental way the grammar student is the source of the authority of the grammar teacher.

The scandal is contained, in the old books, by celebrating and enforcing what *some* people have said, what *some* people have written. One way has to be chosen, since the student has to be told whether he is right or wrong. He has to progress; he has to be tested; he has to get a grade. The way some people have written is the source of the rules. These rules are the basic content of the grammar book, but the rules are always underwritten by examples.

For instance, here is a paragraph from Lindley Murray's *English Grammar*, first published in 1795 and the dominant model for most of the nineteenth century: "The nominative denotes the subject, and usually goes before the verb or attribute; and the word or phrase, denoting the object, follows the verb; as 'A wise man governs his passions.' Here, a *wise man* is the subject; *governs*, the attribute, or thing affirmed, and *his passions*, the object." Sometimes Murray makes up the sentences he uses as examples, but more often he imitates or adapts sentences already out in the world, the Already Written: literature. "A wise man governs his passions" derives from or is related to a family of sentences written throughout the eighteenth century in magazines, in sermons, and especially in books of maxims and rules for living, all of them using and moving around the words Murray italicizes. Murray's adaptation makes it not exactly a quotation, and especially in being presented as a "sentence" this bit becomes a different thing from the originals, a more compressed, more self-sufficient and compact thing. Murray's quotation from the Book of Life is single and self-sufficient, and hence highly suitable for (brief, compact) analysis.

Murray is running rule the other way, imposing rule on literature itself. In absorbing the already written into Education, citing (slightly made-up) "usage," Murray is making written culture what it *should* be in the process. In becoming Education, literature is being rewritten to conform to and hence exemplify the rules for which it is, or should be, the ultimate source.

This re-presentation of the world in adapted and compressed form is just like the selection and adaptation behind so many of the poems in anthologies like Q's *Oxford* book. In the grammar and rhetoric books the unit is the "sentence," which corresponds to the often-clipped or adapted "poem" of the select anthology. The "literature" quoted in the grammar book is also the "best," like that in the select anthologies. So the little self-contained virtual classroom of the grammar book is also a self-contained universe of language and meaning. It has to be. If, in giving an answer, the student can escape from the environment of rule and enforcement, she can't be graded reliably, and she can't be compared to others. As Q makes so clear, institutional literary education is not only a learning of facts: it is a sorting mechanism, in which the best literature is appreciated by the best people.

Bending the real world to fit has an air of cowardice about it, the cowardice any enforcement of cultural standard implies. The grammarian does not accept the simple reality of different forms of usage and makes this point of view resemble reality by rewriting existing sentences and by sorting competing forms of usage into Good and Bad. Bad usage is present, especially, in the exercises, which contain sentences the student is to correct. In some editions the key to the exercises is attached, so the student, with proper self-control, can be her own Teacher. In the exercises the student turns from Bad to Good by turning the bad into the good.

The Complete Moral World of the Textbook

An Approach to Literature very distinctly blends the spirit of the grammar textbook with that of the select anthology, and this blending is the source of its vibrating, hectoring energy. In spite of their stated opposition to thinking about "literature" as the "best," Brooks and Warren are equally interested in confronting and denouncing the Bad. That is—in the poetry section, the book contains both good and (what the editors say are) bad poems. The *College Omnibus* contains only good poems, like most classroom anthologies, and says things like this (about Keats's "Ode on Melancholy"): "One of the shortest, it is one of the most poignant of the odes." *An Approach to Literature* subjects "Ode on Melancholy" to one of its "readings," a several-page essay that takes it apart bit by bit, always with a sharp, unrelenting appraiser's eye. *Approach to Literature* says things like this about Keats's poem: "The poem, as has already been indicated, is not altogether successful, though parts of it are very fine."

Brooks and Warren's textbook, like the old grammar textbook, states the rules by which good and bad can be distinguished, and, as in the old grammar book, formulations of the book's values appear overtly and covertly on almost every page. These values subsequently became famous as the values of the New Critics, a set of Professors and writers whose origins lay in the gatherings of the Fugitives at Vanderbilt (and in the reading of I. A. Richards and T. S. Eliot). About "Ode on Melancholy," for instance, they say, shortly after the bit quoted above, that "the poem does not have enough irony."

By "irony," Brooks and Warren mean essentially the same thing Richards meant by "multiple meanings," and *An Approach to Literature* offers the "training" in multiple meanings Richards insisted would save the world. In *Approach to Literature* "irony" names the forms of language that express multiple meanings, but fundamentally the commentary is constantly after describing the kind of mind or character who is *capable* of irony. This character is the "grownup" referred to above, in the part about sentimentality, and is the hero of the book.

The good poet is also sometimes called "mature" or "tough minded." The good poet, the good poem, the good *reader* of poems, not only can resist presenting the world as simple or singular but also knows that thinking of the world in simple or emotion-driven ways is simply not right. Over and over and over again *An Approach to Literature* insists that people and their culture are complex and multiple, and it condemns any poem or person saying otherwise. Such a person/poem "does not have enough irony."

Just as in the old grammar book, there is no escape from the moral and conceptual world defined by the textbook's pointed promotion of its values and its relentless sorting of good and bad. The student can only breathe a very highly processed air. The correct responses of the reader of poetry are given to her and derive from a sometimes hilariously clearly defined picture of human life. For instance, in the reading that begins the section in which "They Flee from Me" appears, a poem by Thomas Hardy and a poem by Robert Southey are compared. Hardy, of course, wins this one hands down. Among other sins, Southey's poem commits the Great One, the sin of sentimentality, and Brooks and Warren come down hard: "[Southey] says that he has often wept because he thought how much he owed to the past. The reader would be willing perhaps to believe him if he said some *one* particularly tragic or pathetic story have moved him so deeply; but nobody ever wept over the past in *general*." The student may not have thought she could weep in the wrong way, but that is what teachers are for. According to our teachers, Brooks and Warren, nobody has *ever* wept over the past in general. And underneath this urgency about right weeping is the implication that of course you may have wept over the past in general, in your ignorance, but not to worry: you can learn to weep more carefully. The kind of inner life Brooks and Warren recommend and demand is described in the chapter called "Wit and High Seriousness" in *Modern Poetry and the Tradition*, Brooks's first major critical statement, published in 1939 and summing up the decade's work. He is speaking of a poem by the Renaissance poet John Hoskins (once thought to be by Donne): "The ability to be tender and, at the same time, alert and aware intellectually is a complex attitude, a mature attitude, but not necessarily a self-contradictory attitude. Only a sentimentalist would feel it to be so." Or, from a reading of (the much-reviled) Percy Shelley's "Indian Serenade" in Brooks and Warren's next textbook, the endlessly influential *Understanding Poetry*:

> If the reader can be induced to yield himself to the dreamy sweetness of the set-
> ting and if his intellect can be lulled to sleep, he feels that the poem is fine. Good
> love poetry, on the other hand, does not need to resort to such devices. The poet
> achieves an effect of intensity without violating our sense of reality and without
> asking us to stop thinking so that we can exclusively and uninterruptedly "emote."

In the sealed moral and intellectual world created by the textbook, and in the classroom it enables, the badness of giving in to emoting doesn't even need to be actually said. Go ahead, they whisper: do it if you want. You will then enjoy the bad poem "Indian Serenade." If you do, though, not only will you be wrong about the poem's goodness, but you will be stupid, and you won't be like Us.

Some Details, and the Classroom

Questions, and Answers

An Approach to Literature is filled with questions, in the curiously singular "Exercise" attached to many of the poems (as if the questions were a fitness program). In principle it is interesting that authors with such strong opinions, so given to badgering the student into compliance, would also be so interested in questions. The readings are more what we might expect: straightforward intellectual enforcement.

The first question addressed to the reader of "They Flee from Me," about the beings that used to come to the poet's hand, asks for attentive reading: "To what does the word "they" refer in l. 1?" Good question, though it turns out the question is of a type often asked in the seminar classroom created by Brooks and Warren: the book already knows the answer. "It would seem to refer to birds (or any wild, shy, timorous creatures)." So the "question" is in fact an invitation to participate in a small drama of not knowing and then being told. The student is meant to feel the absence of an answer before being given the answer. All of the questions in the "Exercise" are of this type. The student is always invited to be simple before she becomes complex; always invited to feel the presence of a sentimental or intellectually sleepy answer before being told the alert, aware, complex answer, the mature answer.

Some of the questions are barely disguised. The answer is just "yes," as with a multipart one about our poem: "Try to characterize the tone of the last stanza. It evidently involves irony, but what kind of irony? Is it an irony aimed primarily at the expense of the woman for whom love is merely a fashion—a mode of dress to be altered capriciously? Or does the irony also involve the speaker—as if he were intimating 'how foolish of me to have expected anything else'?" The student is saved from sin before he can commit it, prevented from getting it wrong by not being allowed to answer. But he is aware of the possibility and even likelihood of error, since he knows that he probably wouldn't have come up with these answers himself.

The Triumph of Multiple Meanings, and of "They Flee from Me"

The series of questions is thus a Reading in disguise, a reading in the form of ephemeral blank spots created by the questions, quickly but not instantaneously filled in by answers disguised as further questions. The last "question" summarizes the mature reading of the poem and also pointedly expresses why "They Flee from Me," essentially ignored for four hundred years, has suddenly risen to the top of the heap: "4. If this poem does involve a deeply sardonic account of inconstancy how has the poet kept it from seeming passionately bitter or glibly cynical? Does it become a more moving and powerful poem for having been kept free of a more superficial and obvious bitterness?" "They Flee from Me" is not superficial or obvious, like the good student in *An Approach to Literature*. Like the good reader, the poem is capable of holding on to multiple meanings. It doesn't give in to simple emoting, passionate bitterness, or glib cynicism. Like the wise man who controls his passions, the poem keeps being "complex" even when tempted to be simpler. That is why it is a good poem, why it made its way into "Sophomore Poetry Manual" and then into *An Approach to Literature*.

"They Flee from Me" also became, in this period, a kind of Hero of Literature through its textual history. Tottel's changes, for instance, are now an example of weak-minded interest in simplicity, and Tottel's poem is a poster child for what happens when the weak-minded are in charge. In their aggressive and idiosyncratic book *A Pamphlet against Anthologies*, published in 1928 and part of the environment out of which Brooks and his books come, Laura Riding (who published poems in the *Fugitive*) and Robert Graves use "They Flee from Me" to show this very thing. The Tottel poem, the one chosen by Q, is of course the one the "ideal anthologist" would choose. In it he was "giving the public what it could understand" instead of the "vexatious" poem in Wyatt's book. The implication is that Tottel himself was the original soft-minded reader.

Like Q's use of the poem as an invitation to participate in the knowing, faintly but inconsequentially naughty and mildly passionate attitude of the Gentleman, the understanding of the poem's value implied and expressed in *An Approach to Literature* is an invitation to participate in a kind of elite: an elite characterized by a tough-minded, unsentimental, held-off attitude toward a difficult world. *An Approach to Literature* insists that good poems are examples of this attitude and way of thinking. Through the models offered by the readings, and the mock-dramas of learning embodied in the Exercises, the mature attitude is handed over to the students. The students' answers, whether to the questions or in their own essays, written for a class and graded by the teacher, are now like poems. In the old grammarian's way of putting it, the students show their goodness by writing good sentences (about poems).

The world has come around to "They Flee from Me." The poem's little drama of regret about having once given in to feelings demonstrates the fierce virtues characterizing the sealed moral world of *An Approach to Literature*, for one thing. But the specific sense of Thomas Wyatt the person that sneaks into the poem, which seemed to bother people from the start, is now a named, distinct virtue. Wyatt—as a name for the speaker of the poem—is the kind of person Brooks and Warren celebrate. Q may have wanted his students to be like Wyatt, but he wouldn't have said so, and his way of thinking wouldn't have permitted it. Brooks and Warren really do want the student to be like Wyatt. Bitter, maybe, but with a *complex* bitterness, and that complexity is the important thing.

"Elite" Matters

Understanding Poetry, which takes the poetry part of *An Approach to Literature* and extends it into a full stand-alone textbook, was published in 1938 and adopted at Yale in 1946; Cleanth took his place as a member of Yale's English Department in 1947. Yale's English Department was already a high-status department in the world of higher education, and in the next thirty years that stature would only rise, largely because of its investment in Brooks and the methods he and his friends developed. Brooks also entered a department with a continuing connection to government and a (now famous) connection to the intelligence services. This connection came from several sources, most of them the conventional pathways to power associated with elite private colleges.

Yale and Yale's English Department had a special relationship with what became the CIA. A member of the Department, Norman Pearson, had been a central member of the OSS during the war, in charge, specifically, of counterespionage. At Yale he had been a teacher of James Jesus Angleton, also a member of the OSS during the war and a celebrated handler of agents and double agents in the field. Angleton was very interested in contemporary poetry and poets, and in his careful tending of his relationships with modern poets Angleton bears a certain resemblance to the mild-mannered Cleanth Brooks. He corresponded with Eliot, Pound, Cummings, and many others; he was a drinking companion of I. A. Richards's influential student William Empson. He founded a magazine called *Furioso* during his Yale undergraduate days in which he published the poetry of major modernist poets like Pound and Archibald MacLeish, another Yale graduate (who helped form the OSS), and also a review of Brooks's *Modern Poetry and the Tradition*. When the old OSS became the new CIA, in the late 1940s, Angleton became the head of Counterintelligence and an important Cold War Warrior.

Angleton sometimes testified to the relevance of his training in Multiple Meanings. Much later, one of Angleton's own CIA recruits, William Johnson, another Yale graduate who was teaching English at Carleton College when he was recruited, said in his 1987 book *Thwarting Enemies at Home and Abroad*: "I do not require my young CI [counterintelligence] officers to be able to discuss the complexities of a Shakespeare play, but if I catch them studying Brooks and Warren's *Understanding Poetry*, I do not instantly send them off to the firing range. I tell them to go read Cleanth Brooks on 'the language of paradox. . . . '"

The Old Elite

Thomas Wyatt, Gentleman, belonged to an elite that was mostly genetic in its origins but also perpetuated itself through elaborate modes of training, some of which were literary. Wyatt went to Cambridge centuries before I. A. Richards was teaching there. Wyatt also worked in an environment James Angleton would have appreciated, where dealings were at least double on a routine basis and where a misstep in interpreting multiple meanings could lead to a quick (or excruciatingly slow) death.

Thomas Wyatt wrote poetry for multiple reasons, but at least one of them was as practice in his inherited culture of subtlety, and another was to demonstrate his mastery of that culture. Wyatt was accused of treason twice, and was held in the Tower twice, which is once more than most prisoners, since the usual exit route was in a coffin. He left it alive both times, saved, at least partly, and perhaps mostly, by his subtle mobilizations of language and self-interpretation in his own defense.

Many members of Henry's court culture used poetry in their daily lives, even if they did not often author it, like those important women who made what was later called the Devonshire manuscript. Familiarity with poetry other people wrote was a basic expectation of those who participated in Henry's court.

That is: lyric in English has its origins in a culture characterized by clandestine plotting and careful training in multiple meanings. So perhaps it is not so surprising that (centuries later) the study of poetry would be thought of as good training for citizens of a dangerous, multiplotted world, and maybe even good training for a spy.

Reading, Writing, Poetry

Q blurred the difference between the writing and the reading of poetry, a move made necessary by his poorly articulated notion of why reading poetry would be good training as well as a pleasant thing to do. Authors of (good) poems say things in a "noble and high and beautiful" way, and so are easy to celebrate. But why would *reading* such a poem be valuable in a similar way? Ultimately it seems only an exercise of taste, and hence the evasiveness.

This doesn't really work, even at the level of taste. "They Flee from Me" (for instance) has its beauties, but in its sardonic bitterness it is quite specifically not noble or high. If we could ask him, and if he would tell the truth, Q likely would say he liked it for other reasons, because it is subtle and interesting and intimate and a bit off, a bit backbiting and strange.

If the point is to get people to think reading poetry is an important thing to do, especially old poetry, then the closed, intent moral and linguistic universe of *An Approach to Literature* and *Understanding Poetry* is a powerful advance over the earlier formulations. It is not so much the values in play, though Brooks and his friends demonstrate the midcentury interest in dispassionate, scheming analysis and manipulation very clearly, as well as the cold warrior's distanced resistance to passionate single-mindedness. The advance is simpler than that, more direct: *An Approach to Literature* gives reading literature a very specific, practical formulation as a task that can be done poorly or well. By demonstrating a capacity for reading poetry, the student (and the Professor) can demonstrate the capacities Thomas Wyatt demonstrated by writing it. It is a bit of a trick, the consequences of which have reached every corner of the literary world. In Brooks and Warren reading poetry is definitively swapped for writing it.

In particular, the "readings" included in the textbooks not only show the student what he should learn to do but also show the teacher what she is supposed to do—how she should organize her semester and her classroom. The teacher should select the best (short, self-sufficient) poems and then organize short, self-sufficient sessions of analysis that elucidate either goodness or badness but in either case allow both teacher and student to exercise and improve various intellectual and moral capacities.

Saying what "They Flee from Me" means is a good way of demonstrating your alert, intellectually aware maturity. And saying that "They Flee from Me" is a *good* poem is a way to demonstrate a resistance to uninterrupted emoting, as well as an investment in the celebration of this attitude by Brooks and his friends. By learning to be good at saying why "They Flee from Me" is a good poem, the student becomes Good. A good student might get a good recommendation from her teacher, which will help as she moves off into the pathways of power. She might become an English Professor; she might go to work for the CIA.

Séance

The invention of the School of Literature creates the space in which the old poem comes to life. This is true in a conceptual way, but it is also true in plain, even fundamental material ways. The industry of scholarship can feel as if it is powered by its ends, the improvement of knowledge, but the paychecks of the people doing it are made possible by the student, either in an immediate way or at some remove.

The invention of the Student, who comes with the School, also creates a person for the Professor to talk to. Again, this is simple fact, but it is also a larger truth. A rhetorical environment populated by students is an environment in which people are listening, want to listen, need to listen. Or, at least, it is an environment in which it *feels* as if someone is listening. This is what G. F. Nott was missing when he wrote his worried endnotes, heading off the bad reading that wasn't really happening in 1815.

And so, behind the critical essay, the Professor's mono- or multigraph, as both source and target, is the classroom, some kind of classroom, in which students sit and do something in an environment curated by the Professor. Since the student is an Aspirant, the classroom is driven by ambition of various kinds, both the students' ambitions and those of the Professor. Everyone is (at least putatively) trying to be Good.

The Poetry seminars Brooks and his friends invented were and still are Séances in which the inert bodies of printed poems are conjured into life inside the carefully controlled space of the class, drawing on the ambition-fueled energy of the School. By reanimating the past in this way, individual classes mirror (some of) the work "They Flee from Me" did, and does, with the Professor in the place of the Poet, as part of the swap of reading poetry for writing poetry that the New Critics accomplish. The student can do this too, by giving the right answer and by writing Reanimating Readings. How well did these students understand what was going on? Did they like poetry, or did they like Cleanth Brooks, who was a famously easy grader and also a nice man? Did they do their work happily, or was it (later) the source of complex regrets?

Errors and Miracles

The pointed interest in the detailed functioning of individual words in poems modeled by *An Approach to Literature* was an aspect of the new approach people found astonishing, alarming, and potentially weird and bad. Some of Brooks's colleagues at LSU took to calling the book *A Reproach to Literature*, which apparently Brooks and Warren found amusing and adopted themselves.

The Reanimated Readings of the New Critics frequently placed great argumentative weight on the meaning(s) of a single word and frequently used many words to sing the meanings of a single word. In the writing of the New Critics the words of a good poem became the cells of a miraculously detailed, beautiful, densely structured organism. In trying to be convinced by these readings one sometimes thinks: How could a person, the poet, have thought all that up? The good poem, as revoiced in the "reading," looks like the work of a god.

So what happens when the text, the object sponsoring the commentary, is wrong? The version of "They Flee from Me" in *An Approach to Literature* has left the word "heart" out of the fourteenth line. Because this error persisted for decades, generations of students wrote, might have written, responses to exercises that were, in some way, also wrong.

From one point of view this problem is total. Wyatt (putatively) made a miraculous object, and unless that object is present and perfect, the elaborate Reading deriving from its perfect design will be deviant and flawed. How could it be otherwise? From another point of view, this problem doesn't matter at all. If the beauty of the Reading itself is the point, what does the nature of the sponsoring object actually matter in the end? The goal of the Exercise in *An Approach to Literature* is to help students get better by way of enforcing and exercising the New Critical virtues. The poem on which the task is based might be said to be just a kind of scaffolding. The actual interest is the capacity of the reader to spin it into a new song.

Neither of these points of view is very satisfactory, of course. The first is destabilized by the nature of life and the consuming capacity of time. There is more than one contemporary version of "They Flee from Me." Wyatt initialed one of them, but we don't know why, and he himself also has to have been subject to the entropic flux of life, like the rest of us, and so made mistakes every day, perhaps even when writing poems. Wyatt also died, and so manifestly wasn't a god. What sense does it make to treat him like one? At the same time, surely the words, the exact words, do matter. If they don't, then the whole moral and educational structure threatens to be empty of everything except the routines of the training, turning them into something like cognitive calisthenics.

Cleanth Brooks felt this problem deep in his heart. He knew many contemporary poets very well and was not tempted to declare them gods, though he was willing, like I. A. Richards, like T. S. Eliot, to give them a prime place in the manufacture of the meanings of everyday life (as long as they had Professors to help them). Brooks was, however, ready to use the language of miracles when talking about how poems get the amazing density of meaning that his readings purported to make visible. Here he is, in a famous moment, quoting Shakespeare, the original miraculous author, and then fretting over the status of miraculous meaning (at the end of the Preface to *The Well-Wrought Urn*, his next book after *Modern Poetry and the Tradition*):

> Or who [Time's] spoil of beauty can forbid?
> *O none, unless this miracle have might*
> *That in black ink my love may still shine bright.*

> We live in an age in which miracles of all kinds are suspect, including the kind of miracle of which the poet speaks. The positivists have tended to explain the miracle away in a general process of reduction which hardly stops short of reducing the "poem" to the ink itself. But the "miracle of communication," as a student of language terms it in a recent book, remains. We had better not ignore it, or try to "reduce" it to a level that distorts it. We had better begin with it, by making the closest possible examination of what the poem says as a poem.

Is there a miracle, or is it just "what the poem says," which seems uncomfortably akin to Ink? It is a near thing, in his last sentences, as Brooks slides quietly away from a simple declaration of belief in the miraculous capacity of the language in poems, his intensified version of Richards's "Poetry." Without an outright declaration of this faith, Brooks is back with the problem, which is a bad one. If the poem is not full of miraculous, infinite meaning, the Professor's dazzling Séance threatens to be just a peculiar fabrication, a sort of not-very-memorable poetry.

Professors, Critics, and Scholars
The Invention of the "Critical Essay"

Cleanth Brooks and his friends liked to say that one of the things they were doing, in their rather dramatic intervention in the study of literature, was remembering that "criticism" meant judging literary objects as well as describing their beauty and saying when they were written. As in: Thomas Wyatt's poem is better than Percy Shelley's because it has more irony. Brooks and his friends sometimes distinguished between "scholars," the people who explored when and how poems (say) were written, and "critics," who were implicitly more tough-minded and compelling, though Brooks often admitted he needed the help of the scholars. Brooks and his friends wanted Professors and students to pronounce whether the thing in front of them was good or bad. This could only be done with reference to standards, and Brooks took pride in articulating those standards, instead of fudging them as Q did. The injection of these standards (as in: having enough irony) was tremendously invigorating for the ever-intensifying business of English Professoring.

Brooks's values were inherently invigorating, in their focus on vigorous attentiveness, but, again, it was not the values alone that brought the new energy. The advantage of the new methods for the profession was the same as for the student. Brooks's values and standards were fed through a set of tasks that could be used as part of the increasingly detailed and attentive system of evaluation through which Professors were promoted, fired, compensated, and admired. These tasks, like those of the student, also derived from the "readings" that formed the central innovation of *An Approach to Literature*. Professors could write "essays" that were in effect imitations of the "readings" in Brooks and Warren's textbooks.

The professorial essay had been diversifying since its invention in the late nineteenth century. In particular, T. S. Eliot's essays of the 1920s demonstrated a mixture of specificity, generalization, and judgment that was both very different from the Germanic scholars' essays and also much more exciting. Eliot's essays were fun to agree with or hate.

Most Professors could not hope to emulate Eliot's idiosyncratic and irritating brilliance. The new critical "reading," however, offered many possible virtues within the reach of the average educational worker. Such an essay was an opportunity to demonstrate the various intellectual and moral capacities the teacher was encouraging in her classrooms. The essay was also, like the question-driven, analytic class session, relatively short, accomplishable in, say, a summer, or in the midst of the many daily tasks of the professional educator. The critical book, entertainingly called a "monograph," remained the touchstone of accomplishment, but the monograph was almost always a multigraph, with chapters that actually were previously published essays or whose form was an imitation of the essay. This evaluative organization of the labor of the Professor remains entirely in place today.

So there was an explosion of these adapted new critical readings, published in journals curated by card-carrying members of the profession, versions of the book curated by Mary Howard and her friends centuries before. "They Flee from Me," which demonstrates many of the qualities valued by the New Critics, was an excellent subject for this professorial task.

An Example

For instance, "Wyatt's 'They Flee from Me,'" published in the *Sewanee Review* in 1959, written by Arnold Stein, then a Professor at the University of Washington. Stein's essay is an accomplished example of the genre. It exhibits the basic form the reader would be expecting when opening the pages of the journal. At sixteen pages, it is neither short nor long for a thing of its type. It is unusually fluent in its reference to scholarship, and pleasantly humane and elegant in its style.

Stein was a member of the second generation of new critics. His teachers were of the first; he could have used Brooks and Warren's textbooks as an undergraduate, as a teaching assistant in graduate school, and in his years as a Professor himself. The Chair of the department who hired him at UW was Robert Heilman, a close friend and former colleague of Cleanth Brooks (and Red Warren). Heilman had been on the faculty with them at LSU in the heady days of the invention of the new academic world.

The *Sewanee Review* was a cherished asset of the circle of friends and colleagues of which Cleanth Brooks was a part. Recent editors of the journal had all been friends, even good friends. His close friend Alan Tate (from the days of the Fugitives) was the editor for two years in the 1940s, during which he is credited with transforming the journal into one of the most highly regarded literary and critical publications of the day.

The form of Stein's essay is still entirely familiar today, familiar to students from what they are encouraged to write and to Professors from what they read on a regular basis. The first part introduces the poem and the analytic session, praises its New Critical Effects, and voices the Reanimator's ambition: "I am trying to recover some of the feelings these old words should create."

After a glance at previous, putatively flawed and incomplete efforts of the same type, the Séance begins, and the essay moves to an extended discussion of the poem, line by line, stanza by stanza, in the way modeled by *An Approach to Literature*. It uses the structure of the poem to structure its own argument, like two streams flowing side by side. The last steps are attachments to the wider history of lyric love conventions, through quotations of Marvell and Donne, poets at the center of Brooks and his friends' canon of manly, unsentimental, ironic poets.

Stein's Essay Is Beautiful, in Its Own Way

It is hard to do quick justice to Stein's essay, which even though short contains many more words, many more sentences than its central subject. It is subtly learned, sharply alert and attentive and also cheerfully personal: "I may as well admit that I love this poem." His parsing out of what Wyatt's lines mean is generous and convincing without being downright in the way *An Approach to Literature* so frequently is. One quotation will have to serve, a summary of the spirit of the second stanza as Stein moves to discuss the third:

> It was no dream, though he was caught lying down and may have had his reasonable doubts for a while. We take his word for the literal reality, yet even the denial reminds us, as we accept the waking fact, how like a dream it was—the being caught in a delicious passivity, the heart's desire being fulfilled by stealthy grace appearing as easily as thought, and the strange intensity of the separate details as they close in upon the non-dreamer and bring him to the point where he is required to act out his part in the non-dream. And so it was not a dream though it seemed so like one that the denial had to be made.

The quiet inclusion of a quotation without citation ("it was no dream") is diagnostic of Stein's methods and the world which these methods structured. By mixing Wyatt's words with some of his own, Stein emphasizes his partnership with Wyatt in saying what the poem says, and he invites or even coerces his reader into the partnership through the pervasive "we." The shared phrase seamlessly bonds the two writings and serves as evidence for the reanimation of meaning that is the core ambition of such an exercise. Without the Professor the poem (and the poet) will remain dusty and dead. This is quite different from the version of the poem created by the scholars. Stein's reanimation is not halfway in love with death, wanting the poem to be past and present at once. This version is meant to be fully alive, made so by the infusion of the Professor's spirit.

No wonder the Scholars were so disturbed when Brooks and his friends took over. It is one thing to conjure up an ersatz ghost and construct a ruin, as Foxwell does in her antient version of a poem by "Wiat." It is quite another to (claim to) reanimate the corpse itself.

(Another) Song of the Professor

Our first song of the Professor was the footnoted, edited poem produced by Flügel and Foxwell, a version of the poem Wyatt would not have been able to write and apparently did not want to write. Stein's song is rather extraordinary, considered out of context, just as a kind of writing. It is vastly longer and more elaborated than the poem itself. It is built on a tacit assumption that the poem's meaning can sponsor an unlimited commentary, like the biblical text at the heart of one of Brooks's father's sermons (for instance).

Stein strives to make Wyatt's eloquence reavailable by substituting modern words for the old ones, in a line-by-line progress imitating an idealized classroom session. Part of Stein's reanimation is carried out simply by producing more words than the few in the poem, a kind of flowering of alternates that between them allow for a calibration of the (multiple) original. He, Stein, presents himself as a (carefully trained) Oracle through whom the vanished but still vital spirit speaks: Wyatt's spirit, maybe, but more exactly the spirit of the poem, now buried deep in the old words. Deep training in Richards's multiple meanings ("The ironies are broad and vigorous," Stein says) have made him a fit vessel for the speaking spirit of the poem.

In this way Stein's essay strongly resembles the poem it revoices. Mary Howard and her circle sometimes marked poems in their book as songs to be sung, and they changed Wyatt's poem to make it suitable (in some way). Stein's song is located in an academic journal, the latter-day version of that old manuscript: such a journal is a collection of Professorial Songs whose authors are also its audience. Stein's essay sits comfortably and even beautifully within this highly social, professionalized circle of discourse. It forms part of his qualifications for his job and is also verification he is doing his job. Other students—aspiring persons who want to become what he is—can read it and learn from it and cite it in their own songs, citation of previous songs and singers being a convention of this community-based genre. The professionalized Professor sings songs in the Court of Literature, presided over by people like Cleanth Brooks.

Like Wyatt's poem, Stein's essay was written partly as a performance of an inherited culture, partly as a participation in and creation of current culture, and partly as a virtuosic demonstration of Stein's mastery of this culture. In particular, also like Wyatt's poem, Stein's essay demonstrates his qualifications for his role: his good taste, his facility with language, his emotional intelligence, his capacity for analysis and exposition, his awareness of his place within the Court of Literature. And while doing all this Stein's essay is personal and yet also controlled, careful, and sharp. Like Wyatt's poem, and like so many lyrics that come after it, Stein's essay wants to make an experience of the past live again (and again, every time the essay is read).

Like Wyatt's poem, Stein's essay is a celebration of an inherited, carefully supervised culture that it is also helping to create. And: like the poem, its beauties are targeted at insiders, the adepts in the form, who can see that it is both deeply conventional and also just a little bit inventive within the inherited rules it performs.

The Hazards and Rewards of Writing for Those in The Know

Stein's extended song might help a reader notice details she would not notice otherwise, and he tells his readers things that (generally speaking) no one knows, like what "newfangleness" (might have) meant to Wyatt when he put it in a central spot in his poem. Who is this reader? The student, again, for one, the aspirant to the paths to power. But mostly, in the end, like the original audience for Wyatt's poem, people who already know. They know the poem; they *already* know about Chaucer and Marvell and Donne and Petrarch and old love poetry. They can understand sentences like these: "But *newfangledness*, though it suggests promiscuity, also concerns the mind. *Newfangledness* invokes the self-awareness of human consciousness, and so acts out its own degradation under the perjured authority that granted leave from the courtly service." The new circle into which Stein reanimates Wyatt's poem is a version of the world into which the poem was born. This is one reason why the poem makes such a good sponsor of Stein's commentary: "They Flee from Me" is ready, has always been ready, for this reanimation, since it was already cleverly allusive and in need of interpretation by the knowing reader in 1535.

Stein's reproduction of the poem's modes is so complete that his essay has also ended by suffering from a version of the problems Wyatt's poems suffered from before being saved by the much-maligned Tottel. For instance: Stein's essay is entirely, almost perfectly forgotten. It is inside an archive, and available for viewing, but no one, statistically speaking, wants to view it. This has happened because Stein's designed box of beautiful knowing was not designed to travel. It was meant to be heard, not Overheard. It is (has to be) direct where the poem is indirect; it is eloquent, but not slyly revelatory and evasively titillating. It does not want to generate an urge to explain, even though its captivity to time has made some explanation necessary. Stein's essay is Wyatt's poem at one remove.

Wyatt's poem is about he and she, about thin arrays, about irritated awakenings, and Stein can borrow the frankly human interest of the poem to make his own first-person song more interesting; but ultimately his song is about a Professor in his office in Seattle. If we look back at it, Stein's captive lyric eloquence is a little painful. In spite of his faith in reanimation, the melancholy truth is that Arnold Stein is dead, and so is his essay. Stein's generation of Professors has passed away, their methods have passed away, and the delicate back-and-forth of their everyday professional colloquy has passed away. Their successors have their own ways and their own friends, and no one feels any particular need to reanimate the dead.

Moving On, Sort Of

A New Historicism

Stein's reanimated poem has a troubled relationship to the old poem, still resting on its page in the British Library. In its long history of Versions, Wyatt's poem has never been so completely replaced as it is in Arnold Stein's essay. From this point of view Stein's version looks like Frankensteinian madness, the product of a demented instead of beautiful investment in reanimation, and this feature of the New Critical reading began to bother people as time went on. The training the practice of "readings" supported, and the maintenance of the professorial ranks it enabled, did not go out of fashion, being essentially unchanged today, but the ecstatic Parallel Prose Eloquence of the "reading" began, predictably, to seem simply false, and the reanimated poem a kind of monster.

That is, Professors began to worry about the "scholar" who had been left behind by the highly successful "critic." Not in her old wearisome form, certainly, since the opportunity for virtuosity provided by the reading had become deeply necessary in an increasingly competitive professional environment, highly dependent on shared standards of evaluation. Maybe the performative features of the reading could be retained, and history returned? What if a new song could be invented that would be ecstatic and interesting, could be used to demonstrate professorial powers, and could also feel more true to the reality of writing?

Such is the hope of (one of) the next iterations, which came to be called "New Historicism," especially in the writings of Stephen Greenblatt, who received his PhD at Yale in 1969, from a Department still dominated by Cleanth Brooks and his friends.

New, and Improved

"They Flee from Me" appears in Greenblatt's book *Renaissance Self-Fashioning*, published in 1980. This book contains no exercises (though it does contain many [rhetorical] questions), and so is not a textbook in the old sense. It presumes its readers are giving assignments, not completing them. Still, it has many features of *An Approach to Literature*, and it helps to think of it as closely related to a textbook. It is a very highly selected anthology, to start; "They Flee from Me" appears in its entirety. Longer poems and prose appear in selections, now "quotations" embedded in argumentative prose, not unlike the old grammar book's use of examples, or the anthologist snipping out bits of Shakespeare. The book has the familiar hectoring air, the same insistence that its readers should stop doing something bad and embrace the good.

Many features of Greenblatt's use of our poem are familiar. Like Stein, Greenblatt's discussion of the poem uses many more words than the poem itself, and so in part it is still quite cheerfully a "reading" of the Brooksian type. Greenblatt wants to say what the poem means, and is expansive where the poem is compressed, explanatory where the poem is purposefully elusive. Some of what he says would have been at home in Stein's essay of twenty years before:

> "Gentleness" has, by this point, been so charged with inner contradiction and aggression that the speaker's simple attempt at irony turns against him: his "gentleness"—the code that governs his sexual betrayal—may indeed have led to what he perceives as betrayal. "I would fain know what she hath deserved." Excluded from the predominantly male rhetorical culture, "she" has no opportunity to respond, but were she to do so, we might imagine her saying, "Dear heart, what did you expect?"

The old song in a new key: like Stein, Greenblatt mixes his voice in with that of the poem, sifting in his own eloquence as his prose follows the structure of the poem, which provides the lyric skeleton of the eloquent prose body. That Greenblatt's sentences and Wyatt's sentences can mix together so easily is the sign of virtuosity, as every undergraduate composer of an English essay knows. The harmonizing of artist's words and critic's words, their seamless interplay, is a sign of art, of good taste, and a claim to truth. How could they match if what Greenblatt was saying wasn't true?

Slight Sleight of Hand

Though we are unused to thinking of it in such a way, *Renaissance Self-Fashioning* really is a version of a book like *An Approach to Literature*, and this is most visible in the way literature is present in the book. What is admitted into it, what qualifies as "literature," is that which supports the insistent, programmatic claims. Stuff that doesn't harmonize with the argument might be said not to exist, if what is included defines the contours of the depicted world.

What works in practical, simply human ways is also, as always, decisively determinative of what gets in and what is left out. In principle Greenblatt could or even should include all of Thomas More's *Utopia*, since he discusses it at great length. But the book would then be too long, and besides, where would it go? The virtuosic dance of Greenblatt's words with the words of Literature, a central feature of the good reading, demands that literature be included in individual sentences, as he does above with "They Flee from Me." The balls of eloquence need to be kept in the air, and they would all fall while the reader blinked her way through even two pages of quoted prose.

There are four poems quoted in their entirety in *Renaissance Self-Fashioning*, all by Wyatt. It begins to feel inevitable, in the twentieth century, that "They Flee from Me" would be one of them. The electrifying, little-bit-surprising amount of Thomas Wyatt that peeks through it tends to mesmerize the modern Professor, always on the hunt for subtle meanings, hidden meanings, not-obvious things that need her help and that can be used in creating a subtly unfolding Professorial Song. It is also short, in spite of its subtlety, which may, in the end, be the most important thing. The short is substituted for the long, because working with the short thing is easier. It is a trick both Q and Cleanth would have appreciated:

the experience of Wyatt's poem, we may at the same time observe that the *connection* between them remains deeply felt, and not simply as the relatedness of diametrical opposites. I have already spoken of this connection in regard to the penitential psalms with their poetic revelation of the linkage between power, sexuality, and inwardness. This is precisely the nexus of both "Una candida cerva" and "Whoso List To Hunt," where the poet's inner life in each case is shaped by the relation of Caesar and the object of desire. Petrarch's poem, after all, is as much about frustration and loss as Wyatt's, and if the former does not speak of a hunt, it has its own disturbing image for the pursuit: the miser's search for treasure. There is, I suggest, a sense in which this shared emotional state and the structure of relations that brings it about are more important than the contrasting identifications of Caesar with God and with the king. From this perspective, Petrarch's idealism is not *replaced* by Wyatt's sense of weariness and emptiness but rather *fulfilled* by it.[65]

I am not suggesting that the relation between transcendental vision and cynical betrayal was present to Wyatt's consciousness nor that the subtle complicity of the lover in his own failure was fully intended; rather they are intimations at the edges of his finest poems, as if the act of representation itself, in its highest achievements, had its own powers of implication. Few of Wyatt's poems have this resonance, but it seems unmistakably present in moments of the penitential psalms, in "Whoso List," and in his greatest achievement, "They Flee from Me":

They flee from me that sometime did me seek
With naked foot stalking in my chamber.
I have seen them gentle, tame, and meek
That now are wild and do not remember
That sometime they put themself in danger
To take bread at my hand, and now they range
Busily seeking with a continual change.
Thanked be fortune it hath been otherwise
Twenty times better, but once in special,
In thin array after a pleasant guise
When her loose gown from her shoulders did fall
And she me caught in her arms long and small,
Therewithal sweetly did me kiss
And softly said, Dear heart how like you this?
It was no dream: I lay broad waking.
But all is turned thorough my gentleness
Into a strange fashion of forsaking,
And I have leave to go of her goodness,

And she also to use newfangleness.
But since that I so kindely am served,
I would fain know what she hath deserved.

In one of the best recent discussions of this poem, Donald Friedman suggests that we consider the speaker a "fully imagined *persona*" deliberately distanced from Wyatt himself who subjects his creation to a searching "dramatic analysis." This analysis "reveals a man whose sensibility has been warped by subservience to a code he has just learned is false and impermanent."[66] Such an approach enables us to confront the bad faith in the speaker's self-righteous resentment, the ironies that underlie and subvert the claim that "all is turned thorough my gentleness / Into a strange fashion of forsaking." "Gentleness" has, by this point, been so charged with inner contradiction and aggression that the speaker's simple attempt at irony turns against him: his "gentleness"—the code that governs his sexual betrayal—may indeed have led to what he perceives as betrayal. "I would fain know what she hath deserved." Excluded from the predominantly male rhetorical culture, "she" has no opportunity to respond, but were she to do so, we might imagine her saying, "Dear heart, what did you expect?"

The speaker's relations with women are charged with that will to power, that dialectic of domination and submission, whose presence we have viewed elsewhere in Wyatt's poetry.[67] The creatures who now flee from him once put themselves "in danger / To take bread at my hand," a relationship he remembers with bitter satisfaction. But the image is already more than a simple assertion of successful domination; it conveys a complex interweaving of condescension, menace, and entreaty. The wild creatures are induced to place themselves in submissive postures only if the man suspends all signs of aggression and holds himself perfectly still. The paradox of a power suspended, rendered passive, in order to exist at all is intensified in the second stanza where the bravado of "twenty times better" gives way to the highly particularized recollection of a moment of perfect passivity. Friedman finds this stanza "an anticlimax that reveals the poverty of moral imagination that underlies an elaborate, exalted, and idealizing vision of human conduct"; the scene, he writes, is "a sketch of rapacious appetite, its outlines blurred and made glamorous by ritualized manners and by the compressed meanings of a conventional diction."[68] This response is the outcome of the view that the speaker is a *persona* from whom both poet and audience are wholly detached, but I think it is precisely here that

Once Again, the Reprinter Really Means It

Like our previous Correcting Critics, Greenblatt's voice rises, and his volume increases, as he reaches his big points:

> The experience at the heart of the poem is less a matter of individual character, isolated like a laboratory specimen for our scrutiny, than a matter of shared language, of deep cultural assumptions, of collective mentality. Hence the ambiguity of the speaker's passivity has its roots not in the quirks of a complex personality—there is little individuation of this kind in Wyatt's poetry—but rather in the conflicting cultural codes that fashion male identity in Tudor court lyrics.

This is a very pointed argument with Cleanth Brooks and his friends, and might be said to be the central claim of the book. Perhaps because certain features of Greenblatt's methods bear a very close resemblance to a Brooksian Reading, he has to declare his independence very vigorously.

Not a "laboratory specimen," since the elaborate, isolated reanimation of individual poems and poets has now become suspicious, even though the poem is present in its entirety, under some kind of microscope or macroscope. Not a "complex personality," because the implied and overt celebration of the good poet's miraculous genius, which the New Critical reading discerns in his writing, is now an embarrassment, an unconvincing and gendered picture of how life actually goes.

The (now celebrated) ambiguity of the feelings in the poem has its roots in "the conflicting cultural codes that fashion male identity in Tudor court lyrics" instead of the mind of the individual, ironic poet. The poem is no longer about the self, and its abundance of Meaning no longer derives from a hard-to-visualize supercomplex psyche. "Wyatt," as a name for the voice in the poem, is now a construction of the forces of his time, or perhaps a record of their interplay (as is the poem).

Greenblatt's reanimation is a declaration of independence, from Brooks and his friends, and, perhaps more importantly, from the influence of the poet himself. Greenblatt is no longer subject to the hectoring of his undergraduate textbooks, having invented a new sort of hectoring, and he is also no longer under the thumb of the godlike Maker of Miracles, the poet who makes the poems the New Critic can only admire and spin into songs of praise. The poet is not a god. He is not even a full autonomous self, being the product of "conflicting cultural codes."

Human culture, taken as some kind of vaguely outlined whole, is endlessly complicated, or at least so complicated it can't be held in the hand. So if Culture, more generally speaking, made "They Flee from Me," then the poem can have the deep intricacy Greenblatt needs as he creates his Professorial Song, and he doesn't have to make Wyatt a god, since Wyatt didn't really make it. Greenblatt, in his own NewOld mode, asserts himself over the poet, and the past.

Or Does He?

Once the ecstatic rewriting of poems for the purposes of moral instruction that Brooks and his friends invented in the "reading" is seen to be just that, which happened after the values driving the rewriting no longer seemed so obvious as to be invisible, Professors decided it should never happen again, and that they should be above such sordid schooling. They no longer wanted to be Cold Warriors.

And yet you can't hector without being a Hectorer, and so Greenblatt, like so many of his forebears, truly, deeply believes he is right and other people, Cleanth Brooks, say, are wrong. As many readers noticed right away, it is a little off-kilter, saying "Wyatt" is a social construction while acting so much like a highly opinionated Complex Personality yourself. He doesn't let Thomas Wyatt be a superinteresting self, but he wants, in some way, to be superinteresting himself.

If nothing else, graduate education in the study of literature in the later twentieth century taught self-consciousness about methods, and so Greenblatt is painfully aware of this impasse. Readers of books like Greenblatt's would not, in the 1980s and '90s, have been surprised to find an Epilogue in which the Not Cool nature of insisting you are right is addressed, even at the cost of making the whole edifice a bit unstable. The last words in the book describe what amounts to guilt over being so individuated: "I want to bear witness at the close to my overwhelming need to sustain the illusion that I am the principal maker of my own identity."

That is, among the claims being advanced in *Renaissance Self-Fashioning* are the interests of Professor Stephen Greenblatt, now a modestly famous person and a Professor at Harvard, and Stephen Greenblatt knows it, but can't stop doing it. "They Flee from Me" is no longer about the ambitions and subtlety of an interesting manly Man; those ambitions, and those interests, have been transferred to the Reanimator. The ambition of the Aspirant fuels Greenblatt's version as it did the first one, 450 years before. The underlying truth, as important for Greenblatt as it was for Thomas Wyatt, is that "Greenblatt" might name a set of cultural codes, but the paychecks associated with the job at Harvard are made out to Stephen Greenblatt, and he can cash them at his bank. Who better to give those paychecks to than the man who demonstrates such subtlety, such canny, self-conscious understanding of the ways of the literary courtier, in his BookPoem *Renaissance Self-Fashioning*?

The Greatest

As he begins his section on "They Flee from Me," Greenblatt refers to it as Wyatt's "greatest achievement," one of the nicest things anyone has said in the poem's whole long history. The qualities that made it such a perfect sponsor for Arnold Stein's brilliance have, curiously, made the jump over to the new era. Indeed, the very same density of meaning that made it an excellent specimen under the Brooksian microscope now makes it an excellent validator of claims about the suspect nature of critical microscopes. The poem's multiplicity is the quality people noticed right off, hundreds of years before, and it is the same quality that caused readers to ignore the poem for hundreds of years after that. Sometimes we want things and people to be Exceptional, and sometimes we don't.

As for the density of meaning itself, as a quality, either Wyatt put it there on purpose, or he couldn't help putting it there. Factually speaking, Greenblatt's method treats Wyatt's poems as highly exceptional, even if Greenblatt resists declaring Wyatt to have been a highly exceptional person worth emulating or at least worth knowing about. Should we read Wyatt's poems because Wyatt knew more than normal people do about life, and put what he knew in his poems? In the end, Greenblatt isn't clear on this point.

Which Poem? One Last Time

Greenblatt uses the poem from Wyatt's book in creating his reprinting. He has removed some of the tricks of recent editors, like quotation marks and italics. He has modernized the spelling, though, and he pushes the stanzas together, without spacing, in imitation of (one feature of) the way it appears in Wyatt's book, though he also inserts some unauthorized indenting. It is a mixed presentation, in keeping with Greenblatt's mixed mode. He both turns over some old bones, asking us just to look, and also conjures new life from them. His choice of the Authorized version is inherently interesting given Greenblatt's eventual argument about the socially constructed nature of selves and poems. The version in Mary Howard's book, which shows signs of actual group authorship, might have been the better version from a technical point of view, though it doesn't have as much of the stuff he wants. It is possible he didn't know very much about it; no one was thinking particularly seriously about it in 1980, and some factual information has been cleared up since then.

His use of Wyatt's version is, however, the kind of thing Greenblatt ends up fretting over in his epilogue. The poem may not be "about" a complex personality, may not be a production and expression of individual Genius. But Greenblatt has to choose, and he chooses the poem that has the strongest flavor of individual agency, the one with Wyatt's initials next to it.

One More Example

In the early twenty-first century we are in the midst of a Thomas Wyatt uptick, a kind of Renaissance renaissance. The first chapter of the first section of a recent biography of Wyatt, by Susan Bridgen, is entitled "They Fle from Me." It begins with an image of the page in Wyatt's book on which "They Flee from Me" appears, the one with which I began.

Conclusions

Progress in the Arts: Continuity

In spite of Cleanth Brooks's fears, it does begin with the ink. Who wrote the poem into Wyatt's book? Does it matter? What is the Secretary Hand? Who wrote the poems in Mary Howard's book? You can tell by the handwriting, and you need a lot of training before the handwriting will yield its secrets. Where was Thomas Wyatt's book in 1534? What did a secretary do in 1534, anyway? How were the writers in Mary Howard's book related? These questions have answers too. But a lot of cooperative, careful, documented reading of old Ink was necessary before they were found.

The accumulation of knowledge the story of "They Flee from Me" documents is fundamentally social. The remembering of the ink (and the ideas) might be said to have its origins in the letters Thomas Percy wrote to people he had met, to friends of friends, to authors of books he had read, and their letters back. Step by step, this web of interconnected people thinking about similar things leads to the comparatively fine grain of our knowledge about how people thought about poetry almost five hundred years ago, and to our ability to remember it. It can feel like a miracle, but it isn't.

Progress in the Arts: Discontinuity

Is the irregularity of line lengths in "They Flee from Me" a sign of genius or incompetence? For centuries people thinking about this question insisted upon Wyatt's incompetence; they thought Wyatt was simply less good at making poems than (for instance) the Incomparable Surrey. Since Surrey's lines tend to be more regular than Wyatt's, this picture of Wyatt underwrote that curious old notion that Wyatt was the Student and Surrey the Master. And for all those centuries this was wrong.

There are things to know about the traditions of poetry making in English that the people making this mistake often didn't know. But of course you don't need to marshal these facts to know it is silly to say that Thomas Wyatt didn't realize his lines had different lengths, or that he was incapable of adding a syllable or two here and there to make it right. In a basic human way such a picture of Wyatt makes no sense. Everything about "They Flee from Me" demonstrates a refined, detailed, analytic, and purposeful approach to poetry making. If you can read the poem you can know that Wyatt made it that way intentionally.

So why couldn't all those old writers see this truth? It seems dull-witted, but that can't be right. Well: they were thinking about the issue in an abstract way that prevented access to the plain everyday reality behind the names. The writers who made the mistake about Wyatt's capacities were captivated by the idea that culture had progressed in a fundamental way from some Past to their Present; we have seen them say poetry had been "perfected" over time. These writers relied on technical definitions of "poetry" that, while not very interesting, allow for "perfection"; more than that, their investment in nascent imperial culture made the story of perfection feel necessary. Since we occupy a different present, which we admire in our own way, this previous perfection looks imaginary.

These kinds of errors happen all the time, of course, and the difficulty in detecting them derives from the social nature of scholarship: from the tendency or even need to work inside a set of commonly agreed-upon notions. Progress requires, paradoxically, some kind of break. Thus William Minto, in his irritation with Nott's errors, noticed that Surrey could not have been the Master and Wyatt the student. It is obvious. He only had to see it to see it.

Progress in the Arts: Making Poetry, Reading Poetry

There is a good question here, though: Do people get "better" at poetry? In the conceptual world of poetry, do the rich get richer, as they do in mathematics?

Certainly through training and practice a person can get better at making poetry to some shared, teachable standard. And a culture can get better at poetry too: or, at least, a continuing, heritable culture can generate audiences capable of valuing and understanding increasingly fine-grained and nuanced poems, which encourages poets to make such poems, as happened with Thomas Wyatt. The accumulation of previous poems, if they are remembered, creates expressive possibilities that did not exist before.

People might also get better at introspection, which, beginning in poems like "They Flee from Me," becomes the primary focus of shorter poems in English. The development of technologies of self-expression like the lyric poem, and the accumulation of shared vocabularies of interior life so evident in these poems, might well make it easier to keep track of what is happening in human heads. The accumulation of previous examples of introspection might make it easier to be right about other selves, or our own.

Wyatt's poetry undoubtedly made things possible for him in the world of Henry's court. It may also have done things for his understanding of his inner life, but that is lost in time. Perhaps it made him feel better simply because he had expressed distress; perhaps it made him feel better because he revenged himself on some former lover. Perhaps writing the poem made him feel worse by emphasizing his faults and those of others. It is impossible to say.

It is quite possible, though, that Wyatt's poetry made a kind of sophistication about psychology and inner life possible for those that heard him, or those who read him, later. Great teachers can make such things happen. But it doesn't seem right to describe any of this as a persistent improvement—progress—in the sense that algebra (for instance) permits and experiences improvement. Plainly speaking, we are far better at mathematics than Robert Recorde was or could be, but we would hesitate to say we are better at poetry or introspection than Thomas Wyatt.

What about enacting what we learn from making or reading poems? Could people become better in some broad way at containing their bitterness over betrayal or at not being overtaken by self-recrimination? Could we become better at not disappointing the people we love? Gosh—it would be disappointing if the answer was "no," though the evidence on hand indicates that at least we don't start off ahead of our ancestors on these challenges.

This last set of questions is the heart of the matter. If it is possible to get better at being human in some overall, cumulative way, even for just a lifetime, that would be good, and carefully sponsored training in old poems might well be a part of the program, as I. A. Richards and Cleanth Brooks and Arnold Stein and Stephen Greenblatt thought. Old poems, some densely made old poems especially, can serve as the focus of such training, or at least they have served this purpose. Old poems have the advantage of being about people. And they show we have a history of trying.

Progress in the Arts: Getting It Right (or Wrong)

There is no question people have gotten better at reading old poetry accurately. For instance, we know "They Flee from Me" exists; we know about the Egerton and Devonshire manuscripts; we know more than previous readers about what old words mean because we have read more old books. We know about the ink. We know about Mary Howard.

The bad reader, who gets the old poem wrong, haunts the days and nights of the person who thinks he knows. Great effort has been expended in trying to head off wrong thoughts about "They Flee from Me" and old poems more generally. For G. F. Nott, for I. A. Richards, for *An Approach to Literature*, for Stephen Greenblatt, heading off the bad reading is a way of making the world better in some way. What are the limits on and interest of getting it right?

For instance: the meditation on the kind of beings "stalking" in the poem's Chamber, begun in our story by G. F. Nott's note, has been a full one and shows no sign of ending. Various sorts of birds and deer have been nominated regularly; an argument has even been made for the rather unlikely possibility of falcons. How important is this question? So what if some nut thinks it's falcons?

Clearly a Professor's students need to be concerned about being actually wrong or thought to be wrong, enmeshed as they are in a system designed to sort the Wheat from the Chaff. The same can be said of any Assistant Professors within a Senior Professor's administrative or disciplinary orbit, since Assistant Professors also get sorted. Inside the Court of Literature advancement depends upon satisfying those who define the standards of right and wrong. But the writing on the page in the British Library is unaffected by all of this, and will go on generating new versions of itself, made by people getting it wrong in their turn, until it molders away or burns up in the fires of the future.

This is because thinking it's falcons doesn't prevent the word "stalking" from meaning something. Wrong or prudish ideas about Kissing on the part of some reprinter can't really interfere with the pleasures of (reading about) kissing. If you could somehow surprise someone reading this poem—quite possibly in the Tottel form, out on the InterWebs—and ask her to explain it, as I. A. Richards liked to do, no doubt she would often say some absurd things, or not very much at all, but she might also say she really liked it.

And, amazingly enough, you can actually find such a person, since there "They Flee from Me" still is, being handed around by the apparently extraordinarily robust forward-moving forces of literacy and language arts. Its structures and its words are still catching the attention of people who might know nothing about the Tower and might skip over "newfangleness," but who know something about sulky men. Or betrayal. Or confusion. Or regret.

Not all old poems can do this. From a documentary point of view only a very small percentage of old poems have kept our attention in this way. Catching our attention is not what Thomas Wyatt was trying to do, really, but it does seem to be the only thing people could mean when they call it his "finest poem." Wyatt was, however, trying to do a closely related thing: he was trying to both hide and reveal himself. He was trying to create a delicious craving for explanation, and that craving is still being created all these years later. The sexiness helps, of course, but the little space elbowed out by Wyatt's careful resistance to saying too much still opens up every time the poem is read.

"They Flee from Me" was designed, from the start, to be filled in by the interested, imagining reader, which makes the later reader and the initial audience curiously similar. Reading old poems is fundamentally just that: overhearing them, catching some but not all of it. All kinds of things might tumble in—all kinds of Falcons—but not just anything can tumble in. Wyatt's arrangements create a sharply defined area of possible meanings, and this (slight) variety makes for a generosity of engagement, openings for the reader, which time has changed but not diminished.

They Flee from Us

Entropy, which names our universe's love for disorder, its fleeing galaxies, is the subject of "They Flee from Me" and the enemy it pits itself against. Those who were tame now range, and the rhyme with "change" is inevitable, and bitter. The poem's speaker is left in a colder world. Things have fallen apart. They have fled. Still, entropy is apparently held at bay or even diminished when Wyatt turns the disorienting experience of disorder into the arresting expressive order of the poem. The design of "They Flee from Me" is, in this sense, a defiant act. In a universe that seems always to be accelerating toward chaos, little islands of order like this poem are a consolation to the spirit, and so we love them.

An island of order, though, and a temporary one, as if we needed to be reminded of this fact. There is no escaping the rule of entropy. The poem is made, comes to be, sets itself apart, gets written down, and immediately becomes harder to read, more obscure, more distant from the scene of its making, and this all increases with every second. We know more than Thomas Warton did about Wyatt's ink, but Wyatt knew more about it than we do, and we will never recover the entirety of his experience.

But since "They Flee from Me" is also about the way things fall apart and diminish and escape, it catches us coming and going, entropically speaking. The poem dramatizes the difficulty of imposing understanding and order on the chaos of experience, and its evocative rhyme royal is also a beautiful, helpful imposition of understanding and order. The speaker of this poem learns, which is a kind of antientropic mastery, and what he learns is that entropy is inescapable.

The later revoicer of Wyatt's two-handed learning experiences the same multiple. Time has whirled Wyatt's poem away and made the Secretary Hand virtually unreadable, but if we exert ourselves we can pull it back toward us and understand (some of) what it is saying; and if we can say what "They Flee from Me" means, we stake a small claim against the losses of time. The thrilling sense of understanding what the poem says, and the schoolroom benefits of the process of learning about what the poem says, are part of its sturdy persistence.

The seeming permanence of Wyatt's black Ink is and has been thrilling: but any grasp on the fleeing poem is also shot through with error and disobedient Falcons. The revoicer's remembering is always liberally seeded with forgetting. Luckily for us, since it was prepared for this from the start, "They Flee from Me" remains cheerfully ready to move on from any current Getting It Wrong to the next one. It was as ready to adapt to the use of Mary Howard's circle as it was to adapt to the use of Stephen Greenblatt, 450 years later.

Schooling: The Fourth Principle

By not saying what the true big deal is about studying poetry, the fourth principle of his new English School, Q cheated, and the relief he feels as he escapes is palpable. It was no doubt the same sort of relief he felt when he just didn't show up for one of his lectures, which happened more often as time went on. In the end, though, he could have just gone ahead and said it. We shall study poems because we have figured out how to make them excellent subjects of schooling. We have figured out how to give exams in literature that are as hard, in their own way, as the famous Cambridge Mathematics Tripos.

Because, in a way of thinking that Q's eccentric colleague Ludwig Wittgenstein would have appreciated, there is nothing ineffable about poetry. It is not somehow the Highest Form of Human Expression. The meanings of individual poems are not produced by miracle. "Poetry," in that ineffable sense, is imaginary, and poems have always been (just) things people make. Their interest is in what we use them for, and their detailed designs make them suitable for many schemes of human improvement. We might object to what someone else is using poems for or has used them for, but such objections have always been an engaging part of shooing away the falcons and getting it right (for now).

So, then, why *old* poetry, that good question? Because old poems show us we have a history of trying. Because they show us that people were like us, in the past, even if their likeness can be discerned only through an exercise of the imagination. Because the effort of connecting with vanished worlds is salutary. Because working out what someone else was thinking is good practice for knowing other people and treating them humanely. Because literacy is a claim against disorder and dissolution, and we need that claim.

References and Further Reading

Part I

The best immediate entry points for Wyatt's life and the environment of Henry's court are two excellent, recent biographies: Susan Bridgen's *Thomas Wyatt: The Heart's Forest* (London: Faber and Faber, 2012) and Nicola Shulman's *Graven with Diamonds: The Many Lives of Thomas Wyatt* (London: Short Books, 2011). More scholarly but still big-picture approaches can be found in Greg Walker, *Writing under Tyranny: English Literature and the Henrician Reformation* (Oxford: Oxford University Press, 2005); Seth Lerer, *Courtly Letters in the Age of Henry VIII: Literary Culture and the Arts of Deceit* (Cambridge: Cambridge University Press, 1997); and Chris Stamatakis, *Sir Thomas Wyatt and the Rhetoric of Rewriting* (Oxford: Oxford University Press, 2012). Most of my claims about Wyatt can be found in greater detail in these books and in articles by Jason Powell that are listed individually below. There are many handbooks available for this period; my favorite is *A Companion to Renaissance Poetry*, ed. Catherine Bates (Hoboken, NJ: Wiley-Blackwell, 2018); see also *The Oxford Handbook of Tudor Literature, 1485–1603*, ed. Mike Pincombe and Cathy Shrank (Oxford: Oxford University Press, 2009). My modern edited text for "They Flee from Me" and any other Wyatt poems is that of Joost Daalder, *Sir Thomas Wyatt: Collected Poems* (Oxford: Oxford University Press, 1975).

The handwritten manuscript I refer to as "Wyatt's book" is in the British Library, where it is called Egerton MS 2711. "They flee from me" is on page 26v. The whole manuscript can be viewed on the British Library's website: http://www.bl.uk/manuscripts/FullDisplay.aspx?ref=Egerton_MS_2711. My primary source for detailed information about this manuscript is Richard Harrier's *The Canon of Sir Thomas Wyatt's Poetry* (Cambridge, MA: Harvard University Press, 1975), with some reference to later work by Daalder and Powell, mentioned below. For the Secretary Hand, see *Elizabethan Handwriting, 1500–1650*, by Giles Dawson and Laetitia Kennedy Skipton (New York: Norton, 1966); for Wyatt's secretaries more generally, see Jason Powell, "Thomas Wyatt's Poetry in Embassy: Egerton 2711 and the Production of Literary Manuscripts Abroad," *Huntington Library Quarterly* 67, no. 2 (July 2004): 261–82. Detailed discussion of the "Tho" markings can be found in Joost Daalder's "The Significance of the 'Tho' signs in Wyatt's Egerton Manuscript," *Studies in Bibliography*, no. 40 (1987): 86–100, and Jason Powell's extensions of this work in "Marginalia, Authorship and Editing in the Manuscripts of Thomas Wyatt's Verse," *English Manuscript Studies, 1100–1700* 15 (2009): 1–40.

Cathy Shrank discusses Wyatt's interest in translation, and also the problematic nature of the "confessional" in Wyatt's poetry, in "Sir Thomas Wyatt and His Posthumous 'Interpreters,'" *Proceedings of the British Academy* 154 (2008): 375–401. Stephen Greenblatt's *Renaissance Self-Fashioning* (Chicago: University of Chicago Press, 1983) is the originator of the contemporary critical thread on self-consciousness in Wyatt.

The conventional poetic environment in which Wyatt wrote is depicted especially vigorously in John Stevens, *Music and Poetry in the Early Tudor Court* (Cambridge: Cambridge University Press, 1961); see also Seth Lerer's "The Medieval Inheritance of Early Tudor Poetry," in Bates's *Companion to Renaissance Poetry*, referred to above. Stevens is especially good on forms, and Lerer notes the prehistory of the phrase "long and small," along with Wyatt's indebtedness to Chaucer in particular. "Me-think thou art unkind" is found on page 321 in the fifteenth-century British Library manuscript "MS Fairfax 16." My source is the facsimile edited by John Norton-Smith (London: Scolar Press, 1979); for more on this MS and the attribution to Suffolk, see Mariana Neilly and Edelgard E. DuBruck, "The 'Fairfax Sequence' Reconsidered: Charles d'Orléans, William De La Pole, and the Anonymous Poems of Bodleian MS Fairfax 16," *Fifteenth-Century Studies* 36 (2011): 127–36. For more on indirection in Wyatt, see especially Stamatakis, *Sir Thomas Wyatt*, and Walker, *Writing under Tyranny*, noted above. Wyatt is referred to as "deep-witted" by Richard Tottel at the beginning of his anthology *Songes and Sonettes* (1557).

Details about the Devonshire Manuscript can be found on the British Library's web page (https://www.bl.uk/collection-items/the-devonshire-manuscript), which includes information about the provenance of the manuscript, who was writing in it, the function of the book in courtly circles, and many high-resolution images. See also the wiki *Social Edition*, at https://en.wikibooks. org/wiki/The_Devonshire_Manuscript. The Egerton and Devonshire versions of "They Flee" are also helpfully printed side by side in Jason Powell's "Editing Wyatts: Reassessing the Textual State of Sir Thomas Wyatt's Poetry," *Poetica* 71 (2009): 93–104; I have taken my transcription from this text. For a detailed look at Mary Shelton, in particular, and at the functioning of this manuscript on a daily basis, see "Mary Shelton and Her Tudor Literary Milieu," by Paul G. Remly, in *Rethinking the Henrician Era: Essays on Early Tudor Texts and Contexts*, ed. Peter C. Herman (Urbana: University of Illinois Press, 1994), 40–77; other essays in this book discuss relevant material in Wyatt and Surrey. I was first alerted to the presence of the stanzas from Chaucer by John Stevens, *Music and Poetry in the Early Tudor Court*, referred to above.

My basic source for the textual and bibliographical elements of Tottel's *Songes and Sonettes* is Hyder Rollins, *Tottel's Miscellany (1557–1587)*, rev. ed. (Cambridge, MA: Harvard University Press, 1966). There is also a Penguin edition, with some quick introductory materials: *Tottel's Miscellany*, ed. Amanda Holton and Tom Macfaul (London: Penguin, 2011). For discussions of the general context of both the book and the period, see J. Christopher Warner, *The Making and Marketing of Tottel's Miscellany, 1557: Songs and Sonnets in the Summer of the Martyrs' Fires* (Burlington, VT: Ashgate, 2013), as well as the excellent *Tottel's Songes and Sonettes in Context*, ed. Stephen Hamrick (Burlington, VT: Ashgate, 2013). Jason Powell has recently extended this work in "The Network behind 'Tottel's' Miscellany," *English Literary Renaissance* 46, no. 2 (2016): 193–224. Harrier, *The Canon of Sir Thomas Wyatt's Poetry*, noted above, is an excellent source here also.

More information about the discovery and provenance of Harington's manuscript books can be found in Harrier, *The Canon of Sir Thomas Wyatt's Poetry*, cited above, and in "The Harington Manuscript at Arundel Castle and Related Documents," by Ruth Hughey, *The Library: Transactions of the Bibliographical Society* 15, no. 4 (March 1935): 388–444. Important qualifications to this older work can be found in Powell's "The Network behind 'Tottel's' Miscellany," above; Powell has discovered that the Arundel MS is most closely related to the second printing of Tottel rather than MS sources. Tottel's note "To the Reader" is from the first edition (June 1557) of *Songes and Sonettes*. I have used the Scolar Press facsimile edition (London: Scolar Press, 1970) and Rollins's reprinting, *Tottel's Miscellany*, noted above, for my text.

The transcription of Surrey's poem is attributed to Harington by Harrier, *The Canon of Sir Thomas Wyatt's Poetry*, cited above; information on the Psalms may also be conveniently found there. Henry Howard's exciting life and death are available in *Henry VIII's Last Victim: The Life and Times of Henry Howard, the Earl of Surrey*, by Jessie Childs (New York: St. Martin's Press, 2006). For writing in texts as a way of reading them, see Steven N. Zwicker, "Habits of Reading in Early Modern Literary Culture," in *The Cambridge History of Early Modern English Literature*, ed. David Loewenstein and Janel Mueller (Cambridge: Cambridge University Press, 2006), 170–200 (much of this article focuses on later periods). For John Harington the Elder, see Ruth Hughey's *John Harington of Stepney* (Columbus: Ohio State University Press, 1971); the best source for John Harington MP is the introductory and explanatory material associated with *The Diary of John Harington, M.P., 1646–53: With Notes for His Charges*, ed. Margaret Stieg Dalton, Somerset Record Society, vol. 74 (Old Woking, Surrey: Gresham Press, 1977); this is also my source for the diary itself. The curiously partisan *The Harington Family*, by Ian Grimble (Oxford: Alden Press, 1957), provides information not easily found elsewhere (like the date the ancestral manse at Kelston was torn down: 1693).

The Cossicke system and Robert Recorde's *Whetstone of Witte* are described in Vera Sanford's essay "Robert Recorde's *Whetstone of Witte*, 1557," in *The European Mathematical Awakening*, ed. Frank Swetz (Mineola, NY: Dover Publications, 1994), 67–75. The *Whetstone of Witte* itself is available online at https://archive.org/details/TheWhetstoneOfWitte.

Part II

Puttenham's *The Arte of English Poesy* has been reprinted recently in an edition by Frank Whigham and Wayne Rebhorn (Ithaca, NY: Cornell University Press, 2007); the reference to "unmeasureable mountains" is on page 214 of this edition. An excellent overview of editing and scholarship in the eighteenth century can be found in "Literary Scholarship and the Life of Editing," by Marcus Walsh, in *Books and Their Readers in 18th-Century England: New Essays*, ed. Isabel Rivers (London: Leicester University Press, 2003), 191–215. John Leland's book is in Latin: *Naeniae in mortem Thomae Viati equitis incomparabilis* (1542). For more on Leland (and Surrey), see Cathy Shrank, "John Leland and 'the Bowels of Antiquity,'" in *Writing the Nation in Reformation England, 1530–1580* (Oxford: Oxford University Press, 2004), as well as W. A. Sessions's "Surrey's Wyatt," in Herman's *Rethinking the Henrician Era*, referred to above, pages 169–92.

Granville the Polite, by Elizabeth Handasyde (London: Oxford University Press, 1933), describes the life of Granville and his wife's heredity, as well as Granville's connection to Alexander Pope and *Windsor Forest*. Curll's 1717 *Songes and Sonettes* with the 1728 addition, as well as Sewell's 1717 *Songes and Sonettes*, are available at Yale's Beinecke Library. For more on the exceptionally interesting career of Edmund Curll, and on George Sewell, see *Edmund Curll, Bookseller*, by Paul Baines and Pat Rogers (Oxford: Oxford University Press, 2007). Baines and Rogers attribute the actual editing of Curll's volume to Richard Rawlinson, who (like George Sewell) was a member of Curll's publishing team. As it is all conjecture, I refer to the editor as "Curll."

For essentially all the facts of Percy's life on which I rely, see *Thomas Percy: A Scholar-Cleric in the Age of Johnson*, by Bertram Davis (Philadelphia: University of Pennsylvania Press, 1989). There are also rich introductory and explanatory materials in all the volumes of *The Percy Letters* (various presses, of various dates), some of which are referred to below. All definitions from Samuel Johnson's *A Dictionary of the English Language* come from the first edition (London, 1755).

Percy's little pamphlet is stitched into a handmade book called "AN ACCOUNT of the private family of Percy, formerly of Worcester, afterwards of Bridgnorth, Shropshire," now in the British Library, Add. MS 32326. Pages quoted are numbered by the British Library f2 and f3v. The best sources for the complicated genealogies are the Wikipedia entries for the individual figures. In a perfectly suitable convergence, Grenville's wife Mary Thynne, who provided the connection to the Howard family for Pope and Curll, was the Countess/Duchess of Northumberland's aunt. Boswell's comment (and subsequent anxiety about it) are discernible through the associated material in *James Boswell's Life of Johnson: An Edition of the Original Manuscript in Four Volumes*, vol. 3, *1776–1780*, Research ed., ed. Thomas Bonnell (New Haven, CT: Yale University Press, 2012); the entry is for Sunday, April 12, 1778. The wonderfully complex issues behind Henry Howard's execution are described in Childs's *Henry VIII's Last Victim*, referred to above.

The quotations from the *Reliques* are from the London 1765 edition: Dedication, v–viii; Preface, ix–x. *The Making of Percy's Reliques*, by Nick Groom (Oxford: Clarendon Press, 1999), gives a thorough accounting of how Percy went about making his book, including the information about Pitt's MS. The letter to Thomas Warton is in *The Percy Letters*, vol. 3, *The Correspondence of Thomas Percy and Thomas Warton*, ed. M. G. Robinson and Leah Dennis (Baton Rouge: Louisiana

State University Press, 1951). Percy's poem is found on page 233 of *A collection of poems, by several hands*, ed. Robert Dodsley, vol. 6 (London, 1758). The fourth edition of Percy's *Reliques*, printed in 1794, contains the new paragraph on the Minstrels (xlvi–xlvii).

"The Child of Elle" starts on page 90 of the 1765 *Reliques*. Details of Percy's re-creation can be found in *Bishop Percy's Folio Manuscript*, ed. Frederick James Furnivall and John Wesley Hales (London: N. Trubner, 1867–68), 1:132–34. This rather wonderful book also includes a foldout facsimile of a page of the original MS. I take my transcription of the stanza in the MS from this book, as well as the quotation from the note about the finding of the original MS that Percy wrote in that manuscript; Nick Groom also quotes this note. For the letter to Warton, see volume 3 of *The Percy Letters*, referred to above, page 69. *Nugae Antiquae* is described in Harrier, *The Canon of Sir Thomas Wyatt's Poetry*, referred to above; I cite from a reprint of the 1804 edition (New York: AMS Press, 1966).

In addition to Bertram Davis, *Thomas Percy*, cited above, for the details of Percy's attempt to reprint Tottel and his contact with the Haringtons, see Cleanth Brooks's excellent appendix to his edition of the Percy-Farmer letters, *The Percy Letters*, vol. 2, *The Correspondence of Thomas Percy and Richard Farmer* (Baton Rouge: Louisiana State University Press, 1946); my information about Nicols's warehouse fire and the surviving copies comes from Brooks's article. For the intricacies of the editions of Tottel, see Rollins, *Tottel's Miscellany*, referred to above.

The fundamental source for Ritson's life and works is Bertrand Bronson's *Joseph Ritson, Scholar at Arms* (Berkeley: University of California Press, 1994), but see also the earlier *Joseph Ritson: A Critical Biography*, by Henry Alfred Burd (Urbana: University of Illinois Press 1916). Burd presents the full details of Percy's fascinated, vengeful interest in Ritson's last illness. Ritson's lengthy "Dissertation on Romance and Mistrelsy" in *Ancient Engleish Metrical Romanceës* (London, 1802) is on pages v–ccxxiv of volume 1. The book may be viewed through the Internet Archive at https://archive.org/details/ancientengleishm01ritsiala. Percy's letter to Anderson is quoted in Burd's *Joseph Ritson*, above, and is also in *The Percy Letters*, vol. 9, *The Correspondence of Thomas Percy and Robert Anderson*, ed. W. E. K. Anderson (New Haven, CT: Yale University Press, 1988).

Walter Scott was a lifelong admirer of Ritson's work. In an 1807 letter to Robert Surtees he writes: "I was very indignant at the insult offered to [Ritson's] memory" (Bronson, *Joseph Ritson, Scholar at Arms*, referred to above, volume 1, page 296). *An Essay on the Abstinence of Animal Food as a Moral Duty* (London, 1802) is available at the Internet Archive: (https://archive.org/

details/anessayonabstinooritsgoog). The quotation is from page 88. For more on vegetarianism, see Timothy Morton's "Joseph Ritson, Percy Shelley and the Making of Romantic Vegetarianism," *Romanticism* 12, no. 1 (2006): 52–59. The "Advertisement" is on pages i–vi of *The English Anthology*, vol. 1 (London, 1793). "My Lute Awake" is on page 1. "My Lute Awake" in its original dress, without punctuation, is on pages 43v–44r of Wyatt's book. For some history of the British Library, and details on the catastrophic fire, see Andrew Prescott's "'Their Present Miserable State of Cremation': The Restoration of the Cotton Library," in *Sir Robert Cotton as Collector*, ed. C. J. Wright (London: British Library, 1997), 391–454.

Robert Anderson's anthology is *The Works of the British Poets* (London, 1793); the poem is on page 619 of volume 1, and the quotation from the end of his Preface is on page 8. I found the description of Wordsworth's use of Anderson's volumes in Thomas Hutchinson's edition of Wordsworth's *Poems in Two Volumes* (London: Nutt, 1897), xi. For more on the rather remarkable Robert Anderson's long and busy life, see the introductory material in the W. E. K. Anderson's edition of volume 9 of *The Percy Letters*, cited above. Anderson infallibly refers to Percy as "my Lord." Ritson's abuse of Warton is found at *Observations on the three first volumes of the History of English Poetry. In a familiar letter to the author* (London, 1782), page 284. The Wyatt section (XX) of Warton's *History of English Poetry*, vol. 3 (London, 1781), is on pages 28–40. The compliment to Surrey is on page 16 of this volume. A still-excellent overview of the writing of literary histories in English can be found in Rene Wellek's *The Rise of English Literary History* (Chapel Hill: University of North Carolina Press, 1941); I take the descriptor *systematic* for Warton from Wellek.

Part III

A good source for the life of G. F. Nott is the entry by Sidney Lee in the old *Dictionary of National Biography* (Oxford: Oxford University Press, 1895–1900). Lee's article is clearly derived almost entirely from the obituary in *Gentleman's Magazine*, January 1842, 106–7. It is worth noting in passing that Nott's uncle John was at one point the Duchess of Devonshire's physician and that this uncle also (almost) published an edition of Tottel in 1812. "Almost" because the proofs were, of course, destroyed by fire. This information is available in William Courtney's *DNB* entry for John Nott, which in turn is also derived from the obituary in *Gentleman's Magazine*, December 1825, 565–66.

In Nott's *The Works of Henry Howard Earl of Surrey and of Sir Thomas Wyatt the Elder*, volume 1 (1815) is on Surrey, and volume 2 (1816) is on Wyatt. This edition is available online and has also been reprinted (New York: AMS Press, 1965). The Surrey volume contains a "Preface" (9, before the Table of Contents); "Memoirs of the Life of Henry Howard" (i); and a "Dissertation" (ccxxxvii). The Wyatt volume contains another "Preface" (i, before the Table of Contents); "Memoirs of Sir. T. Wiat" (i); and an "Essay on the Poems" (cxv). Puttenham's reference to Wyatt and Surrey is on page 148 of Whigham and Rebhorn's edition of *The Arte of English Poesy*, referred to above.

For the Horace ode, see *The Odes of Horace,* translated by David Ferry (New York: Noonday Press, 1997), 169. An entry into the vast field of the history of education and the teaching of English can be had in the now-classic *Professing Literature* by Gerald Graff (Chicago: University of Chicago Press, 1987) and Franklin Court's *Institutionalizing English Literature* (Stanford, CA: Stanford University Press, 1992). For a history of examinations in Britain, see John Roach's *Public Examinations in England, 1850–1900* (Cambridge: Cambridge University Press, 1971). An evocative way to feel the state of things at midcentury is to look into a handbook for people studying for exams: for instance, *English Literature and Composition: A Guide to Candidates in Those Departments in the Indian Civil Service*, by Robert Demaus (London, 1866) (findable online). A quick sketch of early advanced training, German Universities, and the PhD can be found in the first chapter of D. C. Allen's *The Ph.D. in English and American Literature* (New York: Holt, Rinehart and Winston, 1968). Discussion of the nineteenth-century editions of Tottel can be found in Rollins, *Tottel's Miscellany*, cited above. The quotation from the *Cyclopaedia of English Literature*, ed. Robert Chambers, is in volume 1 (Edinburgh, 1844), 46–47. *The Scottish Invention of English Literature*, ed. Robert Crawford (Cambridge: Cambridge University Press, 1998), is an excellent guide to its titular subject and contains much general information about the establishment of the teaching of English; William Minto's training and context are described in this book. The memorials to Minto are in the "Biographical Introduction" to his *Literature of the Georgian Era* (Edinburgh: William Blackwood and Sons, 1894), xi–1. The Wyatt material is in William Minto, *Characteristics of English Poets from Chaucer to Shirley* (Edinburgh: William Blackwood and Sons, 1874), 157–58, 153. It is worth noting that George Puttenham, back in the 1580s, understood Wyatt's irregular metrics also: he says, somewhat bemusedly, "We must think he did it of purpose" (page 214 of Whigham and Rebhorn's edition of *The Arte of English Poesy,* referred to above).

Information about Nott's rebinding of Wyatt's book, and the Devonshire manuscript, along with information about the post-Tudor journeys of these manuscripts, can be found in Ruth Hughey's *The Arundel Harington Manuscript of Tudor Poetry*, vol. 1 (Columbus: Ohio State University Press, 1960), and in *The Courtly Maker*, by Ryamond Southall (New York: Barnes and Noble, 1964). Southall's book remains an excellent resource, especially for facts of this type. The auction of Nott's effects is described in the January 1842 *Gentleman's Magazine* obituary cited above; Bowker's sale is mentioned in Hughey, *The Arundel Harington Manuscript of Tudor Poetry*, 1:14.

My information about Ewald Flügel comes from the excellent and well-documented Wikipedia article: https://en.wikipedia.org/wiki/Ewald_Fl%C3%BCgel. His articles are: Ewald Flügel, "Die handschriftliche Ulberlieferung der Gedichte von Sir Thomas Wyatt. I"; "II"; and "III"; all in *Anglia*: N.F. 6:18 (1896), pp. 263–290 and 455–516, and N.F. 7:19 (1897), pp. 175–210, respectively. The prose, translated by my friend Christian Thorne, is from I, p. 263; the poem is in II, p. 472. Information on Agnes Foxwell is sparse, in spite of her importance as an editor of Wyatt and other scholars' frequent citation of her work, but an excellent quick sketch can be found coming from another angle in Ellen Ross, ed., *Slum Travelers: Ladies and London Poverty, 1860–1920* (Berkeley: University of California Press, 2007), 72–80. Foxwell made a drastic career change when, during World War I, she worked as a welfare supervisor in the dangerous Woolwich Arsenal on the south side of the Thames. Her Wyatt book is *The Poems of Sir Thomas Wiat* (London: University of London Press, 1913).

A quick introduction to the fascinating and important subject of literature and anthologies can be found in Anne Ferry, *Tradition and the Individual Poem: An Inquiry into Anthologies* (Stanford, CA: Stanford University Press, 2002). The Palgrave quotations are from Francis Turner Palgrave, *The Golden Treasury* (London: Macmillan, 1861). Palgrave's note on "They Flee from Me" is quoted in Patricia Thomson's *Sir Thomas Wyatt and His Background* (Stanford, CA: Stanford University Press, 1964), 143.

For Quiller-Couch's life and work, see Frederick Brittain, *Arthur Quiller-Couch: A Biographical Study of Q.* (Cambridge: Cambridge University Press, 1948); *Q's Legacy*, by Helene Hanff (London: Penguin, 1977), describes Q's methods still at work in the mid-twentieth century. The inaugural address in *The Art of Writing* (London: G. P. Putnam's Sons, 1916), 1–25, can be found at https://archive.org/details/onartwritingooquilgoog; almost all of Q's writing can be found online. The interesting earlier life of "Vixi Puellis" can be seen in an appearance in *Gentleman's Magazine*, July 1836, 57; there is also a quick mention of its use in a Trollope novel in Hugh Osborne's "Hooked on Classics: Discourses of Allusion in the Mid-Victorian Novel," in *Translation and Nation: Towards a Cultural Politics of Englishness*, ed. Roger Ellis and Liz Oakley-Brown (Bristol: Multilingual Matters, 2001), 124. This article also has a very useful discussion of "tagging" more generally. An example of the Mildly Naughty use of the "sublimi flagello" tag can be found in *Gentleman's Magazine,* January 1817, 24. For the Horace text itself, see Ferry's translation of *The Odes of Horace*, cited above, page 241. "They Flee" is on page 245 of *The Golden Pomp*, ed. Arthur Quiller-Couch (London: Methuen, 1895). The Tillyard quotation is from *The Muse Unchained* (London: Bowes and Bowes, 1958), 67. The Tripos questions are listed in Carol Atherton, *Defining Literary Criticism* (New York: Palgrave Macmillan, 2005), 49.

Part IV

"The Geometry of Sunset" is in *New Republic*, November 6, 1929, 318. I learned about this poem and about many other things in Mark Winchell's *Cleanth Brooks and the Rise of Modern Criticism* (Charlottesville: University of Virginia Press, 1996). This book is my basic source for most of the biographical details concerning both Brooks and Robert Penn Warren: for instance, the information about Charles Pipkin. Toward the end of his career, Brooks wrote an article about Thomas Percy that makes the parallels between them very clear: "The Young Thomas Percy," *Forum* 17, no. 2 (1979): 49–56. In this article Brooks defends (in a mild way) Percy's changing of his name. For the Fugitives, see (among many) Louise Cowan, *The Fugitive Group* (Baton Rouge: Louisiana State University Press, 1959). Walter Raleigh's self-description as a Gas Man is quoted in Herbert Davis's "David Nichol Smith," in *Studies in the Eighteenth Century; Papers Presented at the David Nichol Smith Memorial Seminar*, ed. R. F. Brissenden (Toronto: University of Toronto Press, 1968), 4; this essay is an excellent and quick introduction to both the Oxford School and Nichol Smith. Fuller discussion of the Oxford School, Raleigh, and Nichol Smith can be found in *The Rise of English Studies*, by D. J. Palmer (Oxford: Oxford University Press, 1965).

In *Cleanth Brooks and the Rise of Modern Criticism*, Winchell discusses the creation of *An Approach to Literature*; for more details, see Thomas Cutrer's *Parnassus on the Mississippi* (Baton Rouge: Louisiana State University Press, 1984). Graff, in *Professing Literature*, cited above, provides a helpful sketch of the New Critical environment. A near-contemporary discussion of textbooks can be found in "The New Criticism and the New College Text," by Clarence L. Kulisheck, *Journal of Higher Education* 25, no. 4 (April 1954): 173–78, 227–28.

The post-1936 editions of *An Approach to Literature*, including the 1952 edition, are published by Appleton Crofts. The poem is on page 467 of the 1936 (and 1939) editions and page 354 of the 1952 edition. The mimeographed "Sophomore Poetry Manual" is in YCAL MSS 30 in the Beinecke Rare Book and Manuscript Library, Yale University. The "universal favorite" compliment is from Thomson, *Sir Thomas Wyatt and His Background,* cited above, page 141.

I gained a good foothold on I. A. Richards from Chris Baldick's *The Social Mission of English Criticism, 1848–1932* (Oxford: Oxford University Press, 1983); see also *I. A. Richards: His Life and Work*, by John Russo (Baltimore: Johns Hopkins University Press, 1989). Winchell's *Cleanth Brooks and the Rise of Modern Criticism*, cited above, contains a good description of Brooks's encounters with Richards while in England. The Brooks-Warren tapes are in Box 95 of the Cleanth Brooks Papers (YCAL MSS 30) at Yale's Beinecke Rare Books and Manuscript Library. I have used the original New York 1929 edition of *Practical Criticism*; in that volume the quotations are, in order, from pages 3, 345, 350, 320.

The quotation about poetry from J. D. McCallum's *The College Omnibus* (New York: Harcourt Brace, 1936) is on page 1013. The quotations from *An Approach to Literature* are from the 1936 edition. The Introduction is pages 1–9. Hugh Blair's "manliness" formulation is quoted in Crawford's *The Scottish Invention of Literature*, cited above, page 62; see also Miriam Brody's *Manly Writing: Gender, Rhetoric, and the Rise of Composition* (Carbondale: Southern Illinois University Press, 1993). The quotation about Keats in McCallum, *The College Omnibus*, cited above, is on page 1031. Murray's grammar is available in myriad editions online; in the York 1798 edition this passage is on page 114. An example of the "wise man" formulation: "The difference between the wise man and the unwise man is, the one governs his passions, the other's passions govern him." From G. E. Howard, *Apothegms and Maxims on Various Subjects, for the Good Conduct of Life, &c.*, vol. 2 of *The Miscellaneous Works, in Verse and Prose* (Dublin: Marchbank, 1783), 274. Murray's version spreads like wildfire through the nineteenth century. The quotation from *Modern Poetry and the Tradition* (Chapel Hill: University of North Carolina Press, 1939) is on page 23; that from *Understanding Poetry* (New York: Henry Holt, 1938) is on page 322.

The "exercise" appears in the edition of 1952; it begins on page 354. The quotation from *A Pamphlet against Anthologies* (New York: Doubleday, Doran, 1928) is on page 58. For more on Angleton at Yale, see Michael Holzman, *James*

Jesus Angleton, the CIA, and the Craft of Counterintelligence (Amherst: University of Massachusetts Press, 2008); William Johnson, *Thwarting Enemies at Home and Abroad* (Washington, DC: Georgetown University Press, 2009); and Robin W. Winks, *Cloak and Gown: Scholars in America's Secret War* (London: Collins Harvill, 1987). For "reproach," see Herbert Davis, "David Nichol Smith"; for *The Well-Wrought Urn* (New York: Harcourt Brace, 1947), see page xi. The most exciting version of the Scholar/Critic distinction is in Ransom's "Criticism, Inc.," in *The World's Body* (New York: Scribner's and Sons, 1938).

Arnold Stein, "Wyatt's 'They Flee from Me,'" *Sewanee Review* 67, no. 1 (Winter 1959): 28–44. For facts about the *Sewanee Review* itself, see Herbert Davis, "David Nichol Smith," cited above, page 211. Information about Robert Heilman (and a mention of Arnold Stein) can be found in the guide to the collection of his papers at the University of Washington: http://archiveswest.orbiscascade.org/ark:/80444/xv76958/op=fstyle.aspx?t=k&q=WAUUA19_13_1000HeilmanRobert.xml. Heilman's recall of his near-witnessing of Huey Long's assassination, days after he arrived at LSU, is very compelling; see *The Southern Connection* (Baton Rouge: Louisiana State University Press, 1991), 5–6. This collection is an excellent insider view of the heady mid-1930s at LSU.

Stephen Greenblatt, *Renaissance Self-Fashioning* Chicago: University of Chicago Press, 1980). The section on "They Flee from Me" begins on page 150; the Compliment is also on this page.

Conclusions

The best thinking about Ink is in Powell, "Thomas Wyatt's Poetry in Embassy," cited above. A list of several notions about the stalkers, and an angry response, are in Richard Leighton Greene, "Wyatt's 'They Fle from Me' and the Busily Seeking Critics," *Bucknell Review* 12, no. 3 (December 1964): 17–30.

Index

Credit List

SQUARE ONE
First-Order Questions in the Humanities

Series Editor: **PAUL A. KOTTMAN**

Square One steps back to reclaim the authority of humanistic inquiry for a broad, educated readership by tackling questions of common concern, regardless of discipline. What do we value and why? What should be believed? What ought to be done? How can we account for human ways of living, or shed light on their failures and breakdowns? Why should we care about particular artworks or practices?

Pushing beyond the trends that have come to characterize much academic writing in the humanities—increasingly narrow specialization, on the one hand, and interdisciplinary "crossings" on the other—Square One cuts across and through fields, to show the overarching relevance and distinctiveness of the humanities as the study of human meaning and value. Series books are therefore meant to be accessible and compelling. Rather than address only a particular academic group of experts, books in the Square One focus on what texts, artworks, performances, cultural practices and products mean, as well as how they mean, and how that meaning is to be evaluated.

———

Lightning Source UK Ltd.
Milton Keynes UK
UKHW040657230320
360469UK00035B/217